THE BATTLE FOR
NORTH AFRICA

PEN & SWORD MILITARY CLASSICS

We hope you enjoy your Pen and Sword Military Classic. The series is designed to give readers quality military history at affordable prices. Pen and Sword Classics are available from all good bookshops. If you would like to keep in touch with further developments in the series, including information on the **Classics Club**, then please contact Pen and Sword at the address below.

Published Classics Titles

Series No.

1	The Bowmen of England	*Donald Featherstone*
2	The Life & Death of the Afrika Korps	*Ronald Lewin*
3	The Old Front Line	*John Masefield*
4	Wellington & Napoleon	*Robin Neillands*
5	Beggars in Red	*John Strawson*
6	The Luftwaffe: A History	*John Killen*
7	Siege: Malta 1940-1943	*Ernle Bradford*
8	Hitler as Military Commander	*John Strawson*
9	Nelson's Battles	*Oliver Warner*
10	The Western Front 1914-1918	*John Terraine*
11	The Killing Ground	*Tim Travers*
12	Vimy	*Pierre Berton*
13	Dictionary of the First World War	*Stephen Pope & Elizabeth-Anne Wheal*
14	1918: The Last Act	*Barrie Pitt*
15	Hitler's Last Offensive	*Peter Elstob*
16	Naval Battles of World War Two	*Geoffrey Bennett*
17	Omdurman	*Philip Ziegler*
18	Strike Hard, Strike Sure	*Ralph Barker*
19	The Black Angels	*Rupert Butler*
20	The Black Ship	*Dudley Pope*
21	The Argentine Fight for the Falklands	*Martin Middlebrook*
22	The Narrow Margin	*Derek Wood & Derek Dempster*
23	Warfare in the Age of Bonaparte	*Michael Glover*
24	With the German Guns	*Herbert Sulzbach*
25	Dictionary of the Second World War	*Stephen Pope & Elizabeth-Anne Wheal*
26	Not Ordinary Men	*John Colvin*
27	Plumer: The Soldier's General	*Geoffrey Powell*
28	Rommel as Military Commander	*Ronald Lewin*
29	Legions of Death	*Rupert Butler*
30	The Sword and the Scimitar	*Ernle Bradford*
31	By Sea and By Land	*Robin Neillands*
32	Cavalry: The History of Mounted Warfare	*John Ellis*
33	The March of the Twenty-Six	*R.F. Delderfield*
34	The Floating Republic	*G.E. Manwaring & Bonamy Dobree*
35	Tug of War: The Battle for Italy 1943-45	*Dominick Graham & Shelford Bidwell*
36	Churchill & The Generals	*Barrie Pitt*
37	The Secret War	*Brian Johnson*
38	Command on the Western Front	*Robin Prior & Trevor Wilson*
39	The Operators	*James Rennie*
40	Churchill and The Admirals	*Stephen Roskill*
41	The Battle for North Africa	*John Strawson*
42	One of Our Submarines	*Edward Young*

Forthcoming Titles

43	The Battle of Trafalgar	*Geoffrey Bennett*
44	Fire Power	*Shelford Bidwell & Dominick Graham*
45	Sieges of the Middle Ages	*Philip Warner*
46	Haig's Command	*Denis Winter*
47	Hitler's Death's Head Division	*Rupert Butler*

PEN AND SWORD BOOKS LTD

47 Church Street • Barnsley • South Yorkshire • S70 2AS

Tel: 01226 734555 • 734222

E-mail: enquiries@pen-and-sword.co.uk • **Website:** www.pen-and-sword.co.uk

JUN 2 8 2005

THE BATTLE FOR NORTH AFRICA

JOHN STRAWSON

New Lenox
Public Library District
120 Veterans Parkway
New Lenox, Illinois 60451

PEN & SWORD MILITARY CLASSICS

3 1984 00231 4688

First published in Great Britain in 1969 by B.T. Batsford
Published in 2004, in this format, by
PEN & SWORD MILITARY CLASSICS
an imprint of
Pen & Sword Books Limited
47 Church Street
Barnsley
S. Yorkshire
S70 2AS

Copyright © John Strawson, 1969, 2004

ISBN 1 84415 105 0

The right of John Strawson
to be identified as Author of this Work has
been asserted by him in accordance with
the Copyright, Designs and Patents Act 1988.

A CIP record for this book
is available from the British Library.

*All rights reserved. No part of this book may be reproduced or
transmitted in any form or by any means, electronic or mechanical
including photocopying, recording or by any information storage and
retrieval system, without permission from the Publisher in writing.*

Printed and bound in Great Britain by
CPI UK

Pen & Sword Books Ltd incorporates the imprints of
Pen & Sword Aviation, Pen & Sword Maritime, Pen & Sword Military,
Wharncliffe Local History, Pen & Sword Select,
Pen & Sword Military Classics and Leo Cooper.

For a complete list of Pen & Sword titles please contact:
PEN & SWORD BOOKS LIMITED
47 Church Street, Barnsley, South Yorkshire, S70 2AS, England.
E-mail: enquiries@pen-and-sword.co.uk
Website: www.pen-and-sword.co.uk

CONTENTS

ILLUSTRATIONS

1. O'Connor and Wavell
2. Long Range Desert Group patrol
3. The Mediterranean Fleet escorting a Malta convoy
4. Matilda tanks
5. Benghazi harbour after RAF attention
6. Axis Prisoners of War
7. Tobruk falls, January 1941
8. Junkers Ju. 87 dive bombers
9. The Desert Air Force – Hurricanes
10. Rommel in the Western Desert
11. Honey tanks
12. The destruction of battle
13. Auchinleck and Wavell
14. Malta succoured
15. Kesselring and Rommel
16. 50mm anti-tank gun
17. The Free French at Bir Hacheim
18. Montgomery
19. 6pr anti-tank gun
20. German graves
21. *Torch* – US troops landing
22. General Anderson with US divisional commander
23. Men of a US tank destroyer unit in Tunisia
24. Eisenhower with Tuker, Nicholls and Walsh
25. Von Arnim and a divisional commander in Tunisia
26. Montgomery talks to Messe, with Freyberg
27. The end in North Africa – Mateur POW camp, May 1943
28. The armies did not stand idle – Churchill with Leese and Alexander in Italy

MAPS

ACKNOWLEDGMENTS

I wish to thank Mr Peter Kemmis Betty for his advice in the planning of this book and for his suggestions about amendments to its first draft. The literature which deals with this part of the Second World War, and which I have consulted, is very extensive, but I must record a particular debt to the four volumes of the Official History, *The Mediterranean and the Middle East,* by Major-General I. S. O. Playfair and others. I am grateful to Mrs Crawley of Headquarters Northern Ireland Library for her tireless assistance in getting books of reference for me, and I would like to thank my sister, Mrs Margaret Motture, for supplying my deficiency in one of the dead languages. I am, of course, responsible for statements of fact or opinion in the book.

My thanks are due to the following for permission to quote from the books mentioned: Allen & Unwin Ltd, Paolo Caccia-Dominioni's *Alamein 1933–1962* and Martin Blumenson's *Rommel's Last Victory;* B. T. Batsford Ltd, General Sir Michael Carver's *El Alamein*; Ernest Benn Ltd, Jan Yidrich's *Fortress Tobruk*; William Blackwood & Sons, H. P. Samwell's *An Infantry Officer with the 8th Army*; Cassell & Co. Ltd, Winston Churchill's *The Second World War,* John Connell's *Auchinleck,* B. H. Liddell Hart's *The Tanks,* and Major-General von Mellenthin's *Panzer Battles;* Collins, Sons & Co. Ltd, John Connell's *Wavell,* Bernard Fergusson's *Wavell, The Rommel Papers,* and Roy Farran's *Winged Dagger*; Hamish Hamilton Ltd, Alan Moorehead's *A Year of Battle* and *The End in Africa,* and H. F. Wood's *The King's Royal Rifle Corps*; Gale & Polden Ltd, R. H. W. S. Hastings' *The Rifle Brigade in the Second World War*; Harrap & Co. Ltd, Heinz Werner Schmidt's *With Rommel in the Desert*; Her Majesty's Stationery Office, Major-General I. S. O. Playfair's *The Mediterranean and the Middle East;* Hodder & Stoughton Ltd, Major-General Sir Francis de Guingand's *Operation Victory*; Michael Joseph Ltd, Dudley Clarke's *The Eleventh at War*; Kimber & Co. Ltd, Correlli Barnett's *The*

Desert Generals; Macmillan & Co. Ltd, Lieutenant-Colonel R. L. V. ffrench Blake's *A History of the 17/21 Lancers 1922–1959,* and Sir John Wheeler-Bennett's *King George VI*; Maclaren & Sons, G. R. Stevens' *Fourth Indian Division*; Frederick Muller Ltd, Robert Crisp's *Brazen Chariots;* John Murray Ltd, Hector Bolitho's *The Galloping Third*; Oxford University Press, Sir Howard Kippenberger's *Infantry Brigadier;* The Royal United Services Institution, *Journal* August 1962; The Times Publishing Company Ltd, *The Times Literary Supplement*; Weidenfeld & Nicolson, Michael Howard's *The Mediterranean Strategy in the Second World War,* and Fred Majdalany's *The Battle of El Alamein.*

The author and publishers wish to thank Ullstein Bilderdienst for permission to reproduce Plates 15 and 25, and US Army Photograph for Plates 23 and 27. All other illustrations appear by courtesy of the Imperial War Museum.

Author's note

Accounts of the way in which battles are conducted may imply criticism of commanders or units. As I have founded my accounts largely on previously published sources, where such criticism is evident, these sources should perhaps be specified. They are these. In Chapter 4, the *Official History* and John Connell's *Wavell*; Chapter 5 and 6, Correlli Barnett's *The Desert Generals* and Ronald Lewin's *Rommel as Military Commander*; Chapters 10 and 11, the *Official History* and Winston Churchill's *Second World War.*

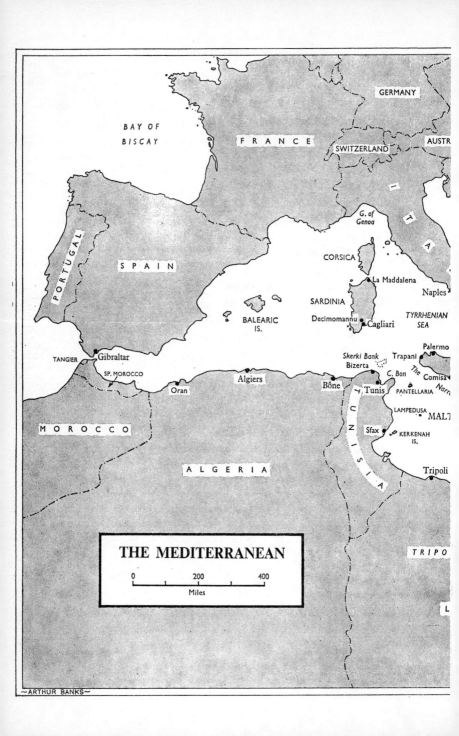

THE MEDITERRANEAN

0   200   400
Miles

~ARTHUR BANKS~

1. Desert crowned in arms*

The author does not seem to consider El Alamein to have been
a decisive battle, but, while one may disagree with him, we can
be thankful for not having to do yet another trip to the desert.

Times Literary Supplement review of Hanson Baldwin, *Battles Lost and Won*

Mr John Knightley held definite views as to the absurdity of dining out in dismal weather. 'A man,' said he, 'must have a very good opinion of himself when he asks people to leave their own fireside, and encounter such a day as this, for the sake of coming to see him.' He went on to ridicule the idea of spending five dull hours away from home where nothing would be said or heard that had not been said or heard yesterday and would not be tomorrow. Anyone who could subject his fellow creatures to such hardship, he concluded, must think himself a very agreeable fellow.

Is there anything about the battle for North Africa which has not been said or heard yesterday? The reviewer whose words are at the head of this page seems to think not and to be on the side of Mr John Knightley. Indeed the accounts of what really happened, whether we are thinking of the campaign as a whole or particular parts of it, are so numerous that if another one is to be welcome, it should at least offer something that has not been attempted before. It may be that there is one way of doing so. Most other books on the subject fall broadly into one of four categories. First comes the personal reminiscence ranging from, say, Robert Crisp's enthralling story of the *Crusader* battles or Heinz Schmidt's recollection of what it was like to be *With Rommel in*

---

* When Dryden claimed that 'desert in arms' should be fittingly crowned, he referred, of course, to deserving. But what better acknowledgement of the special part played by the Western Desert in the struggle for Europe could there be than to suggest that it was crowned in arms.

the Desert to Montgomery's memoirs or Churchill's great work, which in spite of its sweep echoes a former comment on his *World Crisis* to the effect that Winston had written an amusing autobiography about the war. Next there is the biography—John Connell's admirable portraits of Wavell and Auchinleck, for example, in which so much of the Middle East fighting largely figures, or Corelli Barnett's gallery of Desert General. Thirdly we find books about single encounters or a series of them, such as Michael Carver's *El Alamein* and *Tobruk* or von Mellenthin's *Panzer Battles*. Lastly we have the *Official History* and innumerable divisional or regimental histories. But although the ground has been exhaustively covered, there does not in condensed form appear to be an account of the land battles for North Africa which gives proper weight both to those who were in the front line and those responsible for the direction and handling of the armies engaged. Moreover, during almost three years of fighting, the nature and conduct of these battles unavoidably changed. The changes had many causes—commanders, equipment, logistics, support in the air and from the sea, strategic circumstances, tactical needs. The purpose of this volume, therefore, is not to summarize or reiterate previous accounts of the campaign either in general or particular, but rather, against a background of strategic and tactical development, to trace the changes in the way battles were conducted during the three years, 1940 to 1943, and to see from the viewpoint of those who did it what the fighting was actually like. Such a version of events, which have been so often and so fully related before, cannot be original, cannot be comprehensive, cannot even be select, but it can perhaps be representative.

'From noon until three o'clock,' observed Stendhal, 'we had an excellent view of all that can be seen of a battle—i.e., nothing at all.' Wellington put forward a similar sentiment when he likened the history of a battle to that of a ball. Everyone could recall with sharp clarity details here and there, at this time and at that, but few or none could comprehend or describe the whole. There is, however, no shortage among our contemporaries of men who have elected to ignore both Stendhal and The Duke. These men have remembered with advantages what deeds they did that day.

* *

But the advantages have not been, as Henry v meant on Crispin's day, to exaggerate their own exploits. They have been the advantages of communication and recording unknown at the time of the Hundred Days. The airborne camera and the teleprinter have seen to it that much of a battle could be seen and that many of its details could be recorded.

The historian of battles, therefore, may be compared with the historian of literature. His material is to hand. Furthermore, he too deals with reputations, some exploded, some magnified, some unsung, some unequalled. Amongst this last sort, most commentators might agree, would figure Wellington's; not so A. G. Macdonell. In a memorable, but not impartial, estimate of Wellington's task in the Peninsula he declared it to be the easiest one that has ever faced a general. With a mercenary army, assured intelligence, a population wholly hostile to his enemy, abundant supplies, interior lines, and command of the sea, he had 'the game in his hands, and yet it took him nearly six years to advance from Lisbon to the Pyrenees'. There were many daunting tasks which faced British generals during the Second World War, but it might not be unfair to suspect that of them all, those confronting the generals in North Africa were the least complex and the easiest to accomplish. Their logistic resources and main base were for the most part secure; their lines of communication, although long and seriously threatened, were never actually cut; their weapons were plentiful; their intelligence, whilst not always accurate, was well rooted and widespread;* their tactical opportunities were unlimited; their strategic activity urgent; their air and sea support fluctuating, but never totally withdrawn; their reinforcement was largely a matter of arithmetic; their enemies were either half-hearted or inferior in number. Yet in spite of all this it took them nearly three years to advance from Egypt to Tunis.

The two campaigns had other points of resemblance. In writ-

---

* So much so that Rommel recorded in his diary: 'I have maintained secrecy . . . and informed neither the Italian nor the German high command. We knew from experience that Italian headquarters cannot keep things to themselves and that everything they wireless to Rome gets round to British ears.'

ing of Pitt's abilities during the French Revolutionary and Napoleonic Wars, Macaulay was not kind about his handling of military affairs. After many years of war and an enormous expenditure of life and treasure 'the English Army under Pitt was the laughing stock of Europe. It could not boast one single brilliant exploit. It had never shown itself on the Continent but to be beaten, chased, forced to re-embark, or forced to capitulate. To take some sugar island in the West Indies, to scatter some mob of half naked Irish peasants, such were the most splendid victories won by the British troops under Pitt's auspices.' In the early 1800s, therefore, Wellington's victories were overdue. 1940 may have been our finest hour. Sweet are the uses of adversity. But O'Connor's spectacular successes in the winter of 1940–41 were much sweeter. They were the one bright star in a sky almost everywhere dimmed by twilight.

Then there was the extraordinary seesaw of events, the dramatic sequence of advances and withdrawals. In 1810 Wellington defeated Massena at Bussaco, but was soon bundled back to the lines of Torres Vedras; in 1812 he cut up Marmont at Salamanca and took Madrid, only to retire again after a repulse at Burgos; in 1813 he advanced a third time and for once was not required to 'know when to retreat and to dare to do so'. This shuffling to and from Lisbon was to be mirrored in the Benghazi Stakes with El Alamein as another Torres Vedras. In 1940 O'Connor expelled the Italians from Egypt and went on to conquer Cyrenaica; in 1941 Rommel re-took it; later that year Auchinleck forced Rommel back; within a few months the Desert Fox had recaptured it all and more; at last in 1942 the relentless Montgomery–like Wellington, faultless in defence, cautious but not unprodigal in attack –advanced and went on advancing. Right up to the end the resemblance persisted. Wellington's last move forward and Montgomery's first one were made possible only because the enemy's main forces were being engaged by an ally.

But Napoleon was not turned off his throne by Wellington, at least not the first time. Moscow and Leipzig, Blücher's advance to the walls of Paris–these were what induced the Marshals to aban-

don the Emperor and obliged him to abdicate.* Hitler was not
turned out by failure in the Mediterranean. Indeed, Allied objectives in the so-called Mediterranean strategy were by no means
clear cut. A programme was easy enough to draw in general terms.
In essence it was simply to wrest the initiative from the Axis
powers, to halt their advances and gains, to tighten the ring
around their Europe, to enable blows by land, sea and air to be
struck against them. Of course, there were more specific aims.
Amongst them the Allies badly wanted to relieve Malta, eliminate
the threat to Egypt, tap the resources of French North Africa,
open the Mediterranean to their shipping. Nor was it difficult to
produce compelling arguments that the conquest of North Africa
was not just a prerequisite for further offensive action, but that it
would give the Allies a freedom of manoeuvre which up to then
had in the American view been so completely absent that the best
thing they would think of was the establishment of a 'defensive
encircling line'. As early as 3 December 1941, the CIGS General
Sir Alan Brooke, had noted in his diary : 'I am positive that our
policy for the conduct of the war should be to direct both military
and political efforts towards the early conquest of North Africa.
From there we shall be able to reopen the Mediterranean and
stage offensive operations against Italy.' Churchill went further
and conjured with the promises which a successful conclusion of
the North African campaign might hold out, forecasting that, together with invasion from the west, a move northward into Europe would perhaps produce the 'flexible manoeuvres' which he
had always had his eye on. Flank attack and main thrust might
become reciprocal. 'Our second front will, in fact, comprise both
the Atlantic and Mediterranean coasts of Europe, and we can
push either right-handed, left-handed, or both-handed as our resources and circumstances permit.'

The North African coast, in short, was to be a 'springboard,
not a sofa'. In his lucid survey of the Mediterranean strategy,
Michael Howard brings us down to earth, first as to how flexible

---

* How different might have been the plot against Hitler of July 1944 if
someone could have echoed Ney's reply to Napoleon that the Army would
obey its Generals.

this strategy in fact was, secondly as to what was and was not possible and intended. He points out that the concept was one of attrition, not of manoeuvre at all. The whole idea was that for Germany the Mediterranean should become an obligation whose fulfilment would be bound to grind down the Axis strength, but whose abandonment might disrupt the integrity of the *Festung Europa*. It was to be a gigantic distraction, an enforced dissipation of effort, not just to bring relief to the Russian front, but to enable the Allies, by wielding traditionally their superior naval power, to choose the point at which they would strike a concentrated blow with some prospect of its being effective. But Professor Howard emphasizes that, at the time of the Casablanca Conference in January 1943, there was in the minds of the Combined Chiefs of Staff no thought of invading Europe through its 'soft underbelly' or of reaching Central Europe before the Russians did. It was rather that, because of the shortage of shipping, there was nowhere else where British and United States forces could engage the German armies except in North Africa and the Mediterranean. It was not merely expedient to do so. In 1942 there was no alternative. Where it would lead to, however, was far from clear, and in the following year was to result in the strange circumstance, reminiscent of the Allied plans for invading the Crimea some ninety years earlier, 'that when the Allied armies landed in Sicily on 10 July, nobody had yet decided where they were to go next'.

Yet if in 1941 and 1942 strategic objectives and means of exploiting success in North Africa were anything but clearly defined and were in any event subsidiary to the business of defeating the main bulk of the German armies, how dire appeared to be the strategic consequences of failure. To be turned out of Egypt? To lose Palestine, Syria and Iraq, forfeit control of the Persian Gulf and its oil? To allow Turkey to be isolated and the forces of Japan and Germany converge on India? Would not this mean that the main features of Allied Grand Strategy agreed in December 1941 at Washington would collapse in ruins? Communications would be severed; the ring, instead of closing round Germany, would be closing round the British position in the Middle

East; offensive action against Germany would become more
and more difficult to develop. And if this were so, would not
the fundamental doctrine of 'Germany First' itself go by the
board? For Great Britain the question would not be how to prose-
cute the war successfully. It would be whether it could be prosecuted at all. In the 1914–18 war Admiral Sir John Jellicoe, Commander-in-Chief of the Grand Fleet, was once referred to as the
only man who could lose the war in an afternoon. There may
have been times during the winter of 1941 and summer of 1942,
however, when General Auchinleck would have been justified in
thinking that he had stepped into Jellicoe's shoes and that he too
could have lost the war in one short engagement with Rommel.

But for the ordinary soldier in the desert such thoughts were
mercifully far away. For them the war was, as Fred Majdalany
put it, almost a private one. To be 'up the blue' was to be deprived of all life's customary accoutrements–buildings, roads,
trees, towns and villages, shops and inns, ordinary people. Different things became uttermost in their minds, such things as water,
tea, petrol, cigarettes (preferably not of the v variety), the rations,
NAAFI stores, letters from home, leave. The fighting itself was
accepted as an exacting, frightening, exhilarating and somehow
not-to-be-missed adjunct of their nomadic existence. Discomforts
there certainly were. Flies, the heat, gyppy tummy, monotony,
the desert sores, the *khamsin* or *gibleh*, that swirling, driving, penetrating sand-storm which brought all activity to a standstill, to
say nothing of the ever-present reflection that somewhere out
there were Rommel and the Afrika Korps, Rommel whom the
British soldiers admired not only because of his dash and habit of
commanding from the front, but because of his chivalrous attitude to the whole desert conflict. His own words, *Krieg ohne
Hass,** epitomized the British view. Where else did you find Jock
columns swanning about the desert or a man like Campbell himself leading tanks into action standing up in an open staff car?
Where else did you hear the heartening news that divisional headquarters had once again been overrun and the general was once
more a prisoner? Where else did you wear such outlandish kit

* War without hatred.

and wage war with so contradictory a mixture of nonchalance and professionalism? Churchill, as usual, found the telling phrase when he declared that, if a man were to be cross-examined as to his wartime doings, it would be enough for him to say that he had fought with the 8th Army.

No wonder there was a special code of behaviour practised by those who fought this private war. It was left to an officer of the Indian Army to write it down in its most striking and complete form:

Your chief concern is not to endanger your comrade.

Because of the risk that you may bring him, you do not light fires after sunset.

You do not use his slit trench at any time.

Neither do you park your vehicle near the hole in the ground in which he lives.

You do not borrow from him, and particularly you do not borrow those precious fluids, water and petrol.

You do not give him compass bearings which you have not tested and of which you are not sure.

You do not leave any mess behind that will breed flies.

You do not ask him to convey your messages, your gear, or yourself unless it is his job to do so.

You do not drink deeply of any man's bottles, for they may not be replenished. You make sure that he has many before you take his cigarettes.

You do not ask information beyond your job, for idle talk kills men.

You do not grouse unduly, except concerning the folly of your own commanders. This is allowable. You criticise no other man's commanders.

Of those things which you do do, the first is to be hospitable and the second is to be courteous ... there is time to be helpful to those who share your adventure. A cup of tea, therefore, is proffered to all comers ...

This code is the sum of fellowship in the desert. It knows no rank or any exception.

It would be absurd to suppose either that every soldier thought consciously in this sort of way or that all the rules were observed. But there is much in the code which hits exactly the right note. Soldiers in the desert were courteous, they were hospitable, they did proffer cups of tea, and they certainly criticized their own commanders. Of all the commanders who came in for criticism, those concerned with the handling of armour probably came in for most.

The reason for this was simple enough. It was the tank which mattered, and it was the number of them which you could deploy, or destroy, or salvage or keep supplied that determined the outcome of battles. The other arms, artillery, engineers, infantry, transport, indispensable though they might be, were subordinate to the tank. For the armoured soldiers, members of mechanized cavalry regiments, Yeomanry and Royal Tank Regiments, the desert had an even more special flavour, and some of the most agreeable stories of what happened there, however trivial they may be, come from tank crews. There was an intrepid sergeant of a famous Hussar regiment who had been caught by the military police in a forbidden street of Cairo with only his boots on. His explanation that he must have mistaken his way in the black out was not well received by the colonel, who dealt out some suitable justice of fines and threats. The lesson was not wasted on him. A few weeks later, when in command of three Honey tanks, he reported a group of Mark IV Panzers approaching his position and asked for guidance. Curtly told to engage them, his acknowledgement of the order, whilst not observing the radio procedure then in vogue, was a model of courtesy. 'Very good, Sir.' He was as good as his word, beat the enemy off and was subsequently awarded the DCM. For all tank crews, of course, the apotheosis of the day was the brew-up. But battles being what they are, how terrible it was when just as the water was coming to the boil, the dreaded order *Move now* came through the radio headphones. To have the mug so near and yet have it dashed away was unthinkable. It was no surprise that from time to time, as the relentless radio voice asked whether you were in fact moving, the reply –a confident affirmative–would be accompanied by an indication to your driver, who was not even in the tank, to pour the tea out.

Many were the soldiers and many the regiments who saw the whole sequence of ups and downs from the first raids by Western Desert Force across the frontier into Libya to 8th Army's final advance to Tripoli and Tunis. Most renowned of all was the 7th Armoured Division which together with 4th Indian Division was longer in Africa than any other. This is not to say that these two divisions fought harder battles than all the others. Indeed as the story unfolds we shall see how international an arena the desert was. In 1950 Generalleutnant von Ravenstein, who commanded 21st Panzer Division, recorded:

> If the warriors of the Africa Campaign meet today anywhere in the world, be they Englishmen or Scots, Germans or Italians, Indians, New Zealanders or South Africans, they greet each other as staunch old comrades. It is an invisible but strong link which binds them all. The fight in Africa was fierce, but fair. They respected each other and still do so today. They were brave and chivalrous soldiers.

Even von Ravenstein's list is not complete. But of them all certain divisions are better remembered than others, 15th and 21st Panzer, Ariete, 90th Light, the Highland Division, the New Zealanders and Australians. 4th Indian and 7th Armoured Divisions figure high on the list because they were there at the beginning* and at the end. The first meeting between these two fine formations is well recollected:

> They took the road so many came to know so well, turning north at the Pyramids across a hundred miles of hard sand to the causeway over the magenta lagoons behind Alexandria, thence west through the rolling dunes which skirted the bright thunderous Mediterranean, past scattered date oases and fig plantations, until beyond the dusty hamlet of Burgh el Arab the road rose to the crest of the dunes and along the easy valley inland a train snorted up to a sun-bitten drought-stricken halt whose name (which did not matter then) was El Alamein.

---

* 6th Australian Division also took part in Wavell's first offensive.

Forty miles farther on at El Daba Divisional officers met for the first time the bronzed and cheerful officers and men of 7th Armoured Division, who had kept watch for years in the sandy wastes; who knew more about the desert and its ways than anyone alive; who having taken as their emblem the Libyan jerboa, were destined to be known as The Desert Rats as long as memory remains.

Thus 4th Indian Division came to a battlefield on which it was destined to find fame. The Western Desert, between the Nile Delta and the Gulf of Sirte, once a naked and desolate expanse, was no longer empty upon the maps. British officers in search of adventure and against the day of battle had charted its maze of age-old trails, had plotted its contours and defined even its most insignificant features. Of the traditional soft burning sand of the Sahara, they had found little, save in the Great Sand Sea far to the south. But there were vast stretches of hard sand and of stony ground raddled with black basaltic slabs; there were bony ridges and ribbed escarpments and deep depressions; there were flat pans which held water after the rains, where gazelles cropped the coarse grass in midsummer. There were wadi-fed flats which sprang over-night into flowery glory in spring; there were endless undulating sand and gravel dunes whose crests marched in rhythm, like waves at sea.

This last simile was fitting. For war in the desert was in many ways like war at sea. The reconnoitring armoured cars were like the scouting destroyers, the guns and Panzers like battleships and cruisers. Movement was the key to everything, and just as sea power was handcuffed without support from the air, so the tanks and guns and men could only develop their strength to the full if the aircraft above them were on the same side. Little was static. Yet here too there was a parallel. Unsinkable Malta was matched by unmovable Tobruk. Some other pieces of ground were important, but most, like the seas, were not, and for nine tenths of the time were empty. It was not ground or sea you wanted; it was to get at the enemy and sweep him clear of it. In order to get at him, you navigated across the desert with a compass as you did across the sea. But there was no virtue in capturing great tracts of sand unless you could go the whole hog and take it all. The more desert you got, the more you aggravated your own supply problems, and the more vulnerable became your communications. The flanks at sea were land and the desert flanks were seas, salt to the north, sand to the south. Minefields abounded. The very language in which directives were coined had the same ring. 'Search out and destroy' was the traditional naval task. And Churchill told Alexander that his prime duty would be 'to take or destroy at the earliest opportunity the German-Italian army commanded by Field-Marshal Rommel'.

There were to be many changes before this duty was at last done. The tanks and anti-tank guns which British crews manned and fought got better and better although not always fast enough to match their adversary's; the way in which battles were planned, directed and exploited gradually became tighter, although some features, such as the wide armoured turning movements to the south, the only open flank, remained constant; the skies tended to harbour fewer and fewer of the Luftwaffe; commanders came and went, although one, Rommel, called the tune longer than any other; the ordinary soldiers themselves were continually changing, like the fortunes of whichever army they belonged to. Two things, however, did not change. One was the desert itself; and nearly all the most important battles were fought in the same arena; secondly, the struggle for supplies.

What became known as the Western Desert, although its name in origin referred only to a part of Egypt, stretches from El Alamein in the east to Gazala in the west; north lay the Mediterranean coast and some 150 miles to the south the Jarabub and Siwa oases. Western Cyrenaica contained the bulge of the Djebel Akhdar with the towns of Derna and Benghazi, whilst over the desert from the west of El Adem to the south of Agheila coursed an ancient and principal route, the Trigh el Abd. Many of the battles for North Africa were, of course, fought in other places–in Eritrea and Abyssinia, far from the desert but all part of the same struggle, in Syria, in Algeria and Tunisia, to say nothing of the momentous encounters on, above and below the Mediterranean. But it was from Agheila to Alamein and back again that the critical clashes between the Panzerarmee and 8th Army took place. It was there that the 500-feet-high Libyan plateau and the coastal strip were linked by an escarpment descending from one to the other, descending so steeply and roughly that only in a few passes could *all* vehicles negotiate it, passes like Fuka, Halfaya and Sidi Rezegh, which therefore exercised major tactical influence. Apart from the coast road there were no recognized routes other than the Trigh el Abd, the Trigh Capuzzo and a few lesser tracks. But the going was such that in general on the plateau itself tanks and trucks could motor almost anywhere.

This is not to say it was easy to find the way. Argument as to which feature was which on ground and map persisted right up to the time of Montgomery's battle of El Alamein, and it was not always those who had been there longest whose map reading and navigation were best. To the novice the desert seemed largely flat with few features to fix his position by. In fact, sun compass apart, there were many landmarks to steer by–cairns, tombs, potholes, *birs*, mounds, and sometimes inverted, flat-topped craters or miniature escarpments whose possession could be decisive in a battle between tanks and anti-tank guns. The desert's harsh character was at once formed and relieved by these prominences. Of the sinews of war, however, except for the antiquated wells, there were none. Everything required to support and sustain man and machine had to be brought in from outside. It was this which was the second unchanging condition and which made the battle for North Africa principally a battle of supplies.

From the very outset when France's collapse upset the balance of power in the Mediterranean and Middle East, it became clear that the success of any Italian ventures in Africa must be dependent first on the safety of sea routes across the Mediterranean, secondly on air support for the advancing armies. These facts alone, without recourse to the reluctance of their commanders in the field, explain the meagreness of the Italian undertakings. When O'Connor's successes against Graziani further facilitated the reinforcement of Malta and Greece from Gibraltar and Alexandria, the German reaction was swift and effective. Fliegerkorps x arrived in Sicily from Norway early in 1941, and Admiral Cunningham was able to see that air power of the right sort properly employed could within a matter of days transform the situation at sea, and by doing so gravely threaten Malta's continued existence. The pattern of operations throughout the struggle for North Africa, although often jumbled and confused, had a consistent design. The three elements of power were so intermingled in their influence and dependence on each other that it was not always easy, either for the Axis or the Allies, to determine at any precise moment which was predominant, and thus which tactical or strategic aims should be pursued most resolutely. So it was that in February 1941 after O'Connor's lightning campaign in Cyrenaica and in order to stiffen their Italian allies in Tripolitania, the Germans transferred about half of Fliegerkorps x's fighters and bombers to North Africa, granting respite to Malta at the very time when it had to have respite in order to survive at all. At the same time Malta's reduced ability to strike at enemy shipping together with Cunningham's losses had allowed the Italian Navy to transport the Afrika Korps to Tripoli, so giving yet another twist to the kaleidoscope. In 1941 priorities were hard to identify, and the dilemma was slow to disappear.

No sooner had Rommel seized Cyrenaica and invested Tobruk in the spring of 1941, an enterprise which in itself underlined the insufficiency of *his* supplies, and which gave the Royal Navy the exacting, but nevertheless gallantly performed, duty of keeping Tobruk alive—no sooner had the British suffered this reverse, to say nothing of those in Greece and Crete, than Wavell, reinforced by the *Tiger* convoy with its 240 tanks, was being pressed by the Chiefs of Staff to recapture the airfields between Sollum and Derna. These airfields were needed so that Axis sea communications with Cyrenaica via the west coast of Greece could be interrupted and so that Malta could be maintained. The interdependence of land, sea and air battles could hardly be better illustrated. The operation designed to do this, *Battleaxe*, failed, and with its failure Wavell departed. His successor, Auchinleck, had longer to prepare, and the *Crusader* battles, although fortunes in them ebbed and flowed, once more cleared Cyrenaica of Axis forces, and brought relief to Malta. But as each side was to realize in turn, long advances in the desert, whilst spectacular, so multiplied the logistic difficulties that offensive and even defensive strength evaporated. Rommel's shorter lines of communication plus the Luftwaffe's return in numbers led to the British sustaining their severest setback of the whole campaign, including the loss of Tobruk. Yet the resurgence of Malta combined with the growth of both the Desert Air Force and 8th Army to almost overwhelming strength made the Panzerarmee's final extinction a matter only of timing. When Rommel heard that *Torch* was under way and that an armada of 100 or more ships was nearing North West Africa, with all the Allied air and sea mastery which this implied, he knew that the end of his army in Africa was in sight. His comment that 'the African war was being decided by the battle of the Atlantic' reinforced his earlier contention that the Axis would lose control of North Africa unless they captured Malta.

Thus it was that the swing of the desert pendulum was controlled by certain constants–the constant of supplies, of air power, of the struggle at sea, of the two armies' number and quality of tanks–and these constants were themselves wholly interactive. Their respective consequence, however, fluctuated as often and as suddenly as the good or ill fortune of the two contestants. Perhaps no army's fortune took so devastating a dip as the Italian 10th Army's between September 1940 and February 1941. To understand the circumstances in which this came about, we must take a look at the conditions in Libya and Egypt, and more widely in Africa, when Italy declared war on Great Britain.

2. A centre of gravity

But if there were no prospect of a successful decision against Germany herself there was a subsidiary theatre where British forces could be employed to harass the enemy and perhaps inflict serious damage. Italy's entry into the war had turned the Middle East into an active theatre of operations. As a centre of gravity of British forces it was second only to the United Kingdom itself.

Michael Howard

In discussing Hitler's dilemma after his direct attack on England had failed, Major-General Fuller makes a great deal of what he calls the war's centre of gravity and the German Supreme Command's change in its line of operations. He draws attention to Hitler's inability to realize where the true line of operations–that is the direction of strategy in such a way that it yielded decisive strategic prizes–lay. Like Napoleon, he either failed or refused to see that the line ran to London, not Moscow, and that the indirect road to London, a road along which his Italian allies were well placed to be of use, ran through Egypt.* Conquer Egypt, and where would British sea power be, that sea power which enabled England to preserve a degree of initiative and without which she could hardly have conducted offensive operations of any sort? Compared with this target, at this time, the second half of 1940 and the first half of 1941, Russia was an irrelevance. It is just as well that Hitler did take this view for it allowed British forces, as Michael Howard reminds us, to build up a new centre of gravity of their own, and from it to develop a Mediterranean strategy, essentially subsidiary, it is true, to the defeat in Europe of the German armies–which alone could bring the war to an end–but providing none the less a stepping stone to this eventual undertaking.

* When Goering was asked by Ivone Kirkpatrick in June 1945 what Germany's greatest mistake was, he replied: 'Not invading Spain and North Africa in 1940.'

It was also fortunate for the British that at the very time when
the Middle East was to become of such overriding strategic importance to them, they had as General Officer, Commanding-in-
Chief, so stalwart and clear-sighted a soldier as Wavell. Two days
before taking up his appointment on 2 August 1939, he had written a paper, remarkable for its prescience, in which he defined the
object of his work. Starting from the recognition that in war the
Axis powers would enjoy the initiative, he considered that Germany would aim to dominate Eastern and se Europe whilst Italy
would want to do the same in the Mediterranean and North
Africa. He was certain that the Eastern Mediterranean would be
the decisive theatre, and therefore asked himself what use Germany would make of Italy in her plans. Whatever the answer, it
was clear that to secure control of the Mediterranean was indispensable to the British cause and that the longer it took to do this,
the harder it would be to win the war. He concluded, therefore,
that his task was to plan not just for the defence of Egypt and
other Middle Eastern interests, but 'such measures of offence as
will enable us and our Allies to dominate the Mediterranean at
the earliest possible moment; and thereafter to take the counter-
offensive against Germany in Eastern or se Europe'. To effect
this policy he would have four things to do—secure the Canal
base by a bold forward course of action in the Western Desert;
secure control of the Eastern Mediterranean; clear the Red Sea;
and then develop land action in se Europe. During his two years
of command Wavell did much to achieve the first of these things,
was wholly successful in the third, and was heavily committed in
trying with inadequate resources to do the other two. The tragedy
was that, instead of being allowed to get on with them one by
one, he was required to undertake all four at once. Throughout
his spirit never flagged. Rommel thought of him as the only British general who 'showed a touch of genius'. Perhaps at no time
was this more so than in his first audacious offensive against the
Italians when the odds were so heavily against him. Just before the
collapse of France brought about circumstances which led to these
brilliant exploits, Wavell had committed another appreciation to

paper* in which he emphasized just how critical a centre of strategic gravity the Middle East was, and, in view of the thoroughly bleak position in which the Allies found themselves, was notable for its optimism. Despite over-simplification it is so pertinent to the battle of North Africa that meet it is to set part of it down :

1. Oil, shipping, air power, sea power are the keys to this war, and they are interdependent.

   Air power and naval power cannot function without oil.

   Oil, except very limited quantities, cannot be brought to its destination without shipping.

   Shipping requires the protection of naval power and air power.

2. We have access to practically all the world's supply of oil.

   We have most of the shipping.

   We have naval power.

   We have potentially the greatest air power, when fully developed.

Therefore we are bound to win the war.

Wavell went on to argue that as Germany was short of oil, his own principal task might be to prevent oil, from any of the numerous Middle Eastern sources, reaching Germany. When we consider that most of the offensives in the Western Desert had either as a primary or secondary aim the capture of airfields so that our shipping could enjoy the protection of air power and lead to Malta's sustaining its ability to destroy enemy shipping; when moreover we remember that these offensives were themselves only possible because of the support given to them by naval and air power; finally when we remember that every move westwards was altogether conditioned by our having enough oil and petrol, we see what Wavell meant. The Axis lost their grip on North Africa because they did not pursue this line of reasoning far enough. Of course, men were needed too. But in Wavell's offensives not many of them were either to hand or required.

---

* Soldiers spend many hours learning how to write appreciations in the class room. It is often revealing to enquire how many they have written in earnest.

On 10 June 1940 Italy declared war on the United Kingdom. As soon as they heard the news the three Commanders-in-Chief set in motion their plans for striking the enemy. Disparity of strengths was great. Wavell had some 36,000 men in Egypt, but they were neither properly organized nor equipped. 7th Armoured Division had only four regiments of tanks; 4th Indian Division was short of a brigade and of artillery; the New Zealand Division amounted only to a brigade group. In Palestine were 27,500 troops but of these only one British brigade and two battalions were equipped and trained; in any case these units were earmarked either for duty in Iraq or for internal security in Palestine. East Africa was even more lightly garrisoned–a British brigade in the Sudan, two East African brigades in Kenya, and a mere 1,500 local troops in British Somaliland. Against this, and bearing in mind that the fall of France removed the threat from Tunisia and Algeria altogether, Marshal Graziani had about a quarter of a million men in Cyrenaica and Tripolitania, whilst in Italian East Africa the Duke of Aosta commanded a total, white and native, of nearly 300,000 soldiers. As we shall see it was not numbers which worried Wavell. What he lacked was fully trained, properly organized and equipped formations. Without these, battles could not be fought.

Nevertheless on 8 June 1940 General Richard O'Connor took command of all forces in the Western Desert. Wavell had already given orders that offensive action against the Italians at the frontier with Egypt would be taken immediately war was declared, so that Western Desert Force was in action three days after receiving its new commander. O'Connor, who had commanded a brigade on the North West Frontier and had also been in action recently against Arab rebels in Palestine, enjoyed a reputation for originality* and boldness. He was certainly to live up to it. He would not have been able to do so, however, had Wavell long before not established the logistic foundations which were indispensable to military operations of any sort. Wavell had always

---

* Wavell liked the unorthodox. 'Never let yourself be trammelled by the bonds of orthodoxy,' he told Bernard Fergusson, 'always think for yourself . . . and remember that the herd is usually wrong.'

maintained that administration and logistics were the most difficult and yet most necessary accomplishments of generalship. The
battle for North Africa, as we have already noted and will see
confirmed, was a battle of supplies. If Wavell had done nothing
else, his place in this battle would have been assured by the steps
he took first to prepare for and then to establish a huge base in
Egypt and elsewhere able to withstand the endless demands made
on it. The *Official History* underlines the extent to which he himself made the running :

> It was also clear to General Wavell that the land forces in the
> Middle East would sooner or later have to be appreciably
> strengthened if their contribution to the war was not to be con-
> fined to trying not to lose it. He therefore initiated a prelimin-
> ary survey for the creation of a base for fifteen divisions—say
> 300,000 men. This figure was no more than an estimate based
> on a consideration of possible roles, for by the end of October
> (1939), when the survey of ports, railways, roads and sites was
> completed, the long-term policy for the Middle East was still
> being considered in London.

One of the roles that Wavell foresaw was that of invading Libya
and he instructed General Wilson, then Commanding British
Troops in Egypt, to prepare plans for it, including the problem of
supply in the desert. Early in 1940 the War Cabinet gave instructions that the base organizations in Egypt and Palestine were to
be developed. So began the process of building ports, airfields,
roads, railways, water storage wells, workshops, depots, petrol
stores; then of procuring both raw materials to continue their
development and the actual commodities to put in them together
with vehicles to move them about. All these preparations meant
that, by the time O'Connor took over Western Desert Force, units
of 7th Armoured Division positioned near Mersa Matruh were
able, although short of vehicles, to operate right up to the frontier
with Cyrenaica. They were about to show that Italy's declaration
of war was interpreted by the British as actually meaning the start
of hostilities. Almost before some of the Italian soldiers knew they

were at war, the 11th Hussars had taken Fort Maddalena and the 7th Hussars had attacked Fort Capuzzo.

Of all the Desert Rats perhaps the 11th Hussars characterized most completely the troops Churchill had called 'lean, bronzed, desert-hardened and fully mechanized'. Indeed the regiment had had armoured cars since 1928 and been in the Middle East since 1934. They had been training in the Western Desert for five years and were as experienced in desert lore and navigation as anyone. They would have endorsed the comment on their own regiment made by an Army Cooperation pilot that 'the British trooper is really marvellous under any conditions; that the desert offers an enchantment unbeknown to anything else; and that, if romance has gone out of the cavalry, there is something equally fascinating in its newly acquired role'. On the night of 11 June the 11th Hussars were engaged in a skirmish which interrupted the desert's silence for the first time in the three years of shooting which were to follow. Ambushing a column of Italian lorries near Fort Capuzzo, two armoured cars captured some fifty soldiers and seventy weapons, but the squadron did much more than take prisoners. They discovered that the Italians were in no way prepared to start operations against Egypt. O'Connor therefore gave orders on 13 June that Capuzzo and Maddalena would be assaulted.

Armoured cars were not traditionally the sort of troops to use for an assault, but none the less the job of capturing Maddalena was given to A Squadron, 11th Hussars. Next day the squadron set out at 5 am to cross fifty miles of desert to a rendezvous near the fort. There they were to wait until the RAF softened the defences, and on arrival were misled into thinking that this bombing was actually in progress by a rival demonstration of air power—the *Regia Aeronautica* attacking a former Egyptian Army post nearby. The squadron was lucky not to be spotted by the Italian bombers.

Before long RAF Blenheims appeared, and no sooner had they done so than the enemy bombers made themselves scarce. To the watching Hussars, the Blenheim attack seemed rather puny, but as arranged they ringed the fort with their armoured cars and closed in, expecting a fierce action. Far from having a fight, however, the crews were astonished to see the white flag run up. They rapidly made good the fort's capture, and all was over by midday.

Later that month the 7th Hussars were engaged in a different sort of battle at Fort Capuzzo after it had been re-occupied by the Italians. Their task was to advance against the enemy artillery batteries, to destroy them and withdraw—almost a Balaclava affair. It says a good deal for what still had to be learned about the proper use of armour, and in particular about cooperation with infantry, that the regiment was invited to attack an enemy defensive position *at night* without infantry support and with a questionable manoeuvre by which the three squadrons converged from all points of the compass. It was no surprise that the operation, whilst exciting, was not an unqualified success.

The thing began badly. Postponement of the attack meant that it was already too dark when it did get started. The regiment advanced rather slowly and its squadrons were out of position, bunched much too closely together, before they were near enough to the fort to open fire effectively. When they did so, halted only 500 yards away from it, they received a hot rejoinder. Verey lights, multi-coloured tracer, machine guns and, least comforting of all, field guns, apparently on fixed lines, all shot at them. A and C Squadrons, close to these enemy batteries, yet unable to see properly what was happening, were quite helpless to deal with them and had to withdraw. B Squadron, however, attacking from another direction, got quickly across the enemy anti-tank obstacles and into the gun positions. One tank, commanded by Troop sergeant-major Clarke, was hit, then rammed by three enemy tanks, one of whose guns fired point-blank and by some ballistic mystery failed to penetrate even the driver's glass shield. Then Clarke's .5 machine gun jammed, a favourite trick of this particular weapon, so he opened up with the .303, wholly ineffective against armour, but which persuaded the enemy tanks to back away and allowed him to reverse too. Again his tank was hit, and this time caught fire. It looked unhealthy, but another tank rushed up and took Clarke and his crew off. Fort Maddalena with an irresolute garrison had been captured with armoured cars by day easily enough, but Fort Capuzzo, defended by Italian gunners, who almost always fought well, was not going to succumb to an uncoordinated attack by tanks at night.

From such modest beginnings grew the battles which were to ebb and flow up and down the desert. Operations like that at Fort Capuzzo and the 11th Hussars' vigorous patrolling, which resulted in more successful ambushes by themselves and other units of 4th Armoured Brigade, gave these covering troops invaluable knowledge of the frontier areas. The opportunities for bold enterprise were many, and to begin with it was only the British who took them. The desert was something to be used, not feared, and at the end of June General Wavell was to establish an irregular force which made remarkable use of it–the Long Range Desert Group, whose principal tasks were to gather intelligence and harass the enemy. They went on doing so until all North Africa was in Allied hands. But whilst the British might have seized the initiative at the very opening of the campaign, they could not prevent the Italian Army from concentrating its strength between Bardia and Tobruk as a first step to an offensive which everyone expected to be mounted before long.

What was it like to be in the desert behind enemy lines during this period of relative inactivity before the Italian advance got under way?

For the 11th Hussars, keeping their constant vigil, noting every Italian move and change in deployment, getting to know the desert better and better, the days went by in slow time. Just before dawn the patrols would go out, whilst those at squadron headquarters settled down to cook their breakfast. Each armoured car was its own storehouse and own kitchen, and those who have served in regiments of the Royal Armoured Corps will no doubt have observed that the squadron leader's driver was generally the best cook in the squadron. Wonders could be done with a few eggs and some bully beef. In the heat of the morning while the car commanders on patrol searched through their binoculars, the squadron leader would get his administrative work done, walk round the troops in reserve, and keep an eye open for enemy aircraft. It was easy enough to keep armoured cars and men hidden under camel thorn and camouflage nets provided they kept still. But to move about was to be spotted. Every half hour the watching patrols would report, and if it were, as it so often was, a negative report, the midday meal would come as a welcome break to the endless waiting, however tired men might be of hard-tack biscuits, tinned cheese and bully. With air and ground sentries posted, the afternoon was a good time to sleep, for too much of the night was needed for other things. Perhaps at tea-time there would be a hot bully stew, tea, of course, and some sausages. The BBC overseas service would give them the latest news, and even about the very desert activities they were engaged in, its emphasis or purpose could sometimes come as a surprise to them.

A glass of whisky and water was an agreeable prelude to packing up before moving back to a new position for the night. To this position would come all the troops which had been on patrol and they would be joined there by the transport echelons carrying petrol, rations, letters from home, and, if needed, ammunition. Then the bedding would be unrolled, and again with sentries posted the squadron would sleep. Fifty miles inside enemy territory, they could never relax; choosing where to spend the night was an important matter. Ambushes were all too easy to set. Before first light out the patrols would go again, squadron headquarters motored off to one more piece of desert, and yet another long day full of nothing but waiting, monotony, routine, would have begun.

Long and monotonous the days may have been, but they were not wasted, for when the time came that it mattered the 11th Hussars' familiarity with the desert was unrivalled and their reconnaissance record unequalled. Time, in any event, was not on the Italians' side. Before their expected advance materialized there took place the first meeting between Wavell and Churchill which did little to reassure either of them. The collapse of France, whilst bringing to a head Britain's own struggle for survival, had greatly enhanced Italy's ability to concentrate her forces against the British position in Egypt and East Africa, and had upset the balance of sea power in the Mediterranean. Churchill was determined to defend Egypt with whatever could be spared from the more immediate threat at home, and as he put it 'felt an acute need of talking over the serious events impending in the Libyan desert with General Wavell himself'. Both have recorded their impressions of this encounter. Wavell admired Churchill's boldness and foresight in resolving to reinforce the Middle East with tanks at a time when others pressed for their retention at home, and when their passage by sea was in itself a risk. But he did not relish the Prime Minister's interference in detailed matters of troop dispositions–a department he rightly regarded as peculiarly his own– nor had he much respect for the tactical ideas which poured from that ever ready pen.

There was more to it than this. Wavell simply was not one of *Churchill*'s generals, and Churchill for his part was not satisfied that Wavell was making the best use of his resources. The minor triumph of Italian arms in Somaliland irritated him; even more irritating he found Wavell's unwise rejoinder to one of his red-hot cables that heavy casualties were not evidence of tactical sense. Churchill found that he could not *like* Wavell, who was too cool, too unemotional, too independent. What is more he did not wish to leave things to his Commander-in-Chief. He wanted to run them himself. He therefore gave Wavell a directive which contained minutely detailed tactical instructions showing, as Wavell said, that 'Winston did not trust me to run my own show and was set on his ideas'. This document is important in two ways. First, it laid down certain strategic priorities which influenced Wavell in his juggling with limited resources for the simultaneous conduct of numerous campaigns; secondly, as the *Official History* reminds us, it set in train that series of telegrams between Commander-in-Chief and Prime Minister which was to be a persistent feature of the campaign throughout its three year course. Some extracts from it then are relevant here; its date was 16 August 1940.

1. A major invasion of Egypt from Libya must be expected at any time now. It is necessary therefore to assemble and deploy the largest possible army upon and towards the western frontier . . .

2. The evacuation of Somaliland is enforced upon us by the enemy, but is none the less strategically convenient. All forces in or assigned to Somaliland should be sent to Aden, to the Soudan via Port Soudan, or to Egypt, as may be thought best.

3. The defence of Kenya must rank *after* the defence of the Soudan. There should be time after the crisis in Egypt and the Soudan is passed to reinforce Kenya by sea and rail before any large Italian expedition can reach the Tana River. We can always reinforce Kenya faster than Italy can pass troops thither from Abyssinia or Italian Somaliland . . .

10. . . . the Army of the Delta . . . should constitute by October 1, at the latest, 39 battalions, together with the armoured forces; a total of 56,000 men and 212 guns . . .

12. It is hoped that the armoured brigade from England of three regiments of tanks will be passed through the Mediterranean by the Admiralty. If this is impossible their arrival round the Cape may be counted upon during the first fortnight in October. The arrival of this force in September must be deemed so important as to justify a considerable degree of risk in its transportation.

13. The Mersa Matruh position must be fortified completely and with the utmost speed . . .

15. A main line of defence to be held by the whole Army of the Delta, with its reserves suitably disposed, must be prepared (as should long ago have been done) from Alexandria along the edge of the cultivated zone and irrigation canals of the Delta . . .

16. In this posture then, the Army of the Delta will await the Italian invasion. It must be expected that the enemy will advance in great force, limited only, but severely, by the supply of water and petrol. He will certainly have strong armoured forces in his right hand to contain and drive back our weaker forces, unless these can be reinforced in time by the armoured regiments from Great Britain. He will mask, if he cannot storm, Mersa Matruh. But if the main line of the Delta is diligently fortified and resolutely held he will be forced to deploy an army whose supply of water, petrol, food and ammunition will be difficult . . .

two troops turned left and right respectively and began to clear
the perimeter, whilst troops following on made for the defending
guns, and a reserve was held ready to deal with unforeseen resistance, which rapidly made itself felt. It was an unusual, but very
successful way of using tanks which normally fought as a mutu-
ally supporting squadron. But then penetrating and clearing fortresses like Bardia was an unusual assignment. What mattered
was that Jerram made full use of the two cards he had–fire-power
and mobility. Throughout it all, whether in the first assault or
later infiltration, tanks and infantry fought as one.

Bardia yielded 40,000 prisoners, 462 guns, 127 tanks and 700
lorries. A haul like this showed what masterpieces of economy
O'Connor's battles were. They needed to be for he had few resources. But his uncanny knack of attacking Italian defences
from the least expected direction, his insistence on the proper coordination of all arms, his decisive use of the Infantry tanks, his
ability always to think ahead to the next move and be ready for
it, above all his exploitation of the limited mobility which he had,
these things made his campaign at once unforgettable and unique.
By 22 January Tobruk had fallen. Another 25,000 prisoners, another 200 guns and nearly 90 tanks were taken. His progress was
such that Wavell, even though pre-occupied with his forthcoming
offensives in East Africa and concerned about Churchill's intentions with regard to the Balkans, had as early as 5 January, that
is the day Bardia fell, laid down Benghazi as O'Connor's ultimate
objective. Up to this time the campaign had been one of encirclement followed by assault on defended positions. The brilliant
climax was to be the first great left hook of the battles for North
Africa, and the boldest. 7th Armoured Division with the 11th
Hussar group in the lead swept across the desert via Mechili, Msus
and Antelat to Beda Fomm and Sidi Saleh while the Australians
pushed along the coast road. The aim was a simple one–to cut off
and destroy the enemy's entire army. Colonel John Combe, commanding 11th Hussars, with 2nd Rifle Brigade and three artillery
batteries, was in charge of the trap's lower jaw.

It was then that the 11th Hussars showed what all their training in the desert had made them capable of. They had no maps,

17. The campaign for the defence of the Delta therefore re-
solves itself into *strong defence with the left arm from Alexandria inland, and a reaching out with the right hand, using sea-
power upon his communications.* At the same time it is hoped
that our reinforcements acting from Malta will hamper the
sending of further reinforcements–Italian or German–from
Europe into Africa.

18. All this must be put effectively in train by October 1,
provided we are allowed the time . . .

Whatever Wavell may have thought of these detailed instructions
about how the campaign should be conducted–another sphere in
which he regarded the prerogative as his own–and, as we shall
see, he was thinking far more offensively than Churchill, he would
have been obliged to concede that in paragraph 17 the Prime
Minister had put his finger on the nub of the whole struggle for
North Africa. In the event Wavell went his own way, 'carried out
such parts of the directive as were practicable and useful, and dis-
regarded a good deal of it'. In commenting on it by telegram,
however, he made two fundamental objections which pinpointed
the essentials for proper campaigning in the desert–he must have
enough air forces to be able to defend both Egypt and the naval
base at Alexandria (a view naturally endorsed most urgently by
his air and naval colleagues) and he must have a second armoured
division. Churchill's directive had been concerned mainly with the
defence of the Delta. But before Graziani had even begun his advance into Egypt, Wavell was contemplating an offensive into
Cyrenaica, which he thought he could launch either late that
year or early in 1941. He listed its stages as capturing Sidi Barrani, occupying Bardia, taking Tobruk, then advancing on Derna.
As usual he stressed the need for speedy, combined operations and
for denying the enemy the sea routes across the Mediterranean :

Let us avoid as far as we can the slow ponderosity which is apt
to characterize British operations. At the time that we shall be
in a position to take the offensive, we shall presumably have
established a strong enough naval position in the Mediterranean to prevent Libya receiving much in the way of supplies.

We may, therefore, hope . . . to be able to take a certain degree
of risk.

We must have a proper air component with our force, i.e.
one that has been specially allotted to the Army, has discussed
the problems of army support and has trained with the Army.

Whilst still awaiting the long expected Italian advance, O'Connor's troops had constructed defences east of Mersa Matruh, and
all the trained formations available, that is 7th Armoured Division and four brigades, one British, one Australian, one New Zealand and one Polish, were under his command. Brigadier Gott's
Support Group was at the front with orders to observe, and impose delay upon an advancing enemy without becoming heavily
involved. Mussolini meanwhile was prodding the reluctant Graziani, and the battle for North Africa was about to start. Whatever
the outcome of this pending action, one thing was clear. It was
here in Africa and here alone that the British could engage Axis
forces on land. In Somaliland British forces had withdrawn, after
a fight, in the face of greatly superior Italian numbers; in the
Sudan the Italians had achieved minor frontier successes, and
occupied Kassala, Gallabat and Kurmuk; in Kenya there was
little more than patrol activity although the Italians advanced as
far as the two water holes at Dobel and Buna; everywhere the
British were on the defensive. Yet within six months the Italians
were to lose their entire African empire.

At sea, as might have been expected, Admiral Cunningham
was trying to emulate Nelson and his watchword, *touch and take*.
The action off Calabria in July, without yielding great material
results, established the Royal Navy's ascendancy in the Mediterranean in the same way as the Desert Rats had established theirs
in their own environment. But whilst it also showed that at that
stage in the war the Italian fleet could protect military convoys
to Libya, and that the British fleet could similarly safeguard the
passage of its convoys in the Mediterranean, it highlighted what
turned out to be the essence not just of naval operations, but of
the whole progress of the Middle Eastern war at sea and on land.
It was no good Cunningham's pretending that his moral ascend-

ancy plus his freedom to sail ships from Malta to Alexandria and back again added up to *control* of the seas. He would have this only when he could continue to operate freely himself *and* prevent the enemy's doing so. For if the Mediterranean were a centre of gravity for British forces to strike blows at the Axis powers, Malta was a centre of gravity for the Mediterranean itself. And if Malta were the key to naval operations in the central Mediterranean, only when Malta was put to proper use would the British properly develop their striking power. Thus it was demonstrated to the British that they *had* to restore Malta to the point where it could alike savage enemy sea routes and safeguard its own. At this time Malta was almost defenceless. Yet the Italian Commando Supremo failed to see that only the *capture* of Malta would serve their ends. It was luckily a shortsightedness to be echoed by the German Supreme Command later on.

Up to this time then the battle for North Africa had been prosecuted somewhat half-heartedly—by the Italians because it was in their nature, by the British because they lacked resources. But now, one year after the outbreak of war with Germany, in September 1940, there was to be the first of many advances and retirements in the desert, a repetitive process which ended only with the collapse of the whole Axis position there.

3. Fox killed in the open

Egypt's the place ... there we can strike England a shrewd blow.

Emil Ludwig

On 13 September 1940 the 10th Italian Army began its ponderous motor sixty miles into Egypt as far as Sidi Barrani and Sofafi. It was no battle, merely a limited and observed encroachment. Nor was there ever an intention on Graziani's part to achieve more than local success. Ciano recorded in his diary that no commander had ever undertaken a military operation so much against his will. Nevertheless sheer weight of numbers–more than four divisions versus a battalion group–saw to it that despite continual harassing from the air and from light forces of motorized infantry, artillery batteries and armoured cars, the advanced elements of the 1st Blackshirt Division had reached Sidi Barrani by nightfall on 16 September. Graziani then sat down and began to construct a series of defensive camps and to build up his administrative resources and communications, communications which received the Royal Navy's and Royal Air Force's attention whilst the 11th Hussars again took over the task of watching. The only serious drawback to the whole affair from the British point of view was the loss of advanced airfields at Sidi Barrani, which robbed bombers of a refuelling base and all aircraft of range. Hurricanes could no longer be expected to reach Malta; ships could no longer enjoy fighter protection to Bardia; and the enemy inherited those very advantages which the British had lost. Thus attacks on Italian communications became even more important, and for them to be really effective, as we have seen, the strengthening of Malta's defensive and offensive capability was the first requisite. The Chiefs of Staff therefore decided to send to Malta more Hurricanes, Glenn-Martins for reconnaissance, and anti-aircraft guns. But it was not only Malta that was to be reinforced. The whole of the Middle East theatre was receiving regular additions to its strength, and as the threat of invasion at home lessened, so the regularity of these reinforcements steadily grew. It was just as well, for quite apart from Wavell's eagerness to mount an offensive in the Western Desert as soon as he was strong enough, Mussolini was about to take a step which would land him in serious trouble and as a result of Germany's subsequent moves to retrieve the situation, turn Wavell's priorities upside down.

On 28 October the Italian ultimatum to Greece was presented and rejected. From this time forth, nothing went right for Italy. Not only did they have no successes against the Greeks, but early in the following month Admiral Cunningham's Swordfish aircraft from HMS *Illustrious* crippled half the Italian battle fleet in Taranto harbour at a single blow. Whilst this improvement in the balance of sea power enabled the Royal Navy to run convoys through to Malta, the island's striking power was still insufficient to stop Italy's doing the same to Libya. Meanwhile the War Cabinet in London had decided to afford some help to Greece, principally with RAF bombers and fighters accompanied by anti-aircraft batteries–all from Egypt. The British Commanders-in-Chief, Middle East, also became responsible for the security of Crete. Wavell's predictions about SE Europe were beginning to come true. His flair for foreseeing strategic developments was further illustrated when on 17 November he recorded :

I am quite sure Germany cannot afford to see Italy defeated–or even held–in Greece, and must intervene. We shall, I think, see German air assistance to Italy very shortly.* Germany probably does not want, at present, to push Bulgaria into war or invade Yugoslavia, but may be forced to do so. As in the last war, Germany is on interior lines and can move more quickly to attack Greece or Turkey than we can to support them.

In spite of this disagreeable prospect Wavell was still planning to attack the Italian 10th Army before the situation in Greece

* Fliegerkorps x was on the move south through Italy within a month.

became too much of a distraction. He had had the Matilda Infantry
tanks since late September and was pleased with them. They were
to make a major contribution to the fulfilment of his plans. Four
weeks before he foretold what was going to happen in the Balkans,
he had instructed Wilson and O'Connor to consider an attack on
Graziani's positions in the Sidi Barrani-Buqbuq-Sofafi area. He
rated the chances of succeeding high, but at this stage it was a
strictly limited operation that he had in mind, 'a short and swift
one, lasting four or five days at the most, and taking every advantage of the element of surprise'. Wavell went on to suggest all
sorts of tactical possibilities, but, as O'Connor noted, gave no ultimate objective. O'Connor was a man with a mind of his own,
and after re-examining what he knew of the Italian dispositions
he made a plan whose essential feature was penetration between
Sofafi and Nibeiwa, that is the centre of the enemy defences, and
so get into a position where he could attack these defences from
the rear. That this gap between Sofafi and Nibeiwa should be
neither garrisoned nor patrolled was therefore an indispensable
condition of the whole operation. 7th Armoured Division's Support Group saw to it that the critical area was dominated by them.
In one such action Captain William-Powletts of the 3rd Hussars
rejoiced in the carefree, cavalry nature of the engagement. It was
sensible to enjoy it while the going was good for once the Afrika
Korps appeared it would be a different story.

William-Powletts called the episode an 'Iti hunt'. The Italians
were in the habit of sending out strong patrols of up to twenty
medium tanks supported by guns and lorried infantry, and on 19
November he and his squadron encountered one of them. He un-
expectedly found himself in command when the squadron leader
was wounded in an early morning bombing attack. One troop
was forward watching an Italian camp, and were giving such
timely and accurate information that he was able to position his
squadron whilst still out of sight in order to give the enemy a
suitable reception if they made a sortie. When they did come out,
they were so strong that the Colonel of 3rd Hussars sent up another squadron, and during the subsequent manoeuvrings, William-Powletts found himself charging with his squadron to cut off

enemy columns retreating before the other squadron's attack. Opening fire on the Italians at about 800 yards had the effect of speeding them further on their way, and meant another sweep round to get behind them. In the excitement he found that no one paid much attention to his orders, indeed all the dust thrown up made it difficult to see or keep formation. But the rush round succeeded and the squadron had a good shoot. 'We are very pleased with ourselves,' he wrote. 'It was a proper cavalry action. Charging up to the retreating column was wonderful. Rather the same feeling as an old cavalry charge, but safer and not so energetic.'

After various training exercises and rehearsals, during which he concentrated on tank, infantry and artillery cooperation, O'Connor rejected a conventional method of executing his aim and decided on a wholly unorthodox one, involving an approach march which would bring his assaulting forces, the 7th Royal Tank Regiment and a brigade of 4th Indian Division, to the rear, that is the west, of the enemy positions. 7th Armoured Division would first of all protect these moves, then when 4th Indian Division advanced against Sidi Barrani, they would disrupt enemy communications and finally exploit north-west or south. There was no doubt that O'Connor was conforming with Wavell's exhortation to take advantage of surprise. In the event surprise was total and conclusive. O'Connor did more than think of ways to win a first round. He laid plans for exploiting the success he felt sure he would have. It was not a five-day raid he was contemplating, but a campaign which would bring the desert war to an end.

The approach march before the attack on Nibeiwa set the stage for a series of triumphs which were to follow. Captain (now Major-General) Patrick Hobart recalled how 4th Armoured Brigade, whose task was to mask the Rabia-Sofafi area and prevent enemy troops there from interfering in the battle, got going.

The great move westwards began shortly before dusk on 7 December. Hobart remembered that when he looked at the tanks ahead he could see only the turrets, as the rest was hidden by dust floating about in huge clouds. The turrets, however, were sharply outlined against the sky, with their crews' heads and pennants

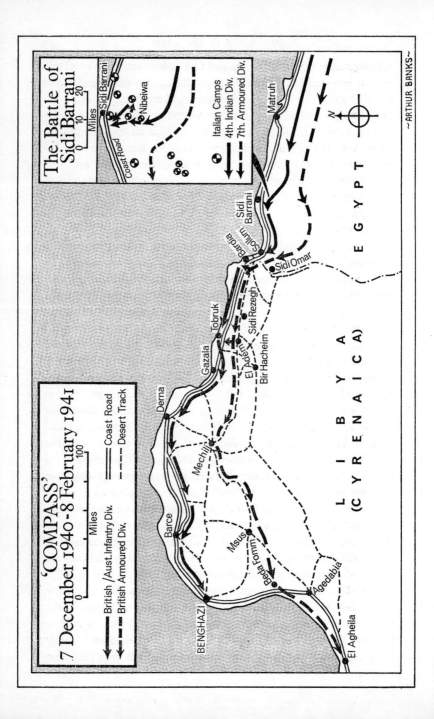

The Battle of Sidi Barrani

Miles
0   10   20

Coast Road

Sidi Barrani
Nibeiwa

Italian Camps
4th. Indian Div.
7th. Armoured Div.

Matruh

'COMPASS'
7 December 1940 - 8 February 1941

Miles
0   100

Coast Road
Desert Track

British / Aust. Infantry Div.
British Armoured Div.

Sidi Barrani
Bardia
Sollum
Sidi Omar

Tobruk
Gazala
Sidi Rezegh
El Adem
Bir Hacheim

Derna

Mechili

Barce

Msus

Beda Fomm

Agedabia

BENGHAZI

El Agheila

L I B Y A
(C Y R E N A I C A)

E G Y P T

N

~ARTHUR BANKS~

sticking up above them. In the morning after a halt for petrol and rest, a fantastic sight was revealed. The entire desert seemed to be monopolized by groups of vehicles, all streaming to the west, tanks, trucks and guns. The columns of dust which such a multitudinous mass of movement sent up needed to be seen rather than imagined. How, Hobart wondered, could they surprise the enemy with such a give-away? But no enemy aircraft appeared.

Weather, sometimes the ally of bold generals, helped by persisting in haziness. At all events on the next morning the Italian defenders of Nibeiwa had no notion of what they were in for. The attack was a model of good timing and proper cooperation between artillery, tanks and infantry. The 4th Indian Division, as so often in the future, was well to the fore.

Nibeiwa Camp was rather more than a mile from their assembled forces, and was itself rectangular, a mile wide, a third again as long. Defences were everywhere except in the north-west corner. Sangars, anti-tank ditches, minefields and so on were concentrated to the east and the south. Machine guns and anti-tank guns abounded. More than 150 emplacements ringed the camp except always in the unsuspecting north-west. In the centre were further field works, tents and hundreds of vehicles.

It would have been hard to find a more attractive target for the artillery of 4th Indian Division. At 7 o'clock, as the guns opened fire, British tanks, closely supported by more artillery, rolled forward. Too late the Italian garrison awoke and tried desperately to man their guns. A charging mass of tanks and Bren carriers rushed through the undefended north-western gap and was upon them. Italian tanks were shot to pieces even before their engines had warmed up, powerless to deal with their more heavily armoured and moving adversaries. The rest of the garrison, however gallantly some of them fought, and, as was their custom, this is just what the Italian artillerymen did, was quickly overwhelmed. The Italian commander himself, General Maletti, was shot down and killed. O'Connor's tanks had struck a mortal blow. It now remained for infantrymen to finish the thing off.

They were only fifteen minutes behind. The Cameron Highlanders, preceded by their carrier platoon and mounted in 3-ton

lorries, followed the route taken by the tanks, dismounted just out
side the camp's perimeter and raced in with the bayonet, while
pipers paced slowly, gravely, to and fro, playing in the charge.
Italian soldiers did not care for the bayonet and hundreds surrendered as they flashed towards them. Hard on the Camerons'
heels were the 1/6 Rajputana Rifles who went on to mop up the
rest of the camp. It was all finished in an hour. Over 4,000 prisoners, 23 tanks, many guns and lorries had been taken. The losses
suffered by the assaulting British and Indian troops had been negligible.

In short the attack had been a triumph, and was soon to be
followed by others–Tummar and Sidi Barrani were the next to
fall; then the Italians abandoned the Sofafi-Rabia and Khur-
Samalus camps. What had begun as a raid had been turned into
a great victory. Two Italian corps had been broken, nearly 40,000
prisoners taken together with 73 tanks and 237 guns. The British
had lost some 600 men. The shrewd blow against England would
never be delivered by the Italian 10th Army. Indeed the threat to
Egypt was gone–for the time being. Yet O'Connor was not satisfied. Although he knew already that he was to lose 4th Indian
Division, which was off to Eritrea, his mind was bent on pursuit.
Churchill, as generous in praise as he had formerly been peevish
in impatience, was quick both to send his congratulations and to
pour out suggestions to Wavell as to how the enemy should be
further hunted along the coast. Wavell was very fond of using
hunting metaphors in his telegrams, and during the advance towards Bardia–O'Connor had been given 6th Australian Division
in place of the Indians–he signalled Dill, the CIGS : 'Hunt is still
going but first racing burst over, hounds brought to their noses,
huntsmen must cast and second horses badly wanted. It may be
necessary to dig this fox.' The Australians and the Matilda tanks
of 7th Royal Tank Regiment did much of the digging. Unlike
Nibeiwa where tanks had led the way in, at Bardia infantry and
engineers cleared lanes first. Jerram, commanding 7th Royal Tank
Regiment, has explained how the leading tank troops then timed
their advance so as to cross the anti-tank ditch at first light just
in front of two further battalions of infantry. Having got in, these

but by the time the main body reached Antelat their leading patrols had already cut the coast road. By midday on 5 February Combe had established his whole force astride the enemy's withdrawal routes near Beda Fomm. What is more he had got there in front of the Italians, but only just, for two hours later leading elements of the garrison retreating from Benghazi came into sight. Numerically the odds were uneven to the point of absurdity. Benghazi's garrison was 20,000 or so and included many regiments of tanks and guns. Combe had fewer than a regiment's worth of guns and at that stage no tanks at all, since 4th Armoured Brigade, albeit making all the speed it could, was hours behind. His total force numbered less than 2,000. Combe's concern, however, was not that he had so many of the enemy to take on; it was that they might slip past him to the south before 4th Armoured Brigade came up. He resolved to fight astride the road.

The battle began when one of the Rifle Brigade companies and c Squadron, 11th Hussars, supported by the RHA batteries, opened fire on the enemy vanguard. Although the company was in a defensive position, it could not by virtue of size alone extend across a broad front, so that c Squadron moved further south to dissuade the Italians from an outflanking movement. They resorted therefore to frontal attacks on the Rifle Brigade. These attacks failed. More difficult to cope with were the hundreds of prisoners who wanted to surrender.

About three hours after the battle started, Combe's force was glad to see 4th Armoured Brigade's leading tanks. It was the 7th Hussars, and they appeared most appropriately to the left and rear of the leading Italian columns. Their commanding officer had no time to waste on complicated operation orders. With the one word, 'Attack!', even that almost superfluous, he launched his regiment at the enemy. The effect on thousands of Italians, on their guns, petrol lorries, civilian refugees and so on of the wholly unexpected appearance of two squadrons of Hussars charging at them with guns blazing may perhaps be imagined. Panic spread amongst the soldiers, fire amongst the trucks. Destruction and prisoners multiplied. Only nightfall prevented the whole thing being finished there and then.

Holding the ring at night was not easy for the small British force, but it was done. Next day the growing Italian strength produced sharper fighting, and they made many an attempt to break their way through with tanks and infantry. But 7th Armoured Division held on, and in doing so knocked out nearly 100 Italian tanks. Again night fell and again the Italians made what was most dangerous of all for so tenuous a trap—strong night attacks by mixed teams of all arms. No less than nine times the Rifle Brigade repelled the enemy, and still they did not give up. At dawn, mustering all the tanks they had got left, about 30, the Italians made a last push to force their way through. This too was held, and at that the entire army surrendered.

It had been that rare thing, the classic armoured pursuit, a battle of annihilation. As O'Connor was later to report: 'I think this may be termed a complete victory as none of the enemy escaped.' No one throughout the years of desert fighting which were to come, not even Rommel, was ever to repeat it. In his message to Wavell on 7 February 1941 O'Connor stuck to the hunting jargon: *Fox killed in the open.* The completeness of the victory was observed by the 1st Battalion of the King's Royal Rifle Corps, who had missed the final phase, but were able to record what the battlefield looked like:

> After we had gone a few miles south . . . we came upon the scene of the campaign's last great battle . . . an imposing mess of shattered Italian tanks, abandoned guns and derelict lorries. There was the familiar sight of hordes of prisoners being rounded up; processions of staff cars, containing General Bergonzoli and his entourage, passed up the road towards Benghazi.

The fruits of victory passed all expectations. In two months two British divisions had advanced 500 miles and had routed an army of ten divisions. In doing so they had suffered about 2,000 casualties, but had captured 130,000 enemy soldiers, nearly 400 tanks and over 800 guns. The Royal Air Force had established mastery of the skies and destroyed about 150 enemy aircraft. But their contribution was not to be measured in numbers of aircraft. They had allowed the tanks and armoured cars of O'Connor's tiny force to outflank the enemy uninterrupted by air attack and to emerge unsuspected behind them.

General O'Connor's own part in it all had been very great. Apart from the tactical success of his early plans to reduce the defences at Sidi Barrani, Bardia and Tobruk, during the pursuit and destruction of the Italian Army, he had displayed just the sort of driving personal leadership at the front that Rommel was to be famous for later. He had the invaluable knack of being where he was most needed at critical moments. He went everywhere over appalling country. He was tireless in maintaining a grip on his small but elusive force. His watchword was offensive action whenever possible. He was always there to make certain that even when the troops were tired out, there was one more effort. He would never allow any relaxation in pressure on the enemy. No wonder the Italians were either paralysed into inactivity or eager only to make good their escape. He kept tight and personal control over the final spearhead across the desert from Tobruk to Beda Fomm by being up at Antelat with the commander of 7th Armoured Division. The Australians got it in a nutshell when one of them said: 'Do you know what we call your general? The little terrier–because he never lets go.' Even after destroying the 10th Italian Army he still did not want to let go, and proposed to Wavell that he be allowed to execute the plan he had already made for an advance to Sirte and Tripoli. In his signal to London of 10 February Wavell backed him as usual, but with reservations:

Extent of Italian defeat at Benghazi makes it seem possible that Tripoli might yield to small force if despatched without undue delay. Am working out commitment involved but hesitate to advance further in view of Balkan situation* unless you think capture of Tripoli might have favourable effect on attitude of French North Africa.

Further advance will also involve naval and air commitments and we are already far stretched. Navy would hate hav-

* German forces destined for Greece began to move through Hungary into Rumania early in January. The attack on Greece was planned for the beginning of April.

ing to feed us at Tripoli and Air Force to protect us. On other
hand possession of this coast might be useful to both.*

Will make plans for capture of Sirte which must be first
step; meanwhile cable me most immediate your views as to
effect on Weygand and war situation generally.

His submission was in vain. The die was already cast. Greece's
acceptance of Britain's offer to aid her had made priorities clear
to Churchill. There was to be no further advance to Tripoli.
Greece was to be 'succoured' and that was the end of it. Dill,
the CIGS, recalls that when he tried to convince the Prime Minister that all the troops in the Middle East were fully committed
and that none could be spared for Greece, Churchill turned on
him, blood rushing to his great neck, eyes darting fury, and began
to talk of Courts Martial and firing squads in Cairo. Dill regrets
not having thought until later of asking Churchill whom he
wanted to shoot.

Even before the redeployment of O'Connor's force had written
finis to any ideas of conquering Tripolitania, Hitler had taken the
steps which would have made the attempt hazardous. The German naval staff's arguments–that Italy's defeat had not simply
removed the threat to Egypt, but had so improved Britain's position in the Eastern Mediterranean that the reinforcement of
Greece would be an easy thing for them–weighed heavily with him.
After Bardia's fall on 5 January, Hitler had made up his mind
that the Italian position in North Africa could not be allowed to
collapse and that North Africa itself, or at least Tripolitania, must
not be lost to the Axis. His Directive No. 22 of 11 January went
further. It laid down not merely that Tripolitania was to be held
and that with this in mind special German forces were to be got
ready to block any further British advance. This was a defensive
precaution. But additionally Fliegerkorps x was to be based in Sicily with a wholly offensive role–to attack British naval forces and
their communications in the Mediterranean (a role their pilots
had been specially trained for); British supply depots and ports in

* It was not long before the strategists in London were directing all their
military and political efforts to the conquest of North Africa.

Cyrenaica and Egypt were also to be attacked. Here was a change
of heart about the war's centre of gravity and the true line of
operations. For if after all the Mediterranean was a theatre where
the British could strike blows at the Axis, as they had so spectacu-
larly demonstrated, it was also one where Hitler, deprived of
strategic decision in the west, and not yet having sought it in the
east, could strike back at the British. Fliegerkorps x's arrival
assisted greatly in making possible the more defensive measures.
Both the Ariete Armoured Division and Trento Motorized Division were to be sent to Tripoli in January and February, whilst
the 5th German Light Motorized Division–strong in anti-tank
guns–would go about the middle of February. By this time the
Luftwaffe had made its presence felt. On 10 and 11 January,
Stukas, in a memorable Mediterranean début, put the aircraft
carrier *Illustrious* out of action and damaged the cruisers *Glouce-
ster* and *Southampton*. Next they concentrated on Malta and
rained heavy blows on it during the next two months. But they
did not finish the job. O'Connor's extraordinary successes in
Cyrenaica drew off part of Fliegerkorps x to North Africa, and
Malta got less attention. The triumph of Beda Fomm, however,
had another effect.

Hitler now decided that the defensive capability of 5th Light
Motorized Division would not be enough and that a complete
Panzer Division, the 15th, should be sent as well so that a properly aggressive policy of defence could be pursued. Here were
the foundations of the Deutsches Afrika Korps, and in February
Lieutenant-General Erwin Rommel was appointed to command
it. Throughout February and March, although Malta's ability to
hit back had not been altogether neutralized, it had been so reduced that there was no interfering with the passage of substantial reinforcements, German and Italian, to North Africa. Supplies and equipment multiplied. 220,000 tons of Axis cargo sailed
across the Mediterranean during these months. Only 20,000 failed
to get to Italian ports. At the same time, when Admiral Cunningham received another aircraft carrier, *Formidable*, on 10 March,
he was able to get a convoy of four ships to Malta without inter-
ruption. Furthermore British reinforcement of Greece was undis-

turbed by the Italian Navy. Even Cunningham's triumph at the battle of Matapan was not conclusive however. Neither side seemed able to wrest mastery of the sea from the other. Yet there was soon to be a demonstration of what air power alone could do, and the British Army and Navy were to know during the campaigns in Greece and Crete the bitterness of fighting without it.

Aid to Greece, of course, meant that O'Connor's corps was dissipated. Churchill's instructions to Eden, whose principal object in going to the Middle East was to provide this aid speedily, identified the central issues:

> What is the minimum garrison that can hold the western frontier of Libya and Benghazi, and what measures should be taken to make Benghazi a principal garrison and air base . . .
>
> The formation in the Delta of the strongest and best-equipped force in divisional or brigade organizations which can be dispatched to Greece at the earliest moment.
>
> The drain to be made upon our resources for the purpose of finishing up in Eritrea and breaking down the Italian positions in Abyssinia. The former is urgent; the later, though desirable, must not conflict with major issues. It may be necessary to leave it to rot by itself . . .
>
> The Foreign Secretary will address himself to the problem of securing the highest form of war economy in the armies and air forces of the Middle East for all the above purposes . . .

There followed further detailed matters into which Eden should look, and his instructions concluded that he was 'to gather together all the threads, and propose continuously the best solution for our difficulties, and not be deterred from acting upon his own authority if the urgency is too great to allow reference home'. In fact Wavell was already gathering the threads together. His reaction to an earlier telegram from London telling him about Eden's mission had been that he must get everything tidied up as soon as possible. The soldier always likes a *tidy* situation. Tidiness is no more than another word for *balance*, a creed which Montgomery later on embraced and voiced so enthusiastically. Wavell's first thoughts were that one division plus an armoured brigade would

be the minimum garrison for Cyrenaica. But the real problem
was which formations to spare for Greece, how to get them there
and supply them, and where the air support was to come from.
By the time Eden arrived in Cairo, Wavell had appointed General
Wilson to run Cyrenaica with headquarters in Benghazi,
transferred O'Connor to Egypt as GOC in C British troops there,
and made up his mind as to what strategic decisions should now
be taken. Whilst he recognized that intervention in the Balkans
was a risky business, both in itself and in denuding Cyrenaica, he
believed that not to do so would jeopardize Britain's position in
the Mediterranean even more–'we are more likely to be playing
the enemy's game by remaining inactive than by taking action in
the Balkans'. The forces at first available for Greece were one
armoured brigade group and the New Zealand Division; later an
Australian division and a Polish brigade; thirdly another Australian
division and a second armoured brigade. To move and support
a force of this size would strain resources to the utmost. Least
satisfactory of all was the shortage of RAF and anti-aircraft units.
But we must follow the fortunes of the Balkan expedition later.

Churchill was never in any doubt that he had been right to go
to Greece. 'I didn't do it simply to save the Greeks. Of course,
honour and all that came in. But I wanted to form a Balkan front.
I wanted Yugoslavia, and I hoped for Turkey. That, with Greece,
would have given us fifty divisions. A nut for the Germans to
crack.' There was nothing unusual about Churchill's having
found himself to be in the right. Wavell's recollections may command
more conviction : 'I am still sure that my instinct, to fight
as far forward as possible in defence of the Middle East, was correct.'
Two questions persist. First, did intervention in the Balkans,
by both diverting attention from Malta *and* prolonging the desert
war, indirectly and ultimately do more damage to the Axis cause
than non-intervention and perseverance with the advance to Tripoli
would have done? Corelli Barnett's answer is uncompromising :

Thus the Greek episode lengthened the campaign in North
Africa by two years–a campaign that sucked in the major

ground efforts of the British Commonwealth, and left the Far East almost undefended against the Japanese.

But, as we have seen, the whole purpose of the Mediterranean strategy was to suck in efforts by the Commonwealth and suck in too efforts by the Axis. It is true that, at the time of intervention in Greece, the British did not know of Germany's intention to attack Russia. Yet without this distraction, is it not likely that a *Barbarossa*, earlier mounted, more strongly supported, more concentrated in shock troops, would have been even more devastating than in fact it was?* Is it not arguable, as indeed it has often been argued, that without the dissipation of German airborne forces in Crete they would have been used to subdue Malta? Is it not certain that the battle for North Africa by virtue of its being protracted, weakened Italy to the point where she wanted only to be rid of her troublesomely steadfast ally and make peace, and at the same time robbed that ally of men and equipment she could ill spare from the Festung Europa? This brings us to the second question. Could Tripolitania have been conquered if, in spite of Greece, the advance after Beda Fomm had been continued?

Rommel thought so. 'If Wavell had now continued his advance into Tripolitania, no resistance worthy of the name could have been mounted against him—so well had his superbly planned offensive succeeded.' O'Connor agreed : 'In my opinion the operation would not only have been possible, but would have had every chance of success provided all three Services gave their maximum support and were not deflected by other commitments.' Leaving aside the rub—the other commitments—there is much to be said for the view that O'Connor could have got to Tripoli. *But could he have stayed there?* Could his corps have been administered, supplied by the Royal Navy, protected by the Royal Air Force, with the Luftwaffe in such strength at Sicily and with Malta at its reduced, albeit defiant, capability? It is to be doubted.

* At the Nuremberg Trials, Jodl. Operations Chief of OKW, stated that Germany had lost the war because she had been obliged to divert divisions to meet the British landing in Greece.

Nothing, however, can take away O'Connor's achievements. Correlli Barnett calls him the *Forgotten Victor* and regrets that his offensive should still be remembered as Wavell's. The truth is that it belonged to them both. Nor is O'Connor forgotten. Nothing can efface his brilliant feats—of preparation, of tactics, of command. He possessed what Professor Marder has reminded us were Nelson's four aces of leadership. He was able to inspire officer and soldier alike; he had creative imagination in planning battles; he could, without forfeiting authority, make use of his subordinates' ideas; above all he was imbued with the offensive spirit.

In all this he resembled Rommel. He had killed his fox in the open. But had O'Connor won the battle for North Africa in February 1941, there might have been no Rommel, or no Desert Fox at least, and no Montgomery, or no Montgomery of Alamein. It hardly bears thinking of. Rommel made one other revealing comment about O'Connor's campaign. 'When, after a great victory which has brought the destruction of the enemy, the pursuit is abandoned on the quartermaster's advice, history almost invariably finds the decision to be wrong and points to the tremendous chances which have been missed.' Rommel was about to win some great victories himself, and he was to find that the quartermaster's voice in the desert was apt to be very persistent and very loud.

4. A different sort of fox

The British were soon to learn—if they did not know it already
—that the means and methods that had done so well against the
Italians were not good enough against the Germans.

Official History

Rommel arrived in Tripoli on 12 February 1941. He was soon to
alarm his enemies and allies alike. There were two main reasons
for Rommel's lightning success in his first African campaign, the
one strategic, the other tactical. In the first place the British miscalculated both the timing and extent of an Axis threat to Cyrenaica and thus the defensive strength required to hold the desert
flank. Secondly, the boldness, energy, tactical skill and implacable
drive of Rommel himself brought a new formula into the game.
Blitzkrieg came to the desert. Wavell's estimate of an infantry
division and an armoured brigade for the defence of Cyrenaica
had been influenced both by his recognition that risks must be
taken somewhere if Greece were to be succoured properly and by
his belief that the Axis would hardly be able to concentrate
enough forces for a counter-offensive there before May, by which
time the British themselves would be stronger, particularly in
tanks out of workshop. The real trouble, however, was that the
troops which were stationed in Cyrenaica were either ill-equipped,
untrained or badly deployed. By the time Rommel was ready to
attack at the end of March, the troops opposite him were dispersed like this: 2nd Armoured Division's Support Group at
Mersa Brega, 3rd Armoured Brigade, with worn out light and
medium tanks plus some captured Italian ones, five miles north-
east, two new brigades of 9th Australian Division east of Benghazi, an Indian motor brigade at Mechili, and a third Australian
brigade in Tobruk. General Neame, who knew nothing of desert
fighting, commanded.

The Afrika Korps contained the German 5th Light Division and the Italian Ariete Armoured Division. 5th Light Division, in spite of its name and lack of desert experience, was powerful. It had strong reconnaissance, artillery and anti-tank units (including 88mm guns), armoured infantry and 5th Panzer Regiment with 70 light tanks and 80 Mark IIIs and IVs. There were also a number of Italian infantry divisions in Tripoli. Even more formidable was the arrival of part of Fliegerkorps X from Sicily. Fifty dive bombers and 20 fighter bombers were under command of General Fröhlich whose task was to destroy the enemy air forces in Cyrenaica and support Rommel's operations.

At this time there was some confusion in the strategic thinking of those responsible for British policy. On the one hand Churchill had made it clear that the primary object of Eden's mission to the Middle East was to send aid to Greece quickly. Eden himself told Smuts: 'I don't think the Germans will do more in Tripoli than make a feint in order to retain our forces in North Africa and prevent their being sent to the Balkans.' In fact on 21 March Rommel was given written instructions that his task was to guarantee the defence of Tripolitania *and to prepare to recapture Cyrenaica*. On the other hand in *The Grand Alliance* Churchill noted that the desert flank was 'the peg on which all else hung' and that there was no question of losing or risking it for the sake of anything that might be done in Greece or elsewhere in the Balkans. Had Wavell been given quite so categoric an order of priorities, it may be doubted whether he would have allowed the situation to develop as it did. As soon as Churchill heard of the German advance to El Agheila on 24 March, he was alarmed and cabled Wavell:

We are naturally concerned at rapid German advance to Agheila. It is their habit to push on whenever they are not resisted. I presume you are only waiting for the tortoise* to stick his head out far enough before chopping it off.

* Tortoise was a poor simile for Rommel. Even fox did not quite get the man. A cross between a rhinoceros and an eagle might have been nearer the mark.

Wavell's reply is significant in three respects. It emphasizes the degree of risk he had taken in order to succour Greece, that is to meet the priorities as they were presented to him; it shows how the pattern of Axis operations was changing the whole strategic balance in the central Mediterranean; and it reveals that Wavell had too many commitments on his hands for the resources at his disposal:

> I have to admit to taking considerable risk in Cyrenaica after capture of Benghazi in order to provide maximum support for Greece...
>
> After we had accepted Greek liability evidence began to accumulate of German reinforcements to Tripoli, which were coupled with attacks on Malta which prevented bombing of Tripoli from there on which I had counted. German air attacks on Benghazi, which prevented supply ships using harbour, also increased our difficulties...
>
> Result is I am weak in Cyrenaica at present and no reinforcements of armoured troops, which are chief requirement, are at present available...
>
> Have just come back from Keren. Capture was very fine achievement by Indian divisions... Platt will push on towards Asmara as quickly as he can, and I have authorised Cunningham to continue towards Addis Ababa from Harrar, which surrendered yesterday.

The battles for East Africa, whilst not properly a part of this story, had great influences on it, and we may perhaps pause a moment to remember them. To have four campaigns on hand at the same time–Cyrenaica, Greece, Eritrea and Somaliland–was a lot for any Commander-in-Chief. Abyssinia had to be conquered quickly in order to get the troops back to North Africa where the threat was potentially and actually so much greater. Moreover the Asmara-Addis Ababa road had urgently to be captured and opened so that troops could then be passed to Egypt via Massawa for Libya and Greece. The battles started in January when General Platt with the 4th and 5th Indian Divisions began to advance from the Sudan into Eritrea. Five days later General Cunning-

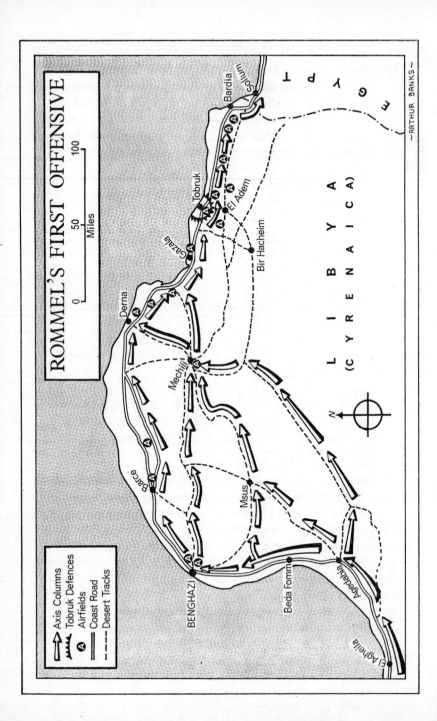

ROMMEL'S FIRST OFFENSIVE

Legend:
- ➤ Axis Columns
- ▲▲▲ Tobruk Defences
- Ⓐ Airfields
- ═══ Coast Road
- ‒ ‒ ‒ Desert Tracks

Scale: 0 50 100 Miles

~ARTHUR BANKS~

EGYPT

LIBYA
(CYRENAICA)

Locations: Sollum, Bardia, Tobruk, El Adem, Gazala, Bir Hacheim, Derna, Mechili, Barce, BENGHAZI, Msus, Beda Fomm, Agedabia, El Agheila

ham with African and South African troops set out on his march
from Kenya. Platt rapidly reached Keren where the most severe
fighting of the whole East African campaign took place.* Late in
March Platt broke the Keren defences and ten days later had
taken both Asmara and Massawa. Cunningham's forces moved
with comparable speed and achieved startling results. He captured Mogadishu together with huge petrol supplies by 25 February, was at Harrar by 25 March, having advanced 1,000 miles in
a month, and then turned on Addis Ababa which fell on 5 April.
The final stage of the campaign was a converging attack, Cunningham from the south, Platt from the north, on Amba Alagi,
where the Duke of Aosta had concentrated what remained of his
armies. On 16 May Aosta surrendered. Wavell's despatch summed the thing up:

> The conquest of Italian East Africa had been accomplished in
> four months, from the end of January to the beginning of June.
> In this period a force of approximately 220,000 men had been
> practically destroyed with the whole of its equipment, and an
> area of nearly a million square miles had been occupied.

The fighting here was very different from the desert. British and
Indian troops had stormed the great mountain barriers at Keren
and Amba Alagi. In parts of Abyssinia the operations had been
largely guerrilla, and their invaluable reward was to tie down
large numbers of Italians who otherwise might have been able to
concentrate against the advancing British columns. These columns
had been as much as 2,000 miles from their bases. It had all been
done with small forces. Yet herein lay the British strength. Dealing
as they were with an enemy who was trying to guard too many
places simultaneously, they were able to cover great distances very
fast and were never burdened with an intolerable supply problem.

* Fighting which was shared by the French Foreign Legion. Members of
4th Indian Division particularly remembered the brave French Commander,
General Montclar, who provided much amusement at conferences because he
was afflicted with hiccoughs. It is diverting to reflect what Montgomery
would have done if, after issuing the 'no coughing' edict, he had been confronted with a hiccoughing French general.

These East African victories spoke loudly for Wavell's strategic and administrative skill, for his planning and direction. Yet they did not alter the fact that in North Africa, because of being generally over-stretched, he was dangerously off balance. Worse, Rommel was aware of it, was convinced that this weakness should be exploited, and was determined to do so off his own bat whatever his masters might say. If the strategic opportunities confronting Rommel were inviting, the tactical ones were nothing short of irresistible. Wavell might have been happy enough to leave things to his subordinate commanders in Abyssinia. He was far from content with what was happening in Cyrenaica. Before sending his signal to Churchill admitting the risks there, he had visited Neame. This meeting on 16 March did nothing to lessen his anxiety. Neame's dispositions were tactically absurd and he was obliged to order changes. The cruiser tanks of 2nd Armoured Division were either in workshops or constantly breaking down. There was no grip, no mobile striking force worth the name, and nothing in reserve to improve the situation. He later gave Neame orders that his task would not be to hold ground, but to keep his forces intact, delay the enemy and inflict losses on them. At about the same time Rommel had been at Hitler's headquarters where he was told that he should not undertake a decisive blow in Africa before 15th Panzer Division reached him in May. But he had already made up his mind about the Agheila attack which so worried Churchill, and was to persist in disregarding the orders he had received. In doing so he instituted a revolution in the nature and conduct of the desert battles.

The history of Rommel's first rush to Tobruk reflects little credit on the British. Rommel, commanding in person right forward in his Storch aircraft, made bold use of his little army, pushing up the coast road with the Brescia Division and across the desert with the Ariete and the German 5th Light Division, driving them on at great speed in widely dispersed small groups of all arms, and then concentrating when it mattered. The German organization, doctrine and training were all peculiarly, indeed purposely, designed for just this sort of circumstance, when grouping and command could be swiftly varied at will. Such an arrangement responded best to the demands and leadership of a Commander who kept himself informed of exactly what was happening at the front and gave orders at once in accordance with a broad tactical aim which was already known and understood by everyone, and this was precisely the sort of commander that Rommel was.

He had more particular tricks up his sleeve. However readily he might brush aside the quartermasters later on, in this his first advance he was conscious enough of the need for fuel *and* the need to deny it to others. Well supported by the Luftwaffe he made a point of destroying British petrol lorries and was assisted by a French motor battalion which set fire to a large fuel dump at Msus when rumour had it that German tanks were approaching. Rumour is dismissed only by reliable information and firm command. And these commodities the British did not have. They suffered then, as so often later in the desert, from a command system which was not just slow in making up its mind what to do, but even slower in giving orders when its mind was made up. There was in this battle no clear tactical aim, and if there had been there were few means of carrying it out. Wavell had told Neame not to hold ground and he certainly obeyed this instruction, for from 4 April onwards the British simply retreated. As for delaying the enemy and inflicting losses, 2nd Armoured Division, short of petrol, harried by enemy aircraft, really contributed nothing to the battle at all, and most of the division, including nearly all the tanks of 3rd Armoured Brigade, was lost. The bulk of the Australian Division, however, succeeded in getting away towards Tobruk which was soon to be reinforced by another brigade. Lack of direction was made final when Neame, during the confused retirement from his headquarters, was captured. O'Connor, who had been sent up by Wavell to advise Neame, was taken too.

How great a contrast we find in Rommel's management of his first great desert battle. He is himself the best illustrator of his own particular methods. On 5 April since it seemed that the British were continuing their withdrawal, he decided to direct his spearheads on Mechili :

At about 1400 hours that afternoon I took off in a Junkers and
flew to Ben Gania. After landing, I heard from the Luftwaffe
that there were no longer any British to be seen in the area of
Mechili and to its south. Schwerin's column thereupon received
the order: 'Mechili clear of enemy. Make for it. Drive fast.
Rommel.' The remainder of our forward troops were also
switched to Mechili. I myself flew off with Aldinger in the
afternoon to take over personal command of the leading units.
Towards evening, we flew back to look for the 5th Light Division columns, which we discovered making good speed to the
north-east. . . . I now sent the Storch back and drove up the
track in my 'Mammoth' to Ben Gania in order to get my own
idea of the difficulty of the march. Two and a half hours later,
completely covered in dust, we reached the airfield where I was
informed that the 5th Light Division had been switched to
Mechili. Shortly afterwards, Lieut. Schulz arrived back from
a reconnaissance flight and reported that Mechili and its sur-
roundings were now held by strong British forces. . . . It was
now night and too late to fly back to Agedabia. In view of the
new and rather less favourable situation, I decided to drive up
to the 5th Light Division and take over command of the operation myself.

Throughout the *Rommel Papers* the man constantly reveals the
way he ran the Afrika Korps and his own insistence on speed and
seeing for himself. There is no time to lose, or the bird will have
flown. It is time to have another look right at the front. Correct
decisions cannot be taken without accurate and timely knowledge
of what is really happening, and so on. General Halder might
later call Rommel 'this soldier gone stark mad', but in two weeks
he had reconquered Cyrenaica, was trying for the first time to
seize Tobruk, and had reached the Egyptian frontier.

What was it like for the British under the impact of this un-
nerving *blitzkrieg*? Roy Farran of the 3rd Hussars recalled his
Colonel's unquenchable spirit and his own unquenchable thirst
at a time when the regiment was unpleasantly positioned near
Msus and had just been dive-bombed:

He was sitting in the top of his Light Tank Mark vib surrounded by the remnants of the regiment. Dour little man that he was with his peaked cap tilted over his eyes, he did not intend to let us share in his depression. The sun was blazing hot and I flopped down on my back in the shadow of his tank while the Squadron Leader discussed the situation. The heat and strain of the march had been most exhausting, especially since we had had no water ration for two days. An impudent little coloured bird hopped on to my chest, but I was too tired to be surprised. A hand stretched down from the turret of the tank, holding a water-bottle. 'Here, Roy, have a drink of this.' Unthinkingly, I took two greedy gulps before I realized what the Colonel had done. There was no more water to be had and yet he, who must have been as thirsty as I was, had given me his last reserve. Such little things lead men to die for one another.

It was while on the march north from Msus that c Squadron of 6th Royal Tank Regiment, like 3rd Hussars part of the unfortunate 3rd Armoured Brigade, had been obliged to abandon its tanks as they ran out of petrol. Its crews then took to lorries and after a series of adventures got back to Tobruk. Sergeant Kennedy has left an account of their escape. Having heard on the bbc that the enemy had reached Derna—where he and his companions were heading—they turned back into the desert.

After a time they again tried to go north, making for the road and a clear run to Tobruk, but as soon as they came in sight of it, enemy vehicles obliged them to sheer off again. It was quite clear that only a bold and long detour into the desert would give them a chance of getting away, so once more they turned south. Even then they would keep bumping into enemy columns and had to take cover in deep wadis for hours on end until it became dark, while the enemy drove by. Forty miles due south by compass and then at last they felt safe to turn eastwards. Sometimes the going was good and they would speed along on hard, level sand, then would come rocky or soft ground which reduced them to a mere crawl. Just as everything seemed to be going really well, two shat-

tering explosions announced that they had run into Italian ther-
mos bombs. The most precious vehicle of all, the water truck, was
blown up.

At this stage they were too tired to care, and slept where they
were. In the morning they were horrified to see enemy trucks
only 500 yards away, but somehow they got out of it, pursued, it
seemed, by German armoured cars, until at last they reached the
outskirts of Tobruk. By this time their petrol was almost finished,
and their hearts sank on observing more armoured cars in front
of them on the El Adem escarpment barring the way to Tobruk.
Determined, however, not to turn back when so near their goal,
they drove headlong at the armoured cars with every weapon they
had at the ready to help them get through. What luck when the
cars turned out to belong to an 11th Hussar patrol. Before long
they were back in their own lines.

In these days, and for the British at almost any time, trained
tank crews were as precious as tanks. 6th Royal Tank Regiment
had plenty of desert fighting still to do. Meanwhile Tobruk had
to be held and another mobile force scratched up to guard the
approaches to Egypt. *Tobruk*–it was to be one of the thorns in
Rommel's side; another was Malta. Each played its part in the
critical battle of supplies; each played its part in wearing down
the Axis strength. The decision to hold, indeed to reinforce,
Tobruk had been Wavell's. It was the one rock in a rapidly worsening Middle Eastern situation. On 6 April Wavell, at a conference in Cairo attended by Eden, Dill and the other two Commanders-in-Chief, had made his intentions clear. Tobruk would
be held as a fortress; he would establish a force on the frontier
ready to interfere with an enemy attempt to take Tobruk; the
defence of Egypt would be rebuilt at Mersa Matruh. On 7 April
Churchill cabled Wavell urging that Tobruk should be held 'to
the death without thought of retirement'. For once the Prime
Minister and his Commander-in-Chief saw eye to eye. That same
day, before he had seen Churchill's cable, Wavell flew to Tobruk
to re-impose the grip which the disappearance of Neame and
O'Connor into captivity had made so necessary. He appointed
General Morshead to command 9th Australian Division in To-

bruk and arranged for more tanks to be sent there by sea. By the time Rommel was ready to attack Tobruk Morshead had six infantry brigades, four artillery regiments, two anti-tank units, 75 anti-aircraft guns and 45 tanks. He was able to repulse all Rommel's attacks. For his part Rommel was beginning to understand that the quartermaster did after all have some say in affairs, that spectacular advances in the desert were usually accompanied by acute logistic problems. What is more, attacking the fixed defences at Tobruk was quite a different thing from rapid, dispersed, encircling movements in the open desert. In his book on Tobruk, Michael Carver draws attention to Rommel's comments after the failure of his assault on the fortress at the end of April. They explain in a few sentences what his battles for North Africa were all about:

> In this assault we lost more than 1,200 men killed, wounded and missing. This shows how sharply the curve of casualties rises when one reverts from mobile to position warfare. In a mobile action, what counts is material, as the essential complement to the soldier. The finest fighting man has no value in mobile warfare without tanks, guns and vehicles. Thus a mobile force can be rendered unfit for action by destruction of its tanks, without having suffered any serious casualties in manpower. This is not the case with position warfare, where the infantryman with rifle and hand grenade has lost little of his value, provided, of course, he is protected by anti-tank guns or obstacles against the enemy's armour. For him enemy number one is the attacking infantryman. Hence position warfare is always a struggle for the destruction of men–in contrast to mobile warfare, where everything turns on the destruction of enemy material.

The importance of Tobruk, quite apart from its value as a 'sally-port', is best understood in relation to the German supply problem. The Axis forces in Libya needed about 50,000 tons of supplies each month. Tripoli was the port to which these supplies would come. Axis shipping could lift only 29,000 tons a month from Italian ports to Tripoli. It followed not only that any attack on Axis communications, land or sea, would pay big dividends. It followed too that Malta's role in doing this assumed even larger proportions than before and that Tobruk's retention by the British was a must. The capture of Tobruk, therefore, a stroke which promised to solve his logistic problems at once, became an obsession with Rommel and monopolized his activities right up until the time of the next great British offensive in November. Meanwhile there were other, unsuccessful attacks by Wavell's forces in the desert, and they were preceded by other, numerous British defeats elsewhere.

During the spring of 1941 the war's centre of gravity lay firmly in the Mediterranean. Amongst the ceaseless minutes and papers which flowed from the Prime Minister's office was a directive dated 14 April on the conduct of the war there. Founded on the need above all else to maintain securely the desert flank, it was primarily concerned with attacking Axis communications between their European ports and Tripoli. It made clear that Cunningham's prime duty was to stop all shipping between Italy and Africa and that the base from which this would be done was Malta. Tobruk was to be defended as strongly as possible. It was as well for the British that this flank of the Middle East did hold fast, for in the centre the Balkan front collapsed almost as soon as it had been established, and the other flank, the northern one, was being threatened for the first time. The battle for Greece began for the British on 8 April and ended with evacuation less than three weeks later. Apart from the hopelessly extended line which General Papagos insisted on trying to hold, the battle was lost because of the overwhelming superiority of German aircraft and tanks and the devastating cooperation between the two. The Royal Navy's evacuation of the army, many of whom went to Crete, was a triumph of organization and defiance in the face of such powerful Axis air forces. During this dismal campaign another, even graver, development nagged at Wavell. Given that the Western Desert was the peg on which everything else hung, he was dangerously short of tanks to be in a position to hold, still less counter-attack, Rommel's forces opposing him. When he heard a report that a German panzer division had landed in

Tripoli, he cabled Dill in London pointing out that if this were so and Rommel could keep his panzers supplied, they would take a lot of stopping. It was then that Churchill showed once more his limitless courage in making decisions at times of crisis. His minute to the Chiefs of Staff began with one of his ringing calls to action :

> The fate of the war in the Middle East, the loss of the Suez Canal, the frustration or confusion of the enormous forces we have built up in Egypt, the closing of all prospects of American cooperation through the Red Sea–all may turn on a few hundred armoured vehicles. They must if possible be carried there at all costs.

The outcome was the *Tiger* convoy which delivered 238 tanks and 43 Hurricanes to Alexandria on 12 May. In spite of the Admiralty's apprehensions Churchill insisted that it should sail through the Mediterranean. His boldness was rewarded. But even whilst cabling Wavell about the despatch of these tanks, he was to give promise of the sort of use he expected them to be put to. 'If this consignment gets through the hazards of the passage . . . no German should remain in Cyrenaica by the end of the month of June.' During naval operations designed to counter the hazards threatening this vital convoy, Admiral Cunningham took the opportunity to re-supply Malta with oil and food; the island also received 15 Beaufighters to assist in providing air cover for the *Tiger* convoy east of Malta. The Royal Navy did more than get Wavell his much needed tanks. In a raid on Benghazi the cruiser *Ajax* and three destroyers had attacked and sunk some enemy ammunition ships. Rommel was already complaining about the gravity of his supply situation. This loss made it worse.

But if the Mediterranean fleet had enjoyed both good fortune and the recompense of daring in protecting their own seaborne traffic and destroying the enemy's, it was now about to suffer grievous losses between 20 and 31 May in the battle for Crete. This was a battle which demonstrated once again–although it was a lesson which the strategists in London seemed reluctant to grasp –that no matter how resolute or skilful troops on the ground or ships at sea might be, and none could have been more so than

General Freyberg's Australian, New Zealand and British soldiers
or the sailors in Admiral Glennie's and Admiral King's destroyers
and cruisers, their operations simply could not prevail against an
enemy air force which enjoyed absolute superiority. Nor had the
Royal Air Force at this time, however willing to comply, mastered
the business of close and rapid cooperation with the army. Yet
losses in Crete, although very great for the British—about 14,000
men, mostly prisoners, out of 32,000 engaged, 17 warships damaged and nine sunk—were not all one sided. The Germans had
suffered 6,000 casualties and General Student's Fliegerkorps xi
no longer existed as a fighting formation. Their airborne invasion,
although novel, had come close to failure, and they never tried it
again. Such near-failure augured well for Malta; and since the
Royal Navy's main task was still to sever sea communications between Italy and Africa and because of their heavy losses in the
Crete evacuations, Malta's role in fulfilling this task was to be
more prominent than ever.

Of all the many strains to which Wavell was subjected, the
worst were perhaps in May 1941. East Africa, although going
well, was not quite over; Crete was lost in ten days' fighting; at
the same time the pro-German Rashid Ali's revolt in Iraq produced yet another commitment; events in Syria led to British invasion and occupation; and throughout, the Prime Minister was
eager to hear what Wavell's plans were for a renewed offensive in
the Western Desert. Interception of a signal sent to Germany by
General Paulus, Hitler's envoy to Rommel, in which it was spelled
out that the Afrika Korps' immediate task was to hold Cyrenaica,
set Churchill off again.

General Paulus' observation of the second battle for Tobruk
did nothing to make him change his mind that the Afrika Korps
was tactically in a bad position and administratively in a worse
one. He recommended that the sea routes to Tripoli and Benghazi should be properly protected, that is to say by the Luftwaffe,
so that urgent needs of petrol, food, ammunition and vehicles
could be met. It was a formidable task. The capacity of the two
ports and their air defence were inadequate, the road from Tripoli
to Tobruk stretched for 1,000 miles, and there were not enough

supply trucks. Halder summed up the situation : 'By over-stepping his orders Rommel has brought about a position for which our present supply capabilities are insufficient.' The quartermaster's voice was growing in volume.

Because of all this Churchill was anxious that Rommel should be harried at Sollum and Tobruk and not left in peace to gather together his fighting and logistic strength for another bound forward. Wavell had already instructed Gott to attack in the Sollum area and had given him what additional tanks he had (the *Tiger* convoy had not arrived at this stage) so that Gott could drive the enemy from Sollum and Capuzzo, savage him as much as possible and exploit towards Tobruk. A successful operation of this sort would be a useful preliminary to the major offensive which Wavell was planning–*Battleaxe*–once he had been able to reconstitute 7th Armoured Division with the tanks from *Tiger*. This preliminary attack, *Brevity,* failed. The plan was for 2nd Royal Tank Regiment with cruiser tanks and some columns of guns and infantry to advance to Sidi Azeiz; for the Guards Brigade and 4th Armoured Brigade with 'I' tanks to clear the top of Halfaya Pass and seize Capuzzo; and for another group to capture the lower Halfaya Pass and Sollum. At first things went quite well. c Squadron, 4th Royal Tank Regiment had a quick success against the Italians at Halfaya.

There were many ways of achieving surprise in the desert, and this time it was done by having no preliminary artillery bombardment. c Squadron reached the enemy position just after first light, perfect shooting conditions. Surprise was complete, and as there were no mines or wire, but only sangars and low stone walls, the tanks were able to get right in amongst the defenders before they could organize resistance properly. Again the Italian gunners fought well, and as the Matilda tanks reared up over the walls, they offered far too attractive and vulnerable a soft under-belly for these gunners. But the all-Italian garrison could not withstand this quickly pressed home attack. Officers in pyjamas, soldiers cooking breakfast were easy meat. The objective was taken, the waiting Scots Guards signalled to follow up, and the top of Halfaya Pass was theirs.

Although Capuzzo was captured a panzer counter-attack under Colonel Herff soon re-took it, whilst Axis resistance at the lower Halfaya Pass was only overcome that first evening. Rommel then reinforced Herff with another panzer battalion, and Gott, concerned about lack of armoured support for his Guards Brigade, withdrew them during the night to Halfaya, leaving 2nd Royal Tank Regiment as covering troops near Sidi Azeiz. Even they retired next day, and *Brevity,* well enough named, had yielded only the capture of Halfaya. Ten days later that too was lost when Herff attacked with 160 tanks. Wavell's first attempt to regain the initiative from Rommel thus ended miserably–a poor omen for the next one which could not now be long delayed as the tanks from *Tiger* were in 7th Armoured Division's hands, and Churchill was pressing again. On the day after *Brevity* was called off he wanted to know when the 'Tiger Cubs' were to be brought into action.

There were urgent strategic reasons for doing so. On 28 May the Chiefs of Staff signalled their instructions to Wavell. German possession of Crete had enabled the Axis to open sea communications with Cyrenaica via western Greece. This route must be interfered with. To do this, to help Malta and to go on attacking the Tripoli route, airfields in Eastern Cyrenaica must be recaptured. Therefore the enemy in the Western Desert must be brought to battle and destroyed. The Chiefs of Staff seemed to have got their priorities right at last. But all this was easily said. There were two drawbacks to doing it. To start with Wavell did not have enough time to make the best use of the resources he had; furthermore the resources themselves were insufficient. It was no use attacking Rommel's Afrika Korps with only two armoured brigades, not matter how much infantry was available. Within a week of taking over command from Wavell, Auchinleck was to state that at least two, preferably three, armoured *divisions* were wanted for the kind of offensive Churchill had in mind, and he did not eventually mount it, despite all the prodding, until November 1941.

Meanwhile preparation for *Battleaxe* went ahead. General Beresford-Peirse's plan was that 4th Indian Division (back from

East Africa) with 4th Armoured Brigade would destroy the enemy in the Bardia-Sollum-Halfaya-Capuzzo area whilst 7th Armoured Division would guard the flank and help 4th Indian Division in dispatching the enemy. Later 7th Armoured Division reinforced with 4th Armoured Brigade would attempt to draw the enemy panzers into a decisive battle. Beresford-Peirse's headquarters was to be at Sidi Barrani–*sixty miles* as the crow flies from the front. Conditioned principally by the time it was taking to re-equip 7th Armoured Division, the attack was to be launched on 15 June, and this date allowed but five days' training beforehand. Maximum air support was to be provided and the Royal Navy would continue to supply Tobruk. It all sounded hopeful. But the Afrika Korps was well disposed to accept an attack. Rommel was expecting one. His defensive arrangements were strong. He had about 200 tanks and was about to show for the first time how effectively they could be employed in a defensive battle in close cooperation with anti-tank guns. One of his armoured formations, 15th Panzer Division, was in the frontier area and the other, 5th Light Division, was in reserve near Tobruk.

Unlike *Brevity, Battleaxe* achieved no surprise. 4th Indian Division was held up on the coast and 88mm guns took heavy toll of both 4th Armoured Brigade's Matildas and 7th Armoured Brigade's cruisers. c Squadron, 4th Royal Tank Regiment, who had started off so well in *Brevity,* soon found that 'the means and methods that had done so well against the Italians were not good enough against the Germans'. The regiment's Commanding Officer, O'Carroll, recalled the destruction of c Squadron.

It could not have been pleasant for him to hear the squadron leader reporting by radio that his tanks were being torn to pieces, and to be powerless to help. The squadron leader himself was soon killed. Well sited, defiladed and concealed 88mm and 105mm guns tucked amongst the sangars, so that their barrels were just clearing the tops, were not what they had been used to at all. Matildas, which previously had enjoyed if not immunity, at least some protection from Italian guns, were simply ripped apart. But the squadron fought on. It fought until all the Matildas but one had been knocked out. This survivor together with a

light tank then withdrew to join the 2nd Camerons who had
been compelled to take refuge in the folds running down from
the top of an escarpment.

The way in which the Camerons had got there illustrates in
how desperate a plight infantry found themselves when deprived
of proper tank or anti-tank support.

They were not easily dismayed. Their reaction to the brewing
up of eleven out of the twelve accompanying tanks was simply to
deploy more widely and go on advancing, ignoring the burning
wrecks all around them. The battalion actually reached its objective and began to reorganize there, but when a complete company of German panzers suddenly appeared and charged straight
at them, there was little they could do except fight on with their
few anti-tank guns. Those Highlanders not killed in the onslaught
made their way back to the wadis behind them and found some
respite from the panzers. Infantry without tanks or *enough* anti-
tank guns simply could not hang on to an objective, even when
captured, if subjected in turn to an armoured counter-attack.

Having held the British attack on 15 June, Rommel began his
counter-strokes the next morning. 15th Panzer Division was the
first to attack, but it made little real progress at Capuzzo where
it was up against 4th Armoured Brigade. 5th Light Division,
however, which was engaging 7th Armoured Brigade between
Sidi Azeiz and Sidi Suleiman, was more successful and fought its
way through to a position north-east of Sidi Omar so that it was
able to continue moving on Suleiman. Rommel was quick to reinforce success. 'This was the turning point of the battle. I immediately ordered the 15th Panzer Division to disengage all its
mobile forces as quickly as possible and, leaving only the essential
minimum to hold the position north of Capuzzo, to go forward
on the northern flank of the victorious 5th Light Division towards
Sidi Suleiman. The decisive moment had come. It is often possible to decide the issue of a battle merely by making an unexpected shift of one's main weight.' This was certainly one way to
get and keep the initiative as Montgomery was later to demonstrate so relentlessly to Rommel. Another was speed, and Rommel, appreciating that the main British effort was about to be

made in the Capuzzo area, got his blow in first, that is very early the next morning, which he believed would be earlier than his enemy's attack. He was right, and the fighting on 17 June resolved the battle's outcome. 'This operation', Rommel wrote, 'had obviously taken the British completely by surprise. In wireless messages which we intercepted they described their position as very serious. The commander of 7th Armoured Division sent a request to the Commander-in-Chief of the desert force to come to his headquarters. It sounded suspiciously as though the British commander no longer felt himself capable of handling the situation.' Rommel also recorded the joy which the Afrika Korps felt in their victory. He considered that stubbornness of defence, sensible grouping and proper use of what mobile forces he possessed were what had enabled him to get the better of larger numbers of tanks. He predicted an even bigger beating for the enemy next time.

5th Light Division's sweep round to the flank and rear of 7th Armoured Division gave the 11th Hussars some uncomfortable moments. One troop leader remembers being shelled whilst observing the battle, shells which followed him as he circumspectly moved further away. Watching an encounter between two mixed groups, he was invited by a tank squadron commander to go forward and have a look for anti-tank guns—not the sort of employment relished by armoured car soldiers interested in living. Nevertheless, when joined by two artillery Forward Observation Officers, who, he noted, were as always totally fearless and who were able to give him some covering fire, forward he went, only to drive straight into the path of about fifty enemy panzers. When he stopped to have a closer look through his binoculars, the shells began to get uncomfortably close, and his driver took a hand in the affair. Trying to get the armoured car into gear without declutching properly, he started, the troop leader says, 'with a jerk which almost broke my neck'.

Even though the troop leader's neck was not broken, the momentum of *Battleaxe* was. Western Desert Force had lost about 1,000 men and nearly 100 tanks. German casualties were fewer —700 men and only 12 tanks destroyed. The Royal Air Force lost some 40 aircraft. What were the causes of failure? Firstly the whole operation had been mounted too quickly. Tank crews had too little time for learning to handle their new tanks, none to practise brigade or divisional operations. And then the two armoured brigades, respectively equipped with cruiser and Infantry tanks, were quite unsuited to fight in support of each other–the one fast with good range, the other slow and restricted to 40 miles radius of action. The Jock columns, which had proved so effective against the Italians, simply did not work against the Germans. What is more the tanks and infantry had not trained together. Worst of all perhaps, the battle commander positioned himself so far back that he was unable properly to coordinate the activities of his two divisions and was so inexperienced in armoured warfare that he did not understand its nomenclature. Brigadier Gatehouse, commanding 4th Armoured Brigade, has told the sorry story about his argument with Beresford-Peirse as to the real meaning of a 'forward rally' for tanks. It is, of course, a place *behind* an objective which tanks and infantry have seized together, to which tanks rally once the infantry are firmly dug in with their anti-tank guns and other supporting weapons. But Beresford-Peirse took it to be an area *in front* of the captured positions, and by insisting that tanks rallied there, exposed them unnecessarily to· enemy anti-tank fire and useless losses. Such amateurism would not do against the professional touch of the Afrika Korps.

There was another serious misunderstanding by the British–about the way the Germans handled their armoured formations. Rommel's panzer groups were quite clear that whereas tanks dealt primarily with the enemy's infantry and soft vehicles, the destruction of tanks was mainly the job of weapons designed for just this purpose, anti-tank guns. This theory was put into practice, and the German 88mm and 50mm anti-tank guns were both powerful in themselves and skilfully manned, but not at the expense of a further fundamental feature of German tactical doctrine–close and permanent integration of tank, gun and infantry teams. In this first requisite of desert, or any other, fighting, the British simply did not match their opponents. Even between the tanks of the two adversaries there were perilous discrepancies in performance. The British 2pr tank gun was no equal to the German 50mm mounted in the Pzkw. III or the 75mm in the Pzkw. IV. Moreover the Afrika Korps had developed a quick, efficient drill for recovering damaged tanks, even under fire, from the battlefield, and Western Desert Force had not.

Battleaxe's failure was a severe blow to Churchill, who had placed such high hopes on his 'Tiger Cubs' and when he heard about it, he wandered disconsolately about the Chartwell valley. The reverse determined him in making the change in Commanders-in-Chief that he had been contemplating for the last month. His cable to Wavell began :

> I have come to the conclusion that public interest will best be served by appointment of General Auchinleck to relieve you in command of Armies of Middle East.

Wavell's reply was characteristic of his generous nature :

> I think you are wise to make change and get new ideas and action on the many problems in Middle East and am sure Auchinleck will be successful choice.

It looked as if Churchill was going to make things easier for Wavell's successor. Oliver Lyttelton became Minister of State, Middle East to deal with political matters, and General Haining, as Intendant-General, was to be responsible for logistics. But none of this could take from Wavell his achievements. Rommel not only thought of him as the one British general in the Middle East who 'showed a touch of genius'. Even after his own triumph in defeating *Battleaxe,* he declared :

> Wavell's strategic planning of the offensive had been excellent. What distinguished him from other British army commanders was his great and well-balanced strategic courage, which permitted him to concentrate his forces regardless of his opponent's possible moves. He knew very well the necessity of avoiding any operation which would enable his opponent to fight on interior lines and destroy his formations one by one with loc-

ally superior concentrations. But he was put at a great disadvantage by the slow speed of his heavy infantry tanks, which
prevented him from reacting quickly enough to the moves of
our faster vehicles.

Such a tribute from the General who had brought a new dimen-
sion to the battle for North Africa and who was to continue to do
so almost until the end, was worth having. There is another which
we will do well to recall. Bernard Fergusson, who served Wavell
so often and so loyally, remembered that at one of his chief's
most difficult moments during the evacuation of Crete, he was
'grim but superb. He seemed quite unruffled, and no more shaken
by these shocking adversities than he had been tempted to maf-
fick during his victories a few weeks earlier.' In short, he treated
those two impostors just the same. In 1939 Fergusson had written of Wavell: 'I believe he is a potential Marlborough, and that
if the chance ever comes his way he will be one of the great commanders of history. He is the only soldier I've ever met of whom
I think that.'

Fergusson's prediction came true. Wavell *was* one of the great
commanders of history, and perhaps his principal misfortune was
that, whilst he was engaged in being a potential Marlborough, he
was serving a man who, family connection aside, thought of himself as an actual one.

5. Crusader

The Honeys did something that tanks don't do in the desert any more. They charged. It was novel, reckless, unexpected, impetuous and terrific.

Alan Moorehead

If there was one thing which the three successive Commanders-in-Chief, Wavell, Auchinleck and Alexander, had in common, it was the misfortune of receiving telegrams from the Prime Minister urging, indeed often requiring, them to attack prematurely. We have seen that in the case of *Battleaxe* hasty preparation, inadequate training, inferior tank performance and the old bogy, which seemed always to dog British operations in the desert, inability to concentrate the armour and integrate it with other arms–these shortcomings added up to failure. The price of failure was not high in numbers, nor was it strategically as grave as it might have been. For in June 1941 Germany had turned away from the Mediterranean. By intervening there earlier that year Hitler had achieved his immediate aim. Italy was still fighting and British forces had been removed from Greece and Crete. His southern flank was tolerably secure so that the *Wehrmacht* could concentrate every fibre on the *Drang nach Osten*. Hitler's decision to invade Russia and win there the decisive objective which had eluded him in the West–this re-orientation of Axis strategy clearly had a major influence on Great Britain's intentions and capabilities. As was customary with a Minister of Defence who had such a passionate grip of detail, combined with a determination that British arms should not stand idle whilst an ally was in distress, these intentions were exhaustively and urgently made known to the Commander-in-Chief in a series of eloquent, closely-reasoned telegrams. Capabilities received shorter shrift. Another common feature of these communications, no matter to whom they were addressed, was that in the end everything boiled down to a question of timing. In July 1941 timing was subject to a myriad of influences. *Barbarossa* had seen to it that the bulk of German resources were drawn away from the Mediterranean. Not only did this mean that the Axis forces in Libya did not receive the material needed to resume the offensive; it meant too that the British were slowly able to strengthen their air forces and armies. On the other hand rapid German success in Russia could remove these advantages at a single stroke, and threaten the British position in the Middle East more seriously than at any time since the war had begun.

For Auchinleck, the pressure was not applied all at once. Churchill's first telegram, dated 1 July 1941, departed so far from character as to suggest to Auchinleck that it was for *him* to decide whether and when to renew the offensive. Nothing could have been further from the Prime Minister's real purpose. In his reply Auchinleck stressed what he regarded as the three prerequisites of a successful attack in the Western Desert—first the security of his base, which included consolidating Syria; secondly air and sea forces of sufficient strength closely cooperating with the Army.; thirdly strong and properly trained armoured units. He concluded that at least two, preferably three armoured divisions and a motor division were needed. As he had but one armoured division at this time, and even this one was neither fully equipped nor trained, all these arguments spelled delay. Furthermore by foreshadowing the deliberate nature of effecting the enemy's complete elimination from North Africa, he made clear where the real difference of opinion about timing was founded. Auchinleck and his colleagues wanted to take the offensive and be sure of winning.* To the Defence Committee in London, and this meant to Churchill himself, there were political and military reasons which made early action in itself more important than later and assured success. The Russians could neither be allowed to win, nor to lose,

---

* Some of Auchinleck's conditions, such as the need for a 50 per cent reserve of tanks, exasperated Churchill. 'This was an almost prohibitive condition', he later wrote. 'Generals only enjoy such comforts in Heaven. And those who demand them do not always get there.'

without the British being engaged; very few German reinforcements were thought to be reaching Libya, and if, therefore, the
West Cyrenaican airfields could quickly be recaptured and used,
this reinforcement might dry up altogether; besides, there was
the unending problem of supplying Malta so that it could further
savage the enemy sea communications.

What is more the Defence Committee regarded September as
the earliest month that a German threat to Syria, Palestine and
Iraq could develop from the north; until that time the British
should enjoy superiority in the air. They further promoted their
contention that September might be the best month for attacking
by arguing that Tobruk, always a thorn in Rommel's side and
always difficult to supply, should be able to support an offensive
most strongly up until then. Auchinleck was not convinced by
these urgent proddings. He was determined that *Battleaxe* should
not be repeated, and he resolutely set his face against what he
looked on as an unreasonable risk. No land offensive, he and his
colleagues signalled on 23 July, was possible in September. But,
the signal went on to say :

> Provided (i) you send us 150 cruisers by mid-September; (ii)
> we still retain air superiority; (iii) enemy land forces are not
> seriously reinforced in the meantime; (iv) a serious enemy
> offensive is not threatened against Syria; we should be able to
> undertake limited offensive to relieve Tobruk in November
> with one armoured division, one armoured brigade group and
> one army tank brigade.

If, however, with the same circumstances prevailing, 150 extra
American tanks were forthcoming by mid-September, together
with trained crews, lorried and air transport, then a decisive
operation to recapture Cyrenaica might be mounted by 15 November. From this initial exchange of telegrams grew the purposes,
promises and at length disappointments and recriminations of
Crusader. But Churchill was not satisfied with the delays which
acceptance of Auchinleck's views imposed until he had had the
opportunity of subjecting him to all the authority of his own per-
sonality. Even this did not move Auchinleck, and the confronta-

tion's result was that November was agreed as the date for the offensive. Thus far, Auchinleck had won the overriding condition he wanted–time. On it depended his other requirements, reinforcement, security and preparation. If for Churchill, raging with impatience, time trotted–and he later recorded his conviction that the 'four and a half months' delay in engaging the enemy in the Desert was alike a mistake and a misfortune'–for Auchinleck, and the battle commander he chose to execute his plans, Cunningham, it galloped.

The problem facing both Rommel and Auchinleck in the summer of 1941 was a recurring one which vexed all desert commanders. Who could reinforce and re-equip faster and therefore be ready to attack first? As so often before and after, the balance was a nice one. Rommel, obsessed with the elimination of Tobruk, was in the event ready to assault it in November, the very month in which his opponent set out to relieve it. Indeed just as Malta was the key to the control of sea communications, so at this time was Tobruk the key to freedom of manoeuvre in the desert. It tied down four Italian divisions and three German battalions, and allowed the British to make their preparations without being interfered with in the frontier area. Even more important the battle of communications was at this period being won by the British. In August the Axis lost 35 per cent of supplies and reinforcements despatched by sea to North Africa, in October 63 per cent. Had this not been so, the progress and outcome of *Crusader* could have been very different. Auchinleck enjoyed another advantage denied to Wavell. The formation in September 1941 of East African Command directly responsible to the War Office relieved him of this distraction, and in the previous month Cunningham had arrived from his triumphs there to take command of the newly formed 8th Army.

8th Army had two corps–13th Corps of 4th Indian Division, the New Zealand Division and a tank brigade; 30th Corps with 7th Armoured Division, 4th Armoured Brigade, 1st South African Division and a Guards Brigade. Tobruk was garrisoned by 70th Division and a tank brigade. There was also an Army reserve of a division and a brigade group. Although each corps con-

tained both infantry and tanks, Cunningham did not think of
their separate activities as complementing each other to form a
single whole. He regarded the first essentially as an infantry corps,
the second as an armoured corps which would operate by itself.
Absolutely from the outset, therefore, Cunningham saw the offensive not as one battle, but as two—the first a decisive tank action
by 30th Corps, which by swinging round to the south of the frontier defences and occupying first the area of Gabr Saleh, then the
critically important escarpment at Sidi Rezegh, would draw Rommel's armour forward to its destruction; the second a primarily
infantry operation against the Axis frontier defences and those
round Tobruk.

The enemy dispositions into which this concept of Cunningham's fitted were: 15th and 21st Panzer Divisions on the coast
east of Tobruk; 90th Light and an Italian division holding the
frontier; four Italian divisions and one German investing Tobruk; the Ariete at Bir el Gubi and another Italian division at Bir
Hacheim. In total numbers of tanks which each side could muster, the British had a superiority. But it was not numbers which
necessarily counted. What did count was their quality, tactical
handling and standard of crew training. The inferiority of the
British Crusader tanks' 2pr* gun to the German 50mm and
75mm has been thoroughly examined and explained.† It was not,
of course, the gun alone which told. It was the gun-armour combination; in other words if your combination of fire power and
protection was such that you could penetrate your enemy's armour
from a range at which he was unable to penetrate yours, your
advantage was alike clear and overwhelming. This was broadly
the advantage which the German panzers enjoyed. But in addition to this, their tactical skill in coordinating the fire power of
tanks and anti-tank guns was not simply greater than the British.
Whereas it was fundamental to their method of fighting, the
British virtually relied on their tanks alone. And the deadly effectiveness of the 88mm and 50mm anti-tank guns needs no empha-

* The American Stuart or Honey tank, of course, mounted a 37mm gun
not a 2pr, but their performance was similar.
† See, for example, *Official History*, Vol. III, p. 27.

sis here. As for training, despite all Churchill's grumbling about delay, Cunningham, who established his headquarters in the desert in September 1941, had but two months to formulate a plan of battle, complete the re-equipping of his armoured formations, and train. His preparations, as we have seen, were based on the operations of two separate groups, an infantry one and an armoured one. The Germans preferred a system of mixed groups.

It is necessary to reiterate here that close and permanent integration of all arms together with concentration of armour were fundamental requirements for success in the desert fighting. In Cunningham's broad plan the first of these had given way to the stronger claims of the other. Yet even during the detailed planning stages, the weakness of subordinating this first requirement produced much apprehension, and efforts to correct this weakness began to undermine the integrity of the second requirement. For the commander of 13th Corps, concerned about his southern flank, insisted so successfully on a degree of protection there that one of 30th Corps' armoured brigades was detailed for the task. Two prime principles of war, singleness of aim, concentration of force, were already, even before the battle had started, being compromised. When it did start, they were to be almost abandoned. But the 8th Army's hopes and spirits were high. This was to be the biggest desert offensive so far. O'Connor had had but one corps. *Battleaxe* deployed only two divisions. *Crusader,* however, with two corps in the front line, the Tobruk garrison and a substantial reserve was a different thing altogether, and would demand different handling. Cunningham's principal object was to destroy the enemy's armoured forces, and when this had been done, he would relieve Tobruk, whose garrison would sally out to assist in defeating the enemy more generally, and clear them out of Cyrenaica. What might not then follow? Churchill was already building his hopes even higher.

He was looking for a victory so decisive that Rommel would be driven right out of Libya and into Tripolitania. A triumph of that sort, he believed, might bring about a change of heart in Tunis, Algeria and Morocco, even in Vichy itself. Whilst conceding that it was no more than a 'hope built upon a hope', he was already toying with the idea of employing four British divisions then in the United Kingdom, which together with appropriate naval forces might, he hoped, descend on some Western Mediterranean objective such as Sicily. Thus would the Second Front become a reality.

The key to it all he saw as the destruction of Rommel and his 'small, audacious army'. Why, with Tripoli in our hands and the German air force busy in Russia, should not eighty thousand British soldiers land on and conquer Sicily? Where else could the Empire engage the Germans on a proper scale? What other scheme would present us with so promising a variety of options? But Churchill admitted that all turned on Auchinleck's offensive and its success, on which he pinned so many of his hopes.

To Rommel the situation appeared far less promising. He had failed to take Tobruk, yet many of his troops were tied up in its siege. His supplies were uncertain. His dispositions had little depth, and might easily be encircled by superior forces. General Bayerlein, the Afrika Korps' Chief of Staff, recalled that Rommel expected the British to take advantage of the tactical opportunities thus presented to them. Tobruk, therefore, had to be taken before they could do so. They had to be forestalled. But in attacking Tobruk there was always the danger of a British force appearing at his back. Therefore the bulk of his mobile forces had to be deployed between Capuzzo and Bir el Gubi. Rommel believed that because a German thrust through the Caucasus would impose so great a threat to their position, the British would be reluctant to take away from Egypt all those forces needed to guarantee success in the Western Desert. He judged that by November they might risk it. In September therefore the Germans strengthened their positions for assaulting Tobruk. But certain drawbacks persisted. If the reinforcements of men, weapons and supplies necessary for this assault were to be forthcoming, Italian shipments across the Mediterranean would have to increase. As usual the Axis High Command's promises were not fulfilled. 'By the end of September,' Bayerlein said, 'only a third of the troops and a seventh of the supplies which we needed had arrived. This was a terrible handicap in our race for time with the British.'

When we remember that the Axis losses at sea in October 1941 reached the astonishing figure of 63 per cent and also that Cunningham did not reach the desert until September, we see how strong the arguments of Auchinleck and his colleagues for not attacking before November really were. What is much more puzzling is that, in spite of Rommel's having calculated that November was a likely month for the British to launch their offensive, he was still not ready to believe that it had started when it did. If there were another principle of combat which might be said to match those of single purpose and concentrated effort, it was surprise; and surprise Cunningham achieved to the full. But he was unable to exploit it. Indeed the extent of surprise was such that it actually detracted from the success of Cunningham's enterprise, for his adversary was not at first convinced that what had taken place was taking place, and so failed to react in the way that Cunningham had expected and hoped. It is a curious fact that neither offensive of the winter of 1941–42, the first Auchinleck's, the second Rommel's, was to begin with taken seriously by the other side. But whereas Rommel's initial refusal to countenance *Crusader* as more than a reconnaissance in force might almost be construed as Socratic irony, the second instance, as we shall later see, inveigled a riposte from which there was to be no quick recover.

The outline of what happened in *Crusader* is, in spite of its complexity, quickly told. It is the way in which things happened, and why, which mainly concern us here. There were broadly four parts to the battle. First on 18 November the British armour advanced and by nightfall three armoured brigades were in position –7th to the north of Gabr Saleh, 22nd to the west, and 4th to the south-east. On the following day 7th Armoured Brigade and 7th Support Group reached Sidi Rezegh, whilst 22nd Armoured Brigade went off to engage the Italians at Bir el Gubi, and 4th Armoured Brigade were in action east of Gabr Saleh. Already the central theme of Cunningham's plan–to take on the German Panzers on ground of his own choosing with the bulk of his own armour–had fallen apart. There followed a series of tank battles near Sidi Rezegh in which both sides suffered heavy losses. On balance, by virtue of their excellent recovery arrangements, the Germans had the better of it. Next came Rommel's dash to the frontier with the Afrika Korps, a gamble certainly, and one which might have come off had Auchinleck not taken a personal grip of the battle, stood fast, and persuaded Rommel that he must return to his supplies between Tobruk and Bardia. The third phase saw Sidi Rezegh again exchange hands with severe encounters between the Germans and New Zealanders. Lastly, Rommel, seeing that he could no longer relieve his Bardia and Halfaya garrisons, which later fell, cut his losses and withdrew to Agheila, not, however, before inflicting further damage on the British armour. *Crusader* cost the Axis about 38,000 killed, wounded and missing; the British losses were some 18,000. Thus the battle, which realized many of its aims, must be counted a British victory. Yet there were times when for the men who fought it, this result was very much in doubt.

On 20 November, Robert Crisp, who commanded a troop in the 3rd Royal Tank Regiment, part of 4th Armoured Brigade, was understandably puzzled. Although their advance seemed to have gone according to plan, the Germans had not reacted as they should have done, and the great battle of annihilating the enemy panzers had not come about. But already he had heard disquieting stories about the effectiveness of German 88mm guns and their Mark III and Mark IV Panzers against the new Honey tanks with which his regiment was equipped. Alan Moorehead observed the first clash.

It began with a gun duel, not gun against gun, but gun against tank. Dust and smoke filled the battlefield and looked like a curtain going up to the sky. Then the tanks closed to a range at which they began to take each other on. It was the first time that the new Stuart tanks, the Honeys, light, fast, with square turrets and 37mm guns, had been in action. How would they do? Moorehead describes how the brigade commander, Gatehouse, sat on the top of his tank, watching the battle develop, judging which ground was to be made use of, how the sun's position would affect things, what the relative strengths were. Having made his mind up, he gave his orders over the radio, and it was

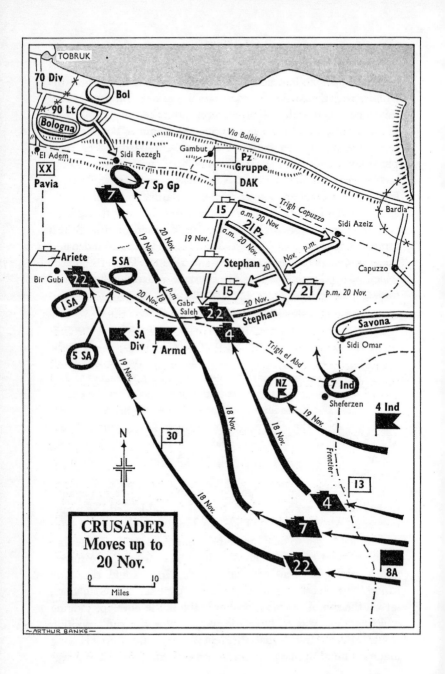

TOBRUK

70 Div

Bol

90 Lt

Bologna

Via Balbia

El Adem · Sidi Rezegh   Gambut   Pz

XX   Gruppe

Pavia   7   7 Sp Gp   DAK

                                    Trigh Capuzzo

Ariete   15   a.m. 20 Nov.   Sidi Azeiz

Bir Gubi   5 SA   19 Nov.   21 Pz

22   a.m. 20 Nov.

1 SA   20 Nov.   Stephan   20   Nov. p.m.   Capuzzo

        p.m Gabr   15   21   p.m. 20 Nov.

5 SA   Saleh   22

            I   20 Nov.   Stephan

            SA   7 Armd   4   Savona

            Div   Trigh el Abd   Sidi Omar

                        NZ   7 Ind   4 Ind

            19 Nov.   Sheferzen

N   30   19 Nov.

                18 Nov.   18 Nov.   Frontier

                            4   13

            18 Nov.   7

CRUSADER   22   8A

Moves up to

20 Nov.

0   10

Miles

~ARTHUR BANKS~

then that the Honeys charged, something as Moorehead pointed
out, that tanks did not do much of after that. But it was no good
being conventional when you knew that you were out-gunned and
out-ranged. Something different was indispensable. The Honey
had one trump up its sleeve. It was agile. Charging at speeds of
forty miles an hour and more, it was an elusive target. Even so to
go within a few hundred yards of the German Mark IIIs and IVs
with their 50mm and 75mm guns was courageous indeed. It
could not be done with impunity.

This action had been fought by the 8th Hussars, one of the
other regiments in 4th Armoured Brigade. But why had it been
fought in this way, which seemed, all the courage and dash notwithstanding, utterly reckless? The answer, of course, was that
the Honey tanks were at so serious a disadvantage because of
their inferior gun-armour combination that, unless they were to
refuse battle altogether, they had to seek protection through speed,
and by jinking fast towards the enemy, get close enough for their
own guns to take effect. They had done so and had knocked out
many enemy tanks, but not without heavy loss to themselves. All
this, Crisp had heard about. Now it was to be the turn of his own
regiment.

We were startled into reality by a frantic call for help from 'B'
Squadron, who screamed that they were being attacked by
over 100 tanks. The desert air was suddenly full of high ex-
plosive and the terrifying swish of armour-piercing shells. Coming in from the west very fast, with the sun behind them shining straight into our gunners' eyes, were scores of the dark,
ominous shapes of German panzers. Going even faster a few
hundred yards ahead of them were 'B' Squadron's Honeys
with half a dozen soft-skinned vehicles.

They came hurtling back through 'A' Squadron, whose commander started yelling into his microphone: 'Halt! Halt! the
lot of you. Turn round and fight, you yellow bastards. I'll
shoot the next tank I see moving back.'

As that rush came abreast of me and the firing began to get

personal, it was desperately hard not to turn round and join
in it. I decided not to. At the same time I didn't particularly
want to die at that moment. Movement was the obvious answer, but movement in a direction which would not be described as running away. I could see the panzers clearly now,
coming down a broad depression in line abreast, 40 to 60 of
them, easy enough to exaggerate into a hundred and more. On
my left was a low ridge, the southern edge of the depression,
and I made for this flat out with my troop conforming, in the
hope of getting on the flank of the advancing juggernauts and
getting out of the direct line of fire.

Once over the ridge I turned back along the crest to see what
was happening, and whether it would be possible to do any
damage. The enemy onslaught was losing some of its impetus,
owing to lack of opposition, and with darkness falling fast the
Germans could not have claimed a great deal of success—although it must have given them a good deal of self-satisfaction.
I noticed that two other Honeys had joined my troop, and I
led them in a wary circle to try and come up behind some of
flank Mark ivs.

Crisp goes on to explain how, catching a glimpse of what he took
to be some enemy armoured cars, much more agreeable assailants
than Mark iv panzers, he went off to investigate, intending to
bring his other tanks forward later. Having positively identified
the armoured cars as German, he was on the point of getting his
troop to engage them when he found himself right in the path of
five Honeys hurtling towards him. Too late to avoid a collision
altogether, he did what he could to moderate its consequences.
Even so his tank became badly entangled with another. When the
other's commander appeared from the turret, Crisp found himself
gazing at his own squadron leader.* The enemy cars got away,
and a somewhat depleted and perplexed regiment began to

* The desert is not always as empty as it seems. I recall colliding with
another tank whilst training in the desert in 1943. My squadron leader
gesticulated bitterly at the miles of emptiness and asked if there were not
enough room.

leaguer† for the night. Crisp and his men had lots of questions
to ask themselves. What was happening? Was this the main battle
or not? Who was winning? But no one knew the answers.

This lack of certainty was to persist. The confused nature of
the armoured battles near Sidi Rezegh and the day to day existence of the tank crews who waged them—these are again best
conveyed by Crisp. Four days later he tells us:

From that moment on I can truthfully say that none of us had
more than the vaguest idea where we were from day to day
and hour to hour, or what was happening either to our own
forces or the enemy's. The campaign swung violently from one
end of the desert to the other. One morning we would be south-
west of Sidi Rezegh; the next afternoon we would be well east
of the point at which we had spent the first night after crossing
The Wire. That I had actually seen the rooftops of Bardia that
second afternoon was an unbelievable dream, part of another
unreal existence. There was no such thing as advance and retreat. We roared off to areas of threat or engagement depend-
ing on the urgency of the information. We chased mirages and
were chased by mirages. Every few hours a landmark or a name
would punch our memories with an elusive familiarity, and we
would recall a forgotten early incident or a battle fought there
days before that was now part of a past so near in time but so
distant in event.

We went without sleep, without food, without washing or
change of clothes, without conversation beyond the clipped talk
of wireless procedure and orders. In permanent need of everything civilized, we snatched greedily at everything we could
find, getting neither enjoyment nor nourishment.

The daily formula was nearly always the same—up at any
time between midnight and 4 o'clock; movement out of the
leaguer into battle positions before first light; a biscuit and a
spoonful of marmalade before the flap of orders and information; the long day of movement and vigil and encounter, death

† Tanks would 'leaguer' or 'laager' at night, in other words make camp
for rest, replenishment and protection.

and the fear of death, until darkness put a limit to vision and purpose on both sides; the drawing in of far-flung formations; the final endurance of the black, close-linked march to the leaguer area; the maintenance and replenishment and order groups that lasted till midnight; the beginning of another 24 hours.

However little some British tank crews may have thought of the 2pr gun and their own artillery compared with that of the Germans, it was not a view always shared by the Germans themselves. On 23 November when Crüwell directed the Afrika Korps against 5th South African Brigade, which, supported by 22nd Armoured Brigade, was holding the ridge south of Sidi Rezegh, they were welcomed with the sort of reception which not only paid tribute to the quality of British guns and the staunchness of their handlers; it showed also that when soundly positioned and controlled, the 8th Army's tanks, infantry and artillery could work together as a team with the best of them. If only the other magic ingredient, concentration, had been present, how different might the Sidi Rezegh struggle have been. Bayerlein described the action in memorable terms :

> Guns of all kinds and sizes laid a curtain of fire in front of the attacking tanks and there seemed almost no hope of making any progress in the face of this fire-spewing barrier. Tank after tank split open in the hail of shells. Our entire artillery had to be thrown in to silence the enemy guns one by one. However, by the late afternoon we had managed to punch a few holes in the front. The tank attack moved forward again and tank duels of tremendous intensity developed deep in the battlefield. In fluctuating fighting, tank against tank, tank against gun or anti-tank nest, sometimes in frontal, sometimes in flanking assault, using every trick of mobile warfare and tank tactics, the enemy was finally forced back into a confined area.

This was the battle of annihilation all right. There was only one thing wrong with it. It was the British who were being annihilated. Each armoured brigade fought with great gallantry and skill, but they always seemed to fight alone. It was as well for the

8th Army that on 24 November Rommel, believing 30th Corps to have suffered even more severely than it had, decided to make his dash to the frontier. Von Mellenthin was deeply critical of this move. He pointed out that the Afrika Korps gained no decisive results at the frontier, but simply frittered away its strength still further whilst giving to the British the opportunity and time to recover tanks, receive reinforcements and reconstitute their armoured brigades. Furthermore, although Rommel's advance had put paid to Cunningham's belief in his ability to persevere with the offensive, this very circumstance had led to his removal and replacement* by the sanguine Ritchie, who, like the old Duke, saw good in everything. Von Mellenthin also observed that the 'Royal Air Force dominated the battlefield', but this did not prevent Rommel's leading the Afrika Korps back and renewing the fight for Sidi Rezegh. If it were difficult for the British armoured brigades to deal with closely cooperating teams of panzers, guns and infantry, how much more so was it for a New Zealand battalion which had only nine officers and 286 men with four 2pr anti-tank guns, when it was attacked at Belhamed on 1 December by forty-eight tanks and several hundred motorized infantry of 15th Panzer Division. Sergeant Macdonald described alike his suprise and chagrin at being obliged to surrender. His battalion was in high spirits, and like all troops who have confidence in their weapons and their leaders, the men were positively looking forward to an enemy attack so that they could chop them up.

When at dawn the battalion was alerted to be ready for an attack by enemy tanks, Macdonald noted that visibility was very poor—not more than 500 yards. But this did not prevent three enemy panzers closing to within 400 yards and firing at the position on Macdonald's flank. He could not understand why his own artillery was not shooting back, and he had nothing to hit them

---

* Robert Crisp recorded: 'General Cunningham had been relieved of his command of the Eighth Army, and had been replaced by General Ritchie. This was a shock to all of us, but not really a surprise. Even right down at the bottom of the ladder, it was impossible not to be aware of the absence of firm direction and purpose from above. Everybody welcomed the change as the beginning of an era of greater decisiveness. Nobody had ever heard of Ritchie.'

with himself. But when German anti-tank guns towed by trucks came into view, he and his platoon opened up quickly enough, and helped to put two big guns out of action by machine-gunning the crews. This was more like it, and they had more successful shoots at motor-cycle and lorried infantry.

But when nine tanks and their supporting weapons turned on his battalion, it was a different story. He suddenly saw during a lull in the battle that some of the men on his left, only a few hundred yards away, were on their feet with hands up. What had happened? His own platoon was still firing at the enemy and getting plenty back. Tanks closed in on them firing their main guns and machine guns. Still Macdonald held on, until one of his own officers shouted to him to put his hands up. Still he could not see why, but a glance to the left told him. Three German tanks were right amongst them. 'Surrendering,' he wrote, 'was something I had never considered possible and yet here it was.'

What is to be made of this jumble of impressions? One point which emerges time after time when examining the way in which British generals conducted their battles is that they almost always did it from the rear. During the crisis at Sidi Rezegh on 22 and 23 November, Rommel was frequently in the battle area, conferring with Crüwell, Commander of the Afrika Korps, or his Panzer Divisional generals; he was never further away than Panzergruppe Headquarters at El Adem. Cunningham was 80 miles from Sidi Rezegh at Fort Maddalena. Later, of course, Rommel put himself at the head of the Afrika Korps and swept to the frontier. This habit of commanding from the front may have led him and his headquarters into difficulties, but at least he never found himself in Cunningham's uncomfortable situation–ignorant of what was really happening and unable to influence events in an immediate, and thus decisive, way. This reluctance to command from a position where the battle's pulse could be frequently and accurately taken was to persist. Auchinleck, it is true, in the great moments of crisis during the winter battles, flew to the front to grip his subordinates, and later on positioned himself at Ritchie's headquarters to give advice as required–an arrangement on which even the impassive *Official History* allows itself to speculate whether advice of this sort did not amount to orders. In the summer of 1942 Auchinleck took over command of 8th Army and placed his austere headquarters in the front line. Yet even these occasions were temporary and at times when the battle was largely static. The idea of having a truly mobile command post for fighting which was after all essentially mobile does not seem to have occurred to them. Even Montgomery, who certainly was not one to relax his grip on events, would retire to his caravan leaving instructions that he was not to be disturbed. This was no way to take tides at the flood. In *Crusader,* whereas Rommel tried to *exercise command throughout the battle,* Cunningham, having made a plan and having launched his army to carry it out, sat back and awaited events. He knew as well as Rommel that no plan survives contact with the enemy, but his plan hardly survived *no* contact with the enemy. Instead of being able to influence events, he allowed events to engulf himself. Circumstances altered so rapidly that only those commanders who were well forward knew of them in time to act upon them appropriately, and in the event appropriately commonly meant concentrating the armour against the enemy's.

What was true at Army and Panzergruppe level seemed to be reflected lower down. Brigadiers like Gatehouse, Kippenberger and Campbell had firm enough control of their own bits of the battle, but unlike 15th and 21st Panzer Divisions, their formations did not seem to be fought as divisions in the way that Cunningham had intended. Nor was this because divisional and corps commanders were not well up in the front. Gott, of 7th Armoured Division, and Norrie, commanding 30th Corps, were very much to the fore. Yet all their efforts to concentrate 4th, 7th and 22nd Armoured Brigades at Sidi Rezegh were frustrated by the almost uncanny instinct shown by Rommel and Crüwell in coordinating their efforts and producing superior strength where it mattered. Crüwell himself was always aiming to integrate the activities of his two Panzer Divisions, and frequently succeeded in doing so.

Further down in the actual regiments and squadrons, the problems which faced the British were easier to understand. We have seen how an inferior gun-armour combination led Gatehouse to

employ his Honeys in the only way which enabled him to bring
fire close enough to the German tanks for it to be effective. It was
to be quite different when the Grants and Shermans with their
75mm guns came along. But the losses sustained during the first
week of *Crusader* were so serious that they afflicted Cunningham,
who up to this time had had no experience of armoured battles,
to the point where he could think only in terms of abandoning
the offensive and withdrawing. The truth was that tanks by themselves, however boldly and skilfully used, could not successfully
combat integrated teams of panzers, anti-tank guns, artillery,
motorized infantry, and tank recovery crews. The reason for Rommel's eventual withdrawal was not his inability to take on roughly
equal numbers of British tanks. It was partly that, whilst Auchinleck was able to reinforce strongly and go on reinforcing, he was
not; then, as von Mellenthin had noted, the RAF dominated the
battle area.

Dominant though the RAF may have been, however, and better
than ever the support which they gave to the soldiers, their use
too underlined the British failure fully to integrate their various
forces into one irresistible whole. Alexander Clifford makes the
point that although the RAF achieved air superiority over the
battlefield, in itself no mean undertaking, it 'did not really know
what to do with it'. New problems of cooperation between the
two elements had received short shrift. It was not merely that new
techniques to solve the business of communications, recognition
and calling for support at the front had not been properly developed. The RAF at this stage were unwilling to recognize that
there was even a need to do so. Their belief in their own integrity
was understandable enough. They had no wish to be subordin-
ated to the land battle. But it was a wholly unrealistic view. The
soldiers rightly saw that the air force was so essentially part of the
ground fighting that it had to be drawn closely into it, and so be
able to provide support which would be fast, accurate and intimate.

There was still a long way to go before the technique was perfected, and, as we shall see, there were new methods of using air
power against ground troops to be developed which would have

major influence on battles still to come. Nevertheless, 8th Army had enjoyed the sort of air support it had never had before, not only in the destruction of enemy weapons and convoys, but also in not being interfered with by the Luftwaffe. If army-air force cooperation was necessary, how much more so was integration within the army. It was to be many months before Montgomery would say of Alam el Halfa that it was to be an 'Army battle', but it was just this sort of control which was missing in *Crusader*. It was one thing to invite tanks to seize an objective. Sidi Rezegh had been seized by 7th Armoured Division quickly enough. It was quite another proposition to hold it, beat off audacious, co-ordinated enemy attacks and in doing so, destroy his armour. For this you needed artillery and infantry *and* the air force as well, all working as one. During *Crusader* 8th Army lost Sidi Rezegh not once, but twice. Destruction of Rommel's Panzer Divisions had been Cunningham's principal objective, and the basic plan of taking a piece of ground so important that he would have to try and get it back was a sound one. What was not sound was that the resources for guaranteeing, as far as anything in war can be guaranteed, the accomplishment of this central object, on which everything else depended, were neither made available nor correctly manipulated.

Battles rarely go as expected, and *Crusader* certainly had not. Yet many of its aims had been realized. Above all Cyrenaica had been retaken. The struggle had been so long and costly, however, that Churchill's hopes for its exploitation were to be disappointed. Perhaps two lessons stand out more than any others. One was that the British had still not mastered the handling of large forces in mobile operations. It was not surprising. They had never done it before. The battle had been a story of gallant piecemeal actions, which was turned from being a failure by Auchinleck's steadfastness. Attrition obliged Rommel to abandon the field. This intervention by Auchinleck emphasizes the second lesson. Command arrangements did not yet seem to be right either in mechanics or personalities. It had still to be shown whether in the next round with Rommel these two shortcomings would be amended. There would not be long to wait for the Winter Battle was not yet over.

6. History repeats itself

The third part of an army must be destroyed, before a good one can be made out of it.

Halifax

At the close of *Crusader* in January 1942 Auchinleck might have been excused for harbouring some satisfaction with its results. It is true that he had been obliged to dismiss one Army Commander and appoint another, whom he regarded, with all the comfort which this entailed, as a protégé of his own. It is true that the 8th Army had suffered heavy losses and was administratively at the limit of its resources. It is true that his plan to destroy the German Panzer force by drawing it on to important, strongly defended ground and his own concentrated armour had not been fulfilled. But he had relieved Tobruk; he had inflicted a defeat upon Rommel; he had reconquered Cyrenaica; and he had made plans—Operation *Acrobat*—to chase the enemy into Tripolitania. Yet within a month, history, the sort that had engulfed the granite-like Wavell, was to repeat itself. Rommel was once more to be within striking distance of Tobruk, and in strategic circumstances which made this repetition far more dangerous than before.

We have seen that, if there were a constant agent at work throughout the desert fighting, it was that of unity in the operation of land, sea and air forces. Their activities were consistently interdependent. In his account of the struggle for the Mediterranean, Donald Macintyre has shown that the key to the battle of supplies was the tiny fortress of Malta; offensive operations by sea and air launched from Malta were able at times to keep the Axis forces in North Africa short of the indispensable sinews of war, and so make it possible for the armoured and infantry divisions of 8th Army to go forward, capture airfields closer to Malta, bring air support to the convoys and thus sharpen Malta's sting. The suppression of Malta, therefore, became for the Axis a matter of great moment. German naval and air reinforcements would then swing the Mediterranean pendulum once more in their favour; Axis blows at the island would multiply; its inability to strike back would allow the Afrika Korps to receive the vehicles, petrol, ammunition and men it so badly needed, and then at the very time when the retention of desert airfields became critical for Malta's survival, the 8th Army would be faced with an enemy adequately supplied and powerfully supported. The dilemma was a simple one. Oversimplified, it was that the British had to keep Malta in order to allow the 8th Army to advance, whilst the 8th Army was compelled to advance if the British were to keep Malta.

There was, of course, a subordinate, but not a less perseverant, agent working in partnership with this joint company charged with winning the battle of resources. It was one equally aggravated by operations in the desert. One side or the other was necessarily closer to its main base; its opponent, therefore, would be at the end of long lines of communication. The first was strong in logistics, strong in air support, strong in balance and strong in offensive capability. The second was likely to be weak in all four. At the end of *Crusader* there was no doubt as to the respective positions in which the two armies stood.

Between January and June of 1942 the desert war, so like an occasionally interrupted game of battledore and shuttlecock, was to reach a previously unknown pitch of speed and violence. For the second time Rommel had the battledore firmly in his hand. 8th Army was the shuttlecock. The reasons for so unenviable a state of affairs were not hard to find. They were broadly twofold. First, and perhaps of most immediate importance, was the situation in the air and at sea. As early as December the balance of air and sea power was moving steadily to the advantage of the Axis. Six months before, Hitler's Directive No. 32, which predicted the outcome of a successful campaign against Russia, had outlined a strategy of strangling the British position in the Middle East by converging attacks from Libya, Bulgaria and Transcaucasia. But Russian resistance and British moves in Syria and Iraq

modified these grandiose ideas and lent weight to von Brauch-
itsch's contention that operations in the Mediterranean itself and
in the Libyan desert should be more closely coordinated as part
of the same problem. This was precisely the view of Rommel and
of Mussolini, and its implementation led to the despatch of no
less than ten U-boats to the Mediterranean between September
and November 1941, whilst in the following month Fliegerkorps
II was transferred from Russia to Sicily. On 28 November Field
Marshal Kesselring reached Rome, charged amongst other tasks
with establishing mastery of the sea and air between southern
Italy and North Africa so that the Axis lines of communication
to Libya would be secured, the British ones with Tobruk and
Malta severed, and Malta itself neutralized. At last it appeared
that the Germans had hit on the very formula which would win
the battle for Egypt. It remained to be seen whether they could
apply it.

At first they had startling successes. In November a U-boat
had sunk *Ark Royal,* the lone aircraft carrier which had enabled
Force 'H' at Gibraltar to bring succour to Malta and for which
there was no replacement. Later that month the battleship *Bar-
ham* was torpedoed and disintegrated. Worse was to come. In
December Force 'K' from Malta, whilst engaged in trying to in-
tercept and destroy an Italian convoy to Tripoli, had run into a
minefield and suffered heavy losses—one cruiser and one destroyer
sunk, two cruisers damaged. Meanwhile three chariots of the 10th
Italian Light Flotilla had in a most daring action severely damaged Admiral Cunningham's two remaining battleships, *Valiant*
and *Queen Elizabeth* at Alexandria. Yet in spite of these grievous
blows, convoys were run from Alexandria to Malta during January 1942. This was possible only because the airfields of Western
Cyrenaica were in British hands so that together with the Hurricanes based at Malta itself, fighter cover could be provided for
the convoys throughout their passage. But although the British
might be able to keep Malta alive, they could not in the face of
heavy attacks upon the island sustain its offensive capability.
They could not, in short, prevent Rommel from being similarly
reinforced, and in that same month of January he received large

quantities of fuel, other supplies of all kinds, no fewer than 55 new tanks with their crews, 20 armoured cars and some anti-tank guns. It was this timely addition to Rommel's strength which made him determine on a spoiling attack whose spectacular success surpassed even his own ebullient expectations. But before we follow the course of this dynamic, we must turn to the second reason for the 8th Army's being less than balanced.

On 8 December 1941, whilst *Crusader* was still in progress, the whole course of the war was altered by the Japanese attacks at Pearl Harbor and Malaya. Britain and the United States at once became allies against Japan and within a few days allies against Germany and Italy. Later that month the first joint designs of this new alliance began to be formed when Churchill and his advisers went to Washington with a memorandum on allied Grand Strategy in their pockets. Whereas the new world might ultimately redress the balance of the old, Japan's entry into the war dangerously and immediately stretched British resources to a degree not previously known or even contemplated. Just as the costly diversion of Greece had written finis to O'Connor's plan for ending the North African campaign in 1941, so the reinforcements desperately required for the Far East stifled any idea that Auchinleck could attack Rommel at El Agheila and push on to Tripoli and victory. Moreover this time there was not to be the consoling reflection that Greece's tragedy had been Malta's reprieve. Malta was to suffer as never before.

Meanwhile the practical effects of war in the Far East were prodigious for the Commanders-in-Chief, Middle East. Of reinforcement on their way to Iraq or Egypt, four fighter squadrons, an anti-tank regiment, four anti-aircraft regiments, and one complete division, the 18th, were swiftly diverted. Also, although General Auchinleck might use 50th Division then in Iraq as he wished, the 17th Division in India, formerly earmarked for Iraq, was now to be exclusively at the disposal of the Commander-in-Chief, India. Not to receive expected reinforcements was one thing. To be obliged to give up what was already there was far more serious. Six RAF bomber squadrons were to be despatched as soon as *Crusader* ended; in fact the first squadron left in Dec-

ember. At least 100 American tanks were demanded, and Auchinleck generously sent 110 manned by 7th Armoured Brigade.
Four more divisions were to be either removed or not forthcoming–the 6th and 7th Australian Divisions and two others from
Iraq and India. While all these reductions in Auchinleck's army
were being made, he and his colleagues were invited to confirm
that the exploitation of *Crusader* would not be affected. This
they did, and there were some grounds for doing so, since the
tangible losses of troops were from Iraq and Persia, not from the
Western Desert. But when Middle East representatives in London
alleged that the withdrawals would not affect *Acrobat* either,
they miscalculated in two respects, first the extent of 8th Army's
over-stretch, secondly the extent of Rommel's reinforcement. The
naval withdrawals were less grave in themselves as they were
mainly small ships from the Red Sea and the Persian Gulf. What
was far more critical was that the Mediterranean Fleet's losses in
battleships and aircraft carriers would not now be made good.

Thus in December 1941 and January 1942 we are confronted
with a contradiction. At the very time when in Washington the
Combined Chiefs of Staff were endorsing a memorandum which
defined the principal features of Allied strategy, and included
statements that Japan would be denied the means to wage war
while the Allies concentrated on the defeat of Germany, and that
in pursuance of this primary object the ring would be tightened
round Germany by sustaining the Russian front, building up
strength in the Middle East and gaining possession of the whole
North African coast–whilst this blueprint for the future conduct
of the war was emerging, for General Auchinleck and the other
Commanders-in-Chief with him, the resources needed to fulfil
the blueprint's first priority were slipping from their grasp. What
is more their charter and responsibilities were being enlarged. It
will be recalled that command of land forces in Iraq passed from
the Commander-in-Chief, Middle East back to his opposite number in India in June 1941. It had always been the Chiefs' of Staff
intention to revert to their previous arrangement if there were
danger of a German attack through Persia and Iraq, a danger
which had been present ever since the German advance into

Russia had started. Now in January 1942 with this threat from the north being diminished by the Russian army and the Russian winter, with General Wavell in India looking firmly eastwards, and with General Auchinleck, never one to eschew responsibility, eager to accept a reorganization which in his view would simplify planning and coordination, the change took place.

Of much more immediate concern to Auchinleck was the tactical situation in the Western Desert. What were the relative prospects of the two armies facing each other in the middle of January? They do much to explain Rommel's striking success. On the British side the Army, which still seemed not to have absorbed the principle of concentration, was spread out between El Agheila and Tobruk, its commanders, Ritchie and behind him Auchinleck, preoccupied with chimerical plans for an advance into Tripolitania, refusing to credit reports of Rommel's growing strength, their minds untuned to the likelihood of an enemy attack. The untried and, as far as the desert went, untrained 1st Armoured Division with only one of its armoured brigades totalling 150 tanks (the other one, 22nd Armoured Brigade, had been exhausted during the *Crusader* battles and was refitting) was widely dispersed in the forward area. 4th Indian Division had one brigade at Benghazi and another at Barce, whilst 7th Armoured Division was far away at Tobruk resting and re-equipping. General Messervy, commanding 1st Armoured Division, had been ordered to reconnoitre and harass the enemy preparatory to the next offensive, *Acrobat*, whilst being ready to fight a defensive battle *should the unexpected happen*. But the truth was that he had neither the means nor the dispositions to do so. There were no prepared defences. His forward troops, 200th Guards Brigade and 1st Support Group, were weakly deployed over a frontage of thirty miles between Mersa Brega and Wadi Faregh. The tanks of 2nd Armoured Brigade were as far back as Antelat trying to do some desert training with inadequate supplies of petrol. Indeed the whole administrative situation was precarious. 250 tons per day too little was reaching the forward troops for daily maintenance alone. Such a shortage did not mean only that an offensive could not be renewed. It meant that the dispositions for meeting an Axis

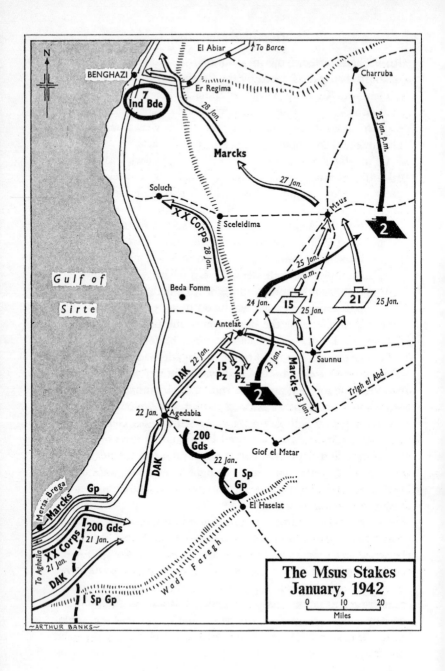

The Msus Stakes
January, 1942

0   10   20
Miles

attack, instead of being determined by tactical requirements, were dictated by the distance from the railhead at Misheifa. The drawbacks of the British might therefore be summarized like this–intelligence was inaccurate, supplies uncertain, training inadequate and adaptability non-existent.

'Look here upon this picture and on this.' How different did the prospect seem through Rommel's eyes. His intelligence staffs not only assessed correctly that during the latter half of January the forces under his command would be more powerful than those immediately opposed to him, but they also gave him the assurance that his opponents' logistic difficulties made them unready for action. Furthermore the Axis air situation was more favourable than it had been for months. Rommel was not a commander who needed nudging into decisive activity. He was above all else an opportunist. And whilst materially his superiority, even locally, over Ritchie's forces might have been marginal, in terms of his own tactical adroitness, his troops' skill and the boldness with which he used them, it was overwhelming. On 18 January he issued his orders for a limited operation. The Afrika Korps was to advance across the desert with its right flank on the Wadi Faregh; 20 (Italian) Corps would attack centrally; on the Via Balbia was a specially constituted group under Colonel Marcks containing units of 21st Panzer Division and 90th Light Division. Subsequent moves would await events. The plan, simple and adaptable, was typical of Rommel who, like Nelson, did not believe in looking too far ahead but in bringing about a pell-mell battle. It was to pay unlooked-for dividends.

For most battles, pursuit is an epilogue; for this one it was the prologue. 1st Armoured Division was simply pushed aside. That it escaped at all was brought about less by its own skill (its courage was not in question) than by a German staff error in orders for encirclement. It was too much to expect that the inexperienced regiments of 2nd Armoured Brigade would be a match for veterans of the Afrika Korps. Heinz Schmidt has explained the Panzer tactics and why they succeeded, particularly against untried troops :

We had our first skirmish with British tanks on the second day of the march [22 January] ... We sighted about thirty tanks stationary at the foot of a rise in hilly ground. When we received the order to attack, we were certain we had not yet been observed. We brought our 50mm anti-tank guns into position in a hollow. The enemy was totally surprised when we opened fire, and a dozen Panzers raced down against the tanks. He decided his position was untenable and pulled out hurriedly with the loss of a few tanks.

We had now developed a new method of attack. With our twelve anti-tank guns we leap-frogged from one vantage-point to another, while our Panzers, stationary and hull-down, if possible, provided protective fire. Then we would establish ourselves to give them protective fire while they swept on again. The tactics worked well and, despite the liveliness of the fire, the enemy's tanks were not able to hold up our advance. He steadily sustained losses and had to give ground constantly. We could not help feeling that we were not then up against the tough and experienced opponents who had harried us so hard on the Trigh Capuzzo ...

We were not entirely happy about our petrol position. Yet one young officer, who said to Rommel, 'Herr General, we need more fuel', received the brisk answer : 'Well, go and get it from the British.'

This close cooperation between tanks and anti-tank artillery was a technique which at that time the British did not seem to take seriously or train in, let alone master or practise in battle. Small wonder that two days after his advance had begun, Rommel had reached Msus. Von Mellenthin has memorably described the result of these whirlwind Panzer tactics–'the pursuit attained a speed of fifteen miles an hour and the British fled madly over the desert in one of the most extraordinary routs of the war'.

General Ritchie, who had judged the Axis advance to be a reconnaissance in force, had neither the practice nor indeed the sources of reliable, timely information to be able to think and act at Rommel's speed. It was not that he was hustled into faulty moves, but rather that he refused to countenance the realities of the *blitzkrieg*. Stubborn optimism might be all very well during a crisis of position warfare when nerve above all else was required; it was dangerous miscalculation when the initiative had been wholly surrendered. The commander of 13th Corps, General Godwin-Austen, reading the battle correctly, wished to withdraw from what seemed to him to be rapidly closing jaws of a pair of pincers. He might have persuaded Ritchie to have allowed him to do so in time had it not been for Rommel's next move in which he feinted towards Mechili, causing the remnants of 1st Armoured Division to follow eastwards, and then, putting himself at the head of Marcks' battle group, pounced north to the coast cutting off 7th Indian Infantry Brigade at Benghazi. The rest of 4th Indian Infantry Division had been ordered to stand on a line in the Djebel Akhdar east of Barce, and it was here that these fine soldiers, veterans of O'Connor's lightning campaign, of Abyssinia, *Battleaxe* and *Crusader*, took part in some of the most exciting encounters of what was in fact a series of encounter battles. Sergeant Grey, DCM, MM, of the Camerons recorded an action at el-Faida against a body of German lorried infantry:

About 1530 they arrived. An armoured car and a tank, followed by lorries came streaming over the top. Twenty Kittyhawks paid no attention and cruised above us, as if on a Bank Holiday. The lorries stopped on the top and the tank and armoured cars came on, watched breathlessly by everyone, until they got neatly picked off by an anti-tank gun as they came round the last corner—nicely within Bren range. The crews only ran a yard or two! Then the party started. The Germans deployed well out of range, got their mortars, machine-guns and a battery going, and rushed stuff over and into our hill without stopping. Meanwhile one could see the infantry dodging about in the bushes on the hillside. Things looked ugly, as presumably we were on a last-man-last-round racket, and it was going to be a night party. No wire and 500 yards to each platoon front.

But as dusk fell word came to thin out at 1915 hours and

leave by 1930 hours—a big relief as there seemed to be a lot of
Germans. By 1930 hours it was dark and I went out to bring
in one of the forward sections. I went off down the hill and
saw some people coming my way. So I shouted 'Is that Mc-
Kay's section?' 'Yes!' came the answer. So I went on to tell
them to sit on top of the hill. When I came nearer I felt that
something was wrong. Something was! A large German jumped out from behind a bush and pinned me before I could think.
Then a German and an Italian officer came running up, took
my rifle and equipment off me, stuck automatics in my stomach
and back, while the Italian, speaking perfect English, said
'Lead us to your comrades; tell them to surrender and you will
be well treated.' I feigned sickness and stupidity and asked for
water, but got kicked in the stomach by the German. There
seemed no alternative, so I pointed to my left and the German
ordered his platoon to go off in that direction, presumably to
do a flanking movement. I started off up the hill, with the
officers on either side, and stumbling in the dark managed to
bring my platoon well on to my flank. Then I aimed for their
position, which I could just distinguish in the dark. I heard a
Jock say 'Here the b——s come.' Then the Italian said 'Shout
to them to surrender!' So I shouted 'McGeough, McGeough!'
(I knew he was a good shot), got within ten yards of them,
shouted 'Shoot!' and fell flat. The boys shot and got the German in the head and the Italian in the stomach. Grand! So off
I ran and rejoined the platoon. By then we were long past our
withdrawal time; so back we went, and after a bit of bayonet
work by the rear platoon, jumped into lorries and drove off
with the Germans lining the road behind us, popping at us at
pointblank range.

When we left Faida we reckoned that by tea-time tomorrow
we would be busy again.

7th Brigade's subsequent break-out from the trap at Benghazi
was no less breathtaking. Even brigade headquarters was in the
thick of it. After leaving Solluch they were obliged to negotiate
fifteen miles of desert which would be alive with enemy. But when

motoring across the desert it was not uncommon to be within easy range of an *enemy* convoy, and yet not see it. Or even if it were seen it was by no means certain that it could be identified. Each side had captured the other's vehicles. Mere proximity often led to the assumption that there was nothing to fear. 7 Brigade Headquarters passed uncomfortably close to a large German convoy escorted by panzers and then through the midst of some halted enemy transport.

There were vehicles in front of them, vehicles to the left of them, vehicles to the right of them. It might almost have been the Valley of Death. This brigadier, unlike Cardigan, grew circumspect. With an eye on both the enemy vehicles and the Axis aircraft overhead, he chose a moment to move forward when least attention would be focused on themselves. Yet as they edged onwards, a motor-cyclist appeared 200 yards away and four tanks halted nearby and started doing maintenance—an ugly sight for soft-skinned lorries. A big gun on tow even stopped to allow their own column to pass just in front of it, the German driver seeming quite unconcerned.

In one of the Brigade Headquarters trucks were five German prisoners. Indian cavalry troopers were ready to bash in their heads if they made a move or yelled out to their tantalizingly near comrades. One actually looked like doing so, but was quickly restrained by his own fellow prisoners. In spite of all these hazards, they got through.

It was the conduct of British and Indian troops during this break-out which did much to redeem the otherwise sorry story of the retreat to Gazala. Audacious ventures with a fair chance of success were the best prescriptions for rousing the best in their spirit and conduct. It confirmed Hobbes' sagacious pronouncement that in war force and fraud are the two cardinal virtues. General Auchinleck, like Wavell a soldiers' soldier, recognized this too when he later commented to 7 Brigade : 'You got through because you were bold. Always be bold.'

On 6 February 8th Army was back on the Gazala–Bir Hacheim line, that is the same line which almost two months earlier the Panzerarmee had abandoned. 8th Army had lost some 70 tanks, 40 guns and 1,400 men. But they had lost much more than this. Where now were the grateful fruits of *Crusader*–the airfields of Western Cyrenaica, the tactical initiative, the promise of *Acrobat* and a successful conclusion of the campaign? Gone! One of the most interesting aspects of this reverse is the wholly different reading of events taken on the one hand by the high command, Ritchie and Auchinleck, and on the other by the actual battle commanders, Godwin-Austen of 13th Corps and his two divisional generals, Messervy and Tuker. It was not difficult to understand, even sympathize with, the robust and sanguine views of the former. The prize offered by *Acrobat*, with its potential effect on French North Africa, was so great, and bearing in mind the setbacks in Russia and the Far East, so necessary. Less easy to comprehend was the failure to take account of the lesson which Rommel had rubbed home a year earlier–that not to have a firm defensible base with appropriate resources and dispositions, and to spread divisions and brigades about with no very clear idea as to how they might be concentrated to support each other–that to make this sort of tactical error was to invite defeat in detail.*

And then the advice of the battle commanders was so very definite. Even before Rommel attacked, Messervy had misgivings about the extent of enemy reinforcements. But his warnings were not heeded. 'General Headquarters,' he said, 'wouldn't believe there were large German tank reinforcements–which infuriated the forward troops who had actually seen them. That was why we were on the wrong foot when he advanced.' During the battle itself there was a tendency at 8th Army Headquarters to fall into the pit of self-deception, a fault which in Napoleon, Marmont had described as that of 'making pictures', and not to accept the real situation. Messervy has also explained how hard it was for him to convince Ritchie that his division had been badly knocked about. 'When I reported the state of 1st Armoured Division to him at a time when he was planning to use it for counter-attack, he flew to see me and almost took the view that I was being subversive.' Tuker, commanding 4th Indian Division, was no less definite as to what went wrong:

* How different it was to be at Alam el Halfa and Medenine.

The reason why Rommel was successful against 13 Corps was because when he counter-attacked from Agheila, 13 Corps was spread out from the sea right round to the south of Agheila in small groups of columns ... The result was that 2 Armoured Brigade, Guards Brigade and Support Group were beaten in detail ... 1 Armoured Division was attacked without a shot being fired by 4 Indian Division and 4 Indian Division was attacked without a shot being fired by 1 Armoured Division ... You will notice also that the principle of security was neglected for nowhere west of Tobruk was there a firm base on which 13 Corps could fall back, or behind which it could rally for a counter-offensive.

In 8th Army's retreat from El Agheila diffuseness of aim led to such dissipation of effort that Hobbes' two recipes for success, force and fraud, were manipulated almost exclusively by the other side. This unhappy state of affairs is perhaps best illustrated by the outcome of Rommel's feint towards Mechili on 28 January which persuaded Ritchie not merely not to concentrate, but to claim 'the enemy has divided his forces and is weaker than we are in both areas. The key word is offensive action everywhere.' Brave words, but the boot was disconcertingly on the other foot. Rommel had started out with a clear but limited aim—a spoiling attack. He had realized his aim almost at once. It was not this, however, which was remarkable. It was his knack of converting limited gains into a major tactical victory. It was, as noted already, like the 'touch and take' of Nelson. Such speed in recon-centration and exploitation was only practicable because he commanded *from the front*. He knew what the situation was as it happened, and was able to act upon it at once. No doubt it led sometimes to such absurdities of higher direction as his receiving permission from Mussolini to enter Benghazi after he had done so. But at this stage, before the British began to enjoy decisive superiority on land and in the air, the desert war was essentially one of opportunity, and you could only seize opportunity if you knew it was there. Command from the rear areas, without immediate and accurate information (which was never forthcoming) could not work. You either had to be there in person or leave decisions to whichever of your subordinates was. The encirclement of 7th Indian Infantry Brigade was the direct consequence of Ritchie's refusal to be guided by Godwin-Austen, and led to the latter's asking to be, and being, relieved of his command.

Panzerarmee Afrika's report to Hitler claimed that during the fighting from 21 January to 6 February 'the British 8th Army was so severely beaten that it was incapable of further large-scale operations for months afterwards'. No report is written without consideration as to who is to read it, but even allowing for this, there was certainly no question of a further British offensive for some months. Yet this is exactly what Auchinleck was being urged to do.

The exchange of telegrams between Churchill and Auchinleck from 25 January to 10 May 1942, which led to what Churchill called 'definite orders which Auchinleck must obey or be relieved', was designed by the Prime Minister to push Auchinleck into attacking as early as possible so that Malta would not fall to the enemy, and by the Commander-in-Chief to gain the time necessary to reorganize, train and supply 8th Army so that its attack could succeed. The dilemma referred to at the beginning of this chapter had once more come full circle. In the event British intentions were again anticipated by the Panzerarmee's advance, but it was the British preparations which had so ambivalent an effect on the subsequent course of the battle for North Africa. The build-up of supplies at Tobruk and Belhamed cabined and cribbed the defensive and offensive courses of the 8th Army to such a degree that its defeat by the dynamic, flexible methods of the Panzerarmee was only a matter of computation; but, and this was all important, the mere condition in which Rommel found himself when so many of these supplies were in his hands was one which caused *him* to misappreciate the true Axis priorities, and to delude himself that the capture of Egypt was a thing to be attempted even though Malta was reviving and active behind him.

It was, of course, only the violence of the Axis attack on Malta that had temporarily redressed the seesaw of supplies and made possible in the first place Rommel's attack at Gazala on 26 May. The pendulum of air and sea power in the central Mediterranean had swung sharply in their favour. Although in March Admiral Vian's skilful conduct at the second battle of Sirte had enabled three merchantmen of a convoy from Alexandria to reach Malta, the Luftwaffe's attack upon them in harbour was so effective that only 5,000 tons of cargo out of the 26,000 which had left Alexandria were unloaded. But the *enemy* cargoes were getting through. Of the freight sailed from Italy to Libya during the months of April and May 1942 between 93 and 99 per cent were safely disembarked. The battle for North Africa had become the battle for Malta. So successful did Kesselring judge the Axis efforts to be that on 10 May he reported the neutralization of Malta to be complete. For this reason and to comply with the demands of the Russian front, he released two bomber and two fighter groups from his Luftflotte. At almost exactly the same time Malta received strong Spitfire reinforcements. The seesaw was a delicate thing, and Malta's agony was to know a turning point before many months were out. Kesselring might have done well to remember Nietzsche's remark that success has always been a great liar. It was not a point which greatly concerned the British desert commanders in the May of 1942 for they were not having any.

The events leading up to the catastrophic fall of Tobruk have been fully described by Michael Carver in his volume, *Tobruk*, and there is no need to repeat them here. It is enough to say here that the battle of Gazala had three distinct phases. From 26 to 29 May Rommel tried to overcome the British defences from the rear; then came the *Cauldron* fighting during which Rommel re-supplied and re-concentrated his forces; thirdly the loss of Bir Hacheim, the British armour's defeat from 11 to 13 June, and 8th Army's withdrawal from the Gazala position. During the lull from February to May Auchinleck had made strenuous efforts to put right what he judged to be the two main failings of 8th Army's organization and training. Firstly he reorganized armoured divisions so that their tanks, infantry and artillery should be able to cooperate more effectively; secondly he ruled that divi-

sions must train to fight as divisions. In other words there was to
be no more piecemeal fighting either by the various components
of brigades or by brigades themselves. The theory was sound
enough. *Übung macht den Meister* ('Practice makes perfect') says
the German grammar book. Just so; but unfortunately 8th Army
did not have the practice which made perfect. Moreover, when
it became clear that it was the Panzerarmee which would attack
first, there was no attempt from the very beginning, and in spite
of all former lessons, to concentrate. 13th Corps in the north was
disposed in a series of dispersed boxes; 30th Corps in the south,
with the bulk of the armour, was strung out in a succession of
scattered brigades. As Rommel's main attack came to the south
of Bir Hacheim and then turned north and north-east, it was well
designed to outflank one corps and roll up the other.

There were nevertheless high hopes among the newly equip-
ping British tank regiments. Lieutenant Colonel G. P. B. Roberts,
who commanded the 3rd Royal Tank Regiment with the new
Grants, has recorded that his tank crews felt they at last had an
answer to the anti-tank gun and anticipated with pleasure the
shock which the German Mark III and Mark IV tanks would
get when the 75mm began shooting at them. Everyone was enthusiastic and when told that Rommel's attack was expected between 25 and 28 May wondered each morning at the pre-dawn
stand-to what that day would hold. His account of what was in
fact in store for them admirably depicts the tank fighting of this
period. On 28 May during the first phase of the battle his regiment, part of 4th Armoured Brigade and 7th Armoured Division
saw heavy fighting to the south-west of El Adem between Trigh
Capuzzo and Trigh el Abd:

We continue to move forward slowly, closing up on the light
squadron and looking for a suitable hull-down position. 'Gosh!
There they are–more than 100. Yes, 20 in the first line, and
there are six, no, eight lines, and more behind that in the distance; a whole ruddy Panzer Division is quite obviously in front
of us. Damn it. This was not the plan at all–where the hell are
the rest of the Brigade? However, no indecision is possible be-

cause no alternatives present themselves. 'Hullo, Battalion–Orders : B and C Squadrons (Grants) take up battle line on the small ridge 300 yards to our front. B Squadron right, C Squadron left. A Squadron (Honeys) protect the right flank from an out-flanking movement and try to get in on the enemy's flank–leave one troop on the left to keep in touch with 8th Hussars who should be coming up on our left at any moment.'

The Grant squadrons were instructed to hold their fire until the Boche tanks were within 1,200 yards or had halted. Meanwhile our gunners, the famous Chestnut troop, had heard the situation on the wireless and were going into action behind us...

The leading enemy tanks had halted about 1,300 yards away; all our tanks were firing, there was no scarcity of targets, certainly two of our tanks were knocked out, but the enemy had also had losses. I could see one tank burning, and another slewed round and the crew 'baling out' ... 'Peter (my adjutant), tell Brigade we are holding our own but I do not anticipate being able to stay here for ever' ... Our instructions were to hold on as long as possible...

Further tank casualties had been inflicted on both sides, but as far as the Boche were concerned as soon as one tank was knocked out another took its place; they merely used their rear lines of tanks to replace casualties in the front line and attempted no manoeuvre. On the other hand, from well in their rear a few tanks and some anti-tank guns were being moved very wide round our right flank and the light squadron was getting more and more strung out keeping them under observation.

'Peter, tell Brigade we cannot hang on here much longer, either there will be nothing left, or we will be cut off, or both.' 'Driver, advance slightly into line with the other tanks.' '75 gunner, enemy tank straight ahead receiving no attention–engage. First shot just over–come down half-a-tank height. Still over–come down a whole tank's height. Good shot–that got him–same again.' Hullo ! there is a dashing Boche on the left, he has come right forward against C Squadron who have withdrawn a little, just the job for the 37mm. '37 gunner traverse left, traverse left, traverse left–on; enemy tank broadside–500–fire. 37 gunner–good–have a couple more shots and then get ready with the co-ax.'

Later in his account Colonel Roberts reveals that the 8th Hussars have suffered heavy losses, that Divisional Headquarters together with the General have been overrun and captured. Rommel had got his pell-mell battle all right. It was to be renewed during the 'Cauldron' phase and reached a new height of ferocity at Knightsbridge. The extent of the British defeat during the Knightsbridge battles of 11–13 June is best comprehended by recourse to mere numbers. On 11 June Ritchie had 300 tanks, about twice as many as the Afrika Korps. Two days later unit strength returns showed the total as 95, whilst on 14 June 8th Army reported that there were only 50 cruiser and 20 Infantry tanks left. Rommel had won, and the only course open to Ritchie was withdrawal to the Egyptian frontier. On 21 June, Rommel's objective, Tobruk, was in his hands. It was then that he overlooked his own previous warning that 'without Malta the Axis will end by losing control of North Africa'. The very magnitude of his triumph (apart from anything else over 2,000 tons of fuel and 2,000 vehicles, his two main deficiencies, were captured) closed his eyes to the rapidly changing strategic and supply situation in the Mediterranean and North Africa. The supreme opportunist, he was disinclined to pause, make sure of Malta, secure adequate resources, and then resume his advance. He could not or would not see that there were times when it was just as important to forego an opportunity as it was to grasp one.

But that lay in the future. So far 1942 had been Rommel's year. The battles fought by the Panzerarmee between January and June had been characterized by simplicity of aim, skill of execution and the grip of a great desert commander at the height of his activity and dexterity. Perseverance and agility had gone hand in hand. As Rommel himself put it in a letter to his wife on 15 June: 'The battle has been won and the enemy is breaking up.' The 8th Army was not exactly breaking up, but *its* record during the same period of five months was almost point for point the antithesis of its opponent's. The courage and skill of individual soldiers and units was never in doubt. But the purpose of operations, except in general terms like that of defeating the enemy, was neither clear nor simple; information was neither timely nor accurate; defensive concepts were too rigid, and there was still no proper means of ensuring that tanks, infantry and artillery fought *one* battle or that the armour concentrated to resist and defeat the Panzer onslaught; the very command arrangements were suspect. On the magnificent support of the RAF, however, the soldiers could count themselves lucky. Without it, the battle for North Africa might have been over. There was perhaps consolation to be found in another direction. If Halifax were right in his declaration that an army must be badly defeated before it became a good one, 8th Army had at least conformed to the premise.

7. 8th Army at bay

The unforeseeable tide of disaster which drove us from Gazala
to Alamein with the loss of Tobruk and fifty thousand men has
now for the time being been stemmed.

Churchill

The partial success of *Crusader,* the grim reverses of its sequel—
these had been the first two instalments of Auchinleck's guardian-
ship of the Middle East. The third and last chapter was to be for
him alike a triumph and an eclipse. The triumph came about because Rommel overreached himself in an attempt to bounce the
8th Army right out of Egypt. The eclipse, a subject for specula-
tion well before the triumph itself materialized, was perhaps inevitable as soon as it became clear that Rommel was in a position to
attempt anything of the sort. On 2 July 1942 Stafford Cripps
produced for the Prime Minister a paper which aimed to summarize principal points of criticism that the Government might
expect to meet during the debate on a motion of censure. This
paper referred to a widespread view that with better generalship
Rommel could have been defeated. Leadership was criticized as
being too defensive in concept, and the paper went on to suggest
that there were serious doubts as to whether either the Commander-in-Chief or the Army Commander really appreciated how to
manage mechanized warfare, and that therefore a complete
change in command might be necessary. Before this, of course,
Auchinleck had already put the question himself. His signal of 23
June to Alan Brooke shows how wholly honest a man he was:

The unfavourable course of the recent battle in Cyrenaica cul-
minating in the disastrous fall of Tobruk impels me to ask you
seriously to consider the advisability of retaining me in my
command. No doubt you are already considering this and quite

rightly, but I want you to know that I also realize the probable effects of the past month's fighting. Personally I feel fit to carry on and reasonably confident of being able to turn the tables on the enemy in time. All the same there is no doubt that in a situation like the present, fresh blood and new ideas at the top may make all the difference between success and stalemate... For this theatre originality is essential and a change is quite probably desirable on this account alone, apart from all other considerations such as loss of influence due to lack of success, absence of luck and all the other things which affect the morale of an army. It occurred to me that you might want to use Alexander...

How accurately he had forecast his successor had yet to be made known. Meanwhile, two days after this telegram he made a change on his own account, a dramatic one in that for the second time in seven months he dismissed an 8th Army Commander whom he himself had chosen. But there was a difference this time. He took personal command of 8th Army. He would pit his own wits against Rommel, and, as he said a few days later: 'I am going to win.'

In the nine days between Rommel's taking Tobruk and reaching the Alamein line, much had happened. In the first place Rommel had overborne the objections of Kesselring and Bastico by appealing to Hitler and Mussolini themselves. His signal to von Rintelen in Rome contained both a statement and a request: 'The first objective of the Panzerarmee–to defeat the enemy's army in the field and capture Tobruk–has been attained... Request you ask the Duce to lift the present restriction on freedom of movement, and to put all the troops now under my command at my disposal, so that I can continue the battle.' There were good reasons for wanting to continue the battle. Just as the British had twice defeated an Axis army and reached the gates of Tripolitania, only to be obliged to pause there and fail to finish the thing off once and for all, so Rommel for the second time found himself on the threshold of the Nile delta and the great complex of ports, airfields and administrative depots whose possession would end the battle of supplies for good. Besides, no commander, particularly one as dashing and opportunistic as Rommel, likes to allow his enemy to get away, re-form, and so start the pendulum swinging yet again. The Napoleonic pursuit with its doctrine of utterly destroying the remnants of a beaten army whilst it was hopelessly off balance–this was the dream of every desert commander. Only O'Connor realized it.

Yet if there were strong tactical and sentimental arguments for conducting a pursuit, how much more powerful were the strategic and logistic ones for not doing so. Kesselring was the first to point out that the advance from Gazala had itself only been possible because Malta's suppression had allowed sufficient supplies to cross the Mediterranean, and that even during the short time since Luftwaffe squadrons had left Sicily to support Rommel in his seizure of Tobruk, Malta was once more reviving its offensive capability and putting the Panzerarmee's supplies into jeopardy. Rommel claimed, however, that the supplies captured at Tobruk were enough to get him to Cairo and that delay, even of a few weeks, would allow the British to recover. All would then be to do again. Yet later even Rommel conceded that it had all been a 'try-on'–a plan with no more than a chance of success. In fact, given the grip which Auchinleck took and the defensive plan he made, it had little chance from the outset. But as Hitler was a gambler too, and as Rommel's bait seemed to do away with the need to mount *Herkules,* the operation to capture Malta, one which with the losses of Crete in mind, the Führer had always jibbed at, he was persuaded to allow Rommel to continue his advance. For Mussolini the prospect of entering Alexandria mounted on a white charger was so alluring that he was able to subdue his former, prudent misgivings.

It is at this point that we see again how critical a part Malta played in the desert fighting. When in May the Prime Minister was pressing Auchinleck to renew the offensive, it was so that an advance in the desert could amongst other things bring relief to a starving Malta. Instead of the desert army's advancing to rescue Malta, however, the exact reverse had occurred. For with this reverse and because of the means by which it had been achieved,

Malta had once more come to the rescue of the desert army. If the battle for North Africa really was one of supplies, never had the interplay of air, sea and land operations been so finely balanced, nor their causes and effects been so decisive. Malta's reinforcement by Spitfires enabled the island to beat off the Axis' renewed assault in July, whilst this assault was itself only made possible because Kesselring withdrew Luftwaffe squadrons from Africa to Sicily, so affording the 8th Army air superiority at a moment when it was most dangerously threatened. Meanwhile the loss of so much Cyrenaican desert and the airfields it contained made the replenishment of Malta—by June gravely overdue—a matter of touch and go. Two convoys sailed for Malta in June. From Gibraltar *Harpoon* had five freighters and a tanker with a powerful covering force, and from the east came *Vigorous* with no less than eleven freighters. Not one of this second convoy's ships reached Malta, and only two of the first, but the islanders were saved from starvation. Thereafter its gradually enhanced ability to resume the offensive against Axis shipping both by sea and air, together with the efforts of the Middle East Air Force, was to be conclusive. For Rommel's supply situation, briefly so promising on capturing Tobruk, was to deteriorate as never before.

All this was to happen at a time when British strength in the Middle East steadily grew and kept on growing. Tobruk's fall may have saved Malta. It did more. It enabled Churchill to extract 300 Sherman tanks and a hundred 105mm guns from Roosevelt, weapons which were greatly to influence future armoured battles. At no time was the disadvantage of being at the end of long and insecure lines of communication more firmly demonstrated than it was to Rommel in the summer of 1942. Moreover, whilst 8th Army received strong reinforcements, the Middle East Air Force was at last achieving parity with the Axis air forces in the Mediterranean and the United States air units were beginning to be active. Further on the credit side was the fact that the Alamein position, where Auchinleck decided to stand, could not be outflanked and would oblige Rommel to fight the sort of battle which the British were best at. Rommel was

always seeking to fight a fluid, fast moving battle where his superior tactics and command arrangements would tell. The British,
on the other hand, were much more likely to be successful when
they were able to rely on material advantages, particularly in
artillery and air power, together with perseverance in a slugging,
head-on encounter. These advantages were to be features of the
Alamein battles in July, August, September and October. But the
British position during the retreat to Alamein, and no euphemism
will do, it *was* a retreat, sometimes a headlong one, was far less
enviable. Indeed it was one which no commander would normally relish. When O'Connor was asked after his campaign of February 1941 what it felt like to be completely successful, he replied
that he would never so consider a commander 'until he had re-
stored the situation after a serious defeat and a long withdrawal.'
Auchinleck was now to have just this opportunity for at Mersa
Matruh he sustained a serious defeat and it was followed by a
long withdrawal. Indeed it says much for his courage and integrity that he decided to take personal command of the battle for
North Africa, and thus total responsibility too, at so difficult a
moment when all was in the balance.

From the start he had disliked Ritchie's plans for Mersa Matruh, another example of trying to combat Rommel's *blitzkrieg*
methods with largely static and dispersed defences–10th Corps in
Mersa Matruh itself, 13th Corps further south as the supposedly
mobile striking force, but in fact having 2nd New Zealand Division at Minqar Qaim and 1st Armoured Division to the south
again. Although Auchinleck quickly determined to fight the decisive battle for Egypt at Alamein, not at Matruh, he was too late
to alter Ritchie's dispositions, and what happened next merely
confirmed his apprehensions. On 26 June, the day after Auchinleck assumed command of 8th Army, Rommel attacked. His plan
was to ward off 1st Armoured Division and encircle the Mersa
Matruh position. In the event both 10th Corps and the New
Zealand Division were cut off and had to break out to the east.
What is more, the two corps once again fought independently and
once again there was no proper coordination between the armoured division and the infantry formations. Kippenberger who

commanded 5 Brigade in the New Zealand Division found the
Minqar Qaim position a great puzzle. He was not at all certain
how it should be occupied. The whole situation was full of uncertainties and difficulties. Although a hundred-foot high escarpment ran east and west, and would stop tanks coming from the
north, there was no reason to suppose that the enemy *would* come
that way. They could just as easily motor straight along it. Information was bad, both as to general intentions and moves of
neighbouring formations. There was no proper tie-up between
the New Zealanders and 1st Armoured Division. Kippenberger's
LOs could not find an Indian Brigade said to be a few miles away.
It was all far too vague. Kippenberger was not at all satisfied, but
could not think how to improve things. When the battle started,
it was not quite as bad as he had feared.

The New Zealanders beat off all attacks made on them, but
they were encircled by 21st Panzer Division, and on the evening
of 27 June, Inglis, temporarily commanding 2nd New Zealand
Division, as Freyberg had been wounded, gave orders for a break
out. It was a brilliant exploit. 4 Brigade made the hole with bay-
onets, and Kippenberger described the excitement of 5 Brigade's
escape :

> I was beginning to think we had found a gap when white flares
> went up close ahead. The column stopped, closely packed.
> More flares went up, no doubt a challenge, to which we had no
> reply to make. The Germans opened fire.
>
> We had bumped into a laager of about a dozen tanks lying
> so closely together that there was no room to break through be-
> tween them. Their fire simply hailed down on us. There were
> tank shells, 20mm shells, and automatics, all firing tracer. A
> petrol truck was hit at once and exploded. An ammunition
> truck was hit and the boxes of cartridges crackled and exploded
> in succession. The most dreadful sight was an ambulance a
> few yards away which blazed furiously, the wounded on the
> stretchers writhing and struggling utterly beyond help.
>
> My car was jammed on all sides and could not move. I told
> Ross and Joe to get out and for a moment we lay flat on the

ground. Many others had done the same. A few seconds later
I saw a truck ahead of us turning to the left, and beyond it
quite clearly saw John Gray standing with his head through
the roof of his car and pointing in the same direction. 'We'll
give it a go, Ross,' I said. 'Very good, Sir,' he replied, as polite
as ever. We scrambled back and followed the trucks ahead, all
bolting like wild elephants. For a few moments we ran on
amid a pandemonium, overtaking and being overtaken by other
frantic vehicles, dodging slit trenches, passing or crashing into
running men, amid an uproar of shouts and screams. I recognized the men as Germans, pulling out my revolver and was
eagerly looking for a target when suddenly there was silence
and we were out running smoothly on level desert. We were
through.

I thought of Joe, who had not got out of the car with us,
turned round and poked him. There was no response. I prod-
ded him again and called anxiously and Joe woke up. He had
slept through the whole affair.

10th Corps fared less well, since the support they had expected
from 13th Corps was not forthcoming, and they had heavy losses.
In spite of defeat at Matruh, Auchinleck succeeded in his principal object of keeping 8th Army in being, indeed in reorganizing
it at a time when it was almost disintegrating. So well did he do
it that on 1 July Rommel was brought to a halt, and from that
moment on the initiative was never really his again. German accounts of the Matruh battle and advance to Alamein underline
the fact that Rommel, whilst at his most impetuous, was frequently mistaken as to the actual situation, and, as so often before,
stuck his neck out in a way which would have proved most costly
had the British been able to react with both speed and coordination of effort. But the British were thinking in terms of retreat,
and retreat they did. Rommel, in a tearing hurry, knew that his
only hope of winning was to bustle 8th Army about in such a way
that it was able neither to stabilize the battle nor draw on its full
resources: the encircling movement, cutting the coast road, preventing the British from concentrating, creating confusion every-

1. O'Connor and Wavell

2. Long Range Desert Group patrol

3. The Mediterranean Fleet escorting a Malta convoy

4. Matilda tanks

5. Benghazi harbour after RAF attention

6. Axis Prisoners of War

7. Tobruk falls, January 1941

8. Junkers Ju. 87 dive bombers

9. The Desert Air Force – Hurricanes

10. Rommel in the Western Desert

11. Honey tanks

12. The destruction of battle

13. Auchinleck and Wavell

14. Malta succoured

15. Kesselring and Rommel

16. 50mm anti-tank gun

17. The Free French at Bir Hacheim

18. Montgomery

19. 6pr anti-tank gun

20. German graves

21. *Torch* – US troops landing

22. General Anderson with US divisional commander

23. Men of a US tank destroyer unit in Tunisia

24. Eisenhower with Tuker, Nicholls and Walsh

25. Von Arnim (left) and a divisional commander in Tunisia

26. Montgomery talks to Messe, with Freyberg (centre)

27. The end in North Africa – Mateur POW camp, May 1943

28. The armies did not stand idle – Churchill with Leese and Alexander
in Italy

where–it was the old pattern. Confusion *was* widespread, and not confined to the 8th Army. Rommel himself recorded how his own headquarters was engaged in 10th Corps' break out from Matruh:

> A wild mêlée ensued, in which my own headquarters, which lay south of the fortress, became involved. . . . One can scarcely conceive the confusion which reigned that night. It was pitch-dark and impossible to see one's hand before one's eyes. The RAF bombed their own troops, and with tracer flying in all directions, German units fired on each other.

Von Mellenthin criticized Rommel's handling of the whole encounter in that he did not pause for proper reconnaissance, but notwithstanding the luck which so frequently accompanies the general prepared to take chances, it is difficult to see what else Rommel could have done if he were to have a chance of breaking right through to the delta. Matruh was a great victory for him, but it was to be his last that summer, for at length 8th Army was to be fought as an army, and not as a series of independent, disjointed formations. The ideas, which Dorman-Smith, Auchinleck's Chief of Staff, put to him for conducting the first battle of Alamein were sound ones and were to persist–to concentrate the army, to fight it in integrated battle groups, to mass the artillery, to husband the armour, to form a light armoured brigade for flank reconnaissance, to attack and wear down the Italian divisions. The result was that during the July battles, Rommel, at the end of his supply lines and with the RAF harassing not only those supply lines but the forward troops as well, was up against an opponent who was not going to be bluffed. Rommel was not simply stopped; he was obliged to go over to the defensive. All his attempts to break through between 1 and 5 July were defeated, but from 10 to 26 July he was himself warding off Auchinleck's counter attacks. The best tributes to Auchinleck's generalship during the first few days of July are those of von Mellenthin and Rommel. Prospects of victory, wrote the former,

were hopelessly prejudiced on July 1. Our one chance was to

9—BFNA

out-manoeuvre the enemy, but we had actually been drawn into a battle of attrition. 1st Armoured Division was given an extra day to reorganize, and when the Afrika Korps advanced on July 2 it found the British armour strongly posted on Ruweisat Ridge, and quite capable of beating off such attacks as we could muster. The South African positions were strong, and 90th Light never had a chance of breaking through them. The Desert Air Force commanded the battlefield.

Rommel's description of what happened on 2 July shows how effective the new methods of Dorman-Smith under the resolute direction of Auchinleck were proving. It was now the Afrika Korps which was beginning to dance to 8th Army's tune–a welcome change from the monotonous measures of the former six months. Reaction to a northward thrust by 13th Corps tied down most of Rommel's armoured force:

> The 15th Panzer Division was pulled out to parry this attack and its armour was soon involved in violent fighting with the British. The 21st Panzer Division's units were also forced increasingly on to the defensive in the sandy, scrubby country, until by evening the whole of the Afrika Korps were locked in violent defensive fighting against a hundred British tanks and about ten batteries... General Auchinleck, who had meanwhile taken over command himself at El Alamein, was handling his forces with very considerable skill and tactically better than Ritchie had done. He seemed to view the situation with decided coolness, for he was not allowing himself to be rushed into accepting a second best solution by any moves we made.

In other words Auchinleck was keeping *balance,* a requirement which Montgomery was later to make so much of. By keeping this balance and by refusing to be thrown off it, Auchinleck was able to make decisive use of the advantages inherent to his position–important ground, assured supplies, superior fire power, ready reinforcements. Spengler maintained that victory's secret lay in organizing the non-obvious. Desert commanders would have had little patience with such sophistry. Auchinleck, however,

did more than harness the obvious; he beat the Afrika Korps at
their own game, and succeeded in drawing their panzers on to
his own armour and artillery fire posted firmly on strong ground
of their own choosing. How well he continued to exploit this technique was demonstrated during the battle fought by 5th Indian
Brigade near the Deir el Shein depression. The opening moves
were familiar.

Stukas and artillery pounded 5 Brigade's positions during the
afternoon of 16 July. Then when the sun was well down in the
sky and shining into the eyes of those manning the defences, the
panzers appeared from the west and north-west. But this time the
British and Indian troops were more than ready for them. Dug-
in six-pounders, the new anti-tank guns, hull-down tanks, artillery
fire–all were directed against the advancing panzers. For three
hours the battle raged, and ended with the Germans abandoning
the field.

Morning showed how well the defenders had done. The battlefield was strewn with wrecked tanks, field guns, anti-tank guns.
Some suspicious looking panzers were subjected to furious artillery
fire, stopped shamming dead, and scuttled away. After the remaining prizes had been finally blown up in case the enemy re-
occupied the area, the count was impressive–24 tanks, six armoured cars, 25 guns. The new 6pr anti-tank gun had won its spurs
all right. It was for 8th Army 'a case of love at first sight'. But it
signified much more than this.

Here at last was a change in the nature and conduct of desert
fighting. In their use of the Ruweisat Ridge the British were de-
monstrating that they too could integrate their teams of armour,
infantry, anti-tank guns and artillery together with air power.
But the first battle of Alamein was memorable not only for this.
Auchinleck systematically attacked the Italian formations, which
fought well enough but were overwhelmed by superiority in infantry and fire power. 'It's enough to make one weep', wrote
Rommel. If there were any doubts as to how gallantly the Italians
could fight, however, a glance at the accounts of some of these
encounters would dispel them.

In his book about Alamein, Paolo Caccia-Dominioni has many

such tales to tell. One of them is about the Australians' attack towards Bir el Maqtua on 17 July, an attack with two brigades, preceded by RAF strikes and supported by strong artillery and armour. Part of this assault fell on the 32nd Battalion, African Combat Engineers, who were in position between the Trieste and Trento Divisions. Although this battalion was down to 100 men out of its normal 500, it fought with great courage, and tenaciously held on to its positions in the face of repeated and determined attacks. The result was that the battalion ceased to exist. When at the end of the day its remnants eventually withdrew, there were only two officers and 14 men left.

It was not quite a last-man-last-round affair, but 16 out of 100 was close to it. In the same action the 3rd/61st Trento Infantry so distinguished itself in defending the Miteiriya ridge that Rommel not only gave them proper recognition in his daily bulletin but was furious that the Italian communiqué (through ignorance, not neglect) failed to do so. For the Germans to draw attention to the gallantry of their allies was hardly an everyday feature of the desert fighting.

Although 8th Army had both stopped the Panzerarmee and conducted a number of successful attacks, Auchinleck had not achieved his aim of making the enemy crack. Furthermore there were disquieting criticisms of the armour's inability either to be up with the infantry at first light after a night attack or to exploit the infantry's gains. The coalition of anti-tank guns and mines so inhibited the armour's freedom of manoeuvre, and sometimes the determination of its commanders, that Kippenberger, in commenting on the regularity with which tanks failed to be where they were wanted in time, went as far as referring to the 'distrust, almost hatred' felt by other arms. 23rd Armoured Brigade, however, did much to remove this feeling and won golden opinions for their courage and keenness to engage the enemy. But this did not mean that the problem of tank-infantry cooperation in *attack* had yet been solved. There was still much to do, it seemed, before 8th Army would be ready to take the offensive again, and win.

July, therefore, ended in stalemate, and once again there was to be a pause during which each side would look to its defences and prepare for an attack. Much has been written about who was responsible for designing the defensive battle of Alam el Halfa which finally put a stop to Rommel's ability to conduct anything but delaying operations, but few would now dispute that the *design* was Auchinleck's.* Execution is another thing, and Montgomery's great contribution to victory was the way in which he conducted battles. Before we come to that it will be as well to pause, and assess how the nature and conduct of battles developed during Auchinleck's command. There were a number of consistent threads which weaved their way in and out of the events between July 1941 and August 1942–the Year of Battle, as Moorehead named it. Firstly, Auchinleck was singularly unfortunate, and, it might be added, injudicious in his choice of commanders for 8th Army. Cunningham had commanded small forces in East Africa with conspicuous dash and success, but he knew nothing of large-scale armoured warfare, so that to select him for a theatre of operations in which the handling of armour dictated the way battles went was odd, to say the least of it. Auchinleck's second choice, Ritchie, was equally strange, particularly when it is remembered that unlike Cunningham he did not even have recent experience of command in war. His last command had been that of a battalion in the First World War. Ritchie was strong and confident, and seemed decisive, but his decisiveness was often based on misappreciation of what was really happening, and at no time did he seem able to think or act with the speed and anticipation which the seesaw of fighting from January to June 1942 demanded. During Ritchie's command subordinate generals always seemed to be asking themselves and each other what the Army Commander's intention really was.† Within three months of appointing Ritchie, Auchinleck was thinking of replacing him. How unthinkable would such a state of affairs have been (the wholly different circumstances notwithstanding) during the Alex-

---

* Based on Dorman-Smith's appreciation.

† In *The Desert Generals,* Corelli Barnett gives amongst other instances Gott's saying: 'I *think* Ritchie is going to do this or that', and Renton's question: 'What is the main idea in the battle now?' being answered with Messervy's: 'I wish I knew.'

ander-Montgomery régime, although, of course, Montgomery had
no hesitation in choosing his own team of subordinates, who, he
knew, would fight battles *his* way without argument. Thus we see
that as far as the *conduct* of battles went, neither conductor
chosen by Auchinleck was really up to the job.

The next thread, which followed automatically from the first,
was that in all three phases of the desert fighting during his year
as Commander-in-Chief–*Crusader,* Gazala to Tobruk, and Alamein–Auchinleck intervened personally, and each time demonstrated his own superior generalship. Firstly by insisting during
Crusader, at a juncture when Cunningham was thinking defensively, that the attacks be renewed, he managed to wear Rommel
down; then by striving in June 1942 to keep 8th Army, above all
else, in being, he saved Egypt; lastly his own conduct of the first
battle of Alamein destroyed Rommel's ambitions of conquest for
ever. Auchinleck's battles were ones of attrition, and twice he got
the better of Rommel. Whereas the first, *Crusader,* left 8th Army
so off balance that it was quickly countered by Rommel, the
second, Alamein, enabled the British finally to wrest the initiative
from him and so sustain their balance that they never lost it again.
What is more Dorman-Smith's plans, accepted and supported by
Auchinleck, for running operations from August 1942 onwards
were a continuation of the theme adopted by Auchinleck on first
taking command of 8th Army. These plans predicted the events
that were to follow–both the way in which Alam el Halfa would
be fought, that is by having strong, deep defences based on the
Ruweisat and Alam el Halfa ridges, combining 'fluidity and mobility and massive use of artillery fire' with strong armoured and
artillery forces able to strike an advancing enemy's flank; and
also how the second battle of Alamein would be conducted, that
is as a set-piece affair making full use of the substantial reinforcements which were coming and exploiting the British qualities of
disciplined perseverance rather than thrusting agility. No general
could have been better fitted to execute these ideas than Montgomery with his maxim of no advance without security.

Here perhaps it is possible to point to a third consistent thread
in Auchinleck's command, for it was so unlike Montgomery's and

was characterized by *in*consistency. There seemed always to be too much chopping and changing in methods of training and tactics. One day it was battle groups; next divisions were to be fought as divisions; then Jock columns were the fashion; after that battle groups were again in vogue. But no matter what the current idea was, brigades, particularly armoured brigades, too often were committed to battle piecemeal. It was no good constantly changing organization and tactics. It was no good constantly altering plans and switching units and formations here and there. It led to confusion, uncertainty and loss of confidence in higher direction. The need for a master plan and a persistent design was clear, and this need was to be properly recognized and satisfied by Montgomery.

On balance, however, Auchinleck must stand high in the gallery of desert generals. In a note at the beginning of his biography, John Connell asks himself whether Auchinleck passed Wavell's test of being fit for inclusion in the Sixth Form of generalship–a hard test which demanded that large forces should be handled independently in more than a single campaign, that the two impostors, success and adversity, should be suitably treated, that strategic and tactical skill, political acumen, training ability should all accompany what ultimately matters–energy and drive in conducting battles. Perhaps the surest confirmation that he passes the test comes from General Bayerlein, who was Chief of Staff at the headquarters of both the Afrika Korps and the Panzerarmee: 'If Auchinleck had not been the man he was–and by that I mean the best Allied general in North Africa during the war–Rommel would have finished the Eighth Army off.'

Auchinleck was, of course, always under tremendous political pressure, as Dill had predicted he would be, but he had never allowed it to stampede him into premature attack. He stood firm against the assaults of Churchill and Rommel alike, and in doing so he had been one of the instruments which turned the tide. In his biography of King George VI, John Wheeler-Bennett wrote:

The actual turning of the tide in the Second World War may be accurately determined as the first week of July 1942. After

Rommel was repulsed at El Alamein on July 2 and turned
away in deference to British resistance, the Germans never
again mounted a major offensive in North Africa; while in
Russia the summer offensive of the Red Army marked the beginning of their ruthless and remorseless progress from the Don
to the Elbe.

If Wheeler-Bennett was right to fix the first week of July 1942
as the turning of the tide, there was no doubt that during subsequent weeks of July and August, many were those who were able
to take the tide at its flood. Three currents of this flood intermingled–Middle East strategy; changes in the British command
to carry it out; and President Roosevelt's decisions for employing
United States forces against Germany that year. As early as the
second week of July the Middle East Defence Committee was
seeking guidance from London as to the future conduct of the
war. They pointed out that up to this time, of the two fronts for
which they were responsible, the northern one in Persia, Iraq
and Syria had consistently taken second place to the other front
in the desert, where most battleworthy forces were concentrated.
If a situation arose when the campaign in Russia went badly and
the northern front were seriously threatened, one front or the
other would, unless further reinforcements materialized, have to
go. Either the Persian oilfields must be defended at the risk of
losing Egypt, or the other way round, but there were not enough
forces to do both. Therefore a choice must be made.

The Prime Minister's reaction was foreseeable, and does much
to explain his ceaseless impatience for a renewal of the offensive
against Rommel. Defeat Rommel, he argued, and then forces
could be redistributed to meet the northern threat should it come.
The answer which the Chiefs of Staff sent to the Middle East
Defence Committee was more explicit.

It laid down that the security of the Middle East could best be
ensured by capturing Cyrenaica and Tripolitania. At the same
time a dispersal of the various administrative installations in case
things went wrong might be judicious. Priorities were clarified.
To hold Abadan must be the first consideration. If the worst

came to the worst and it could only be held by letting other things go, even the Egyptian Delta could be relinquished. But always the central point reasserted itself. Whatever happened at the southern front in Russia, success against Rommel was what mattered. It was this to which every effort must be turned. He had to be defeated and then victory was to be exploited to the utmost. All of Italian Africa must be taken.

From the British point of view, therefore, all turned on the struggle with Rommel. No wonder that at the Cairo conference Churchill asked what else mattered but beating him. As October was thought to be the month when German successes in Russia could most dangerously threaten the Middle East, Churchill's impatience knew no bounds when he saw a telegram from Auchinleck on the eve of his departure for Cairo which stated that mid-September would be the earliest date for renewing offensive operations. It confirmed the Prime Minister's conviction that he must see for himself what was 'wrong' with Middle East Command; it settled his determination to put it right.

Before he left for Cairo, however, he had pulled off one of the greatest strategic coups of his five years in power. As he explains in *The Hinge of Fate* he was at this time politically weak and still unable to offer any positive hopes of military success. Yet the decision he obtained from the United States—to drop any idea of a cross-Channel invasion in 1942 and to adopt instead the joint Anglo-American occupation of French North Africa—dominated the course of the war from then on. In a telegram to Roosevelt of 8 July he urged that *Gymnast* (later renamed *Torch*) offered the best chance for relieving the Russian front. It was the 'safest and most fruitful stroke' that could be delivered that autumn. It accorded with the President's own ideas. It was to be the second front of 1942. Such eloquence did not go unrewarded. In spite of great opposition from the American Joint Chiefs of Staff, who feared that all such diversions would delay preparations for the main invasion of France, Roosevelt gave orders that planning for *Torch* was to go ahead. Churchill received this welcome news from Dill just before setting out on his journey to Cairo.

When he had seen things for himself and consulted with

Brooke, Smuts and Casey, he quickly made up his mind. Alexander was to succeed Auchinleck, and Gott to command 8th Army. Gott's death, of course, enabled Brooke to persuade the Prime Minister that Montgomery was the man for 8th Army. Churchill's directive to Alexander, who became responsible for a smaller command of Egypt, Syria and Palestine only, was strictly in accordance with the strategic policy outlined by the Chiefs of Staff. It read simply:

> Your prime and main duty will be to take or destroy at the earliest opportunity the German-Italian Army commanded by Field-Marshal Rommel together with all its supplies and establishments in Egypt and Libya.

Both Alexander and Montgomery were concerned about 8th Army's morale, and at once set to work in putting it right. Montgomery's extraordinary impact on soldier, commander and politician is well established. In its most plain form it was that he seemed to know exactly what to do, explained it in terms which made everyone both clear as to what was required and convinced that it was right, and then went on actually to do it. Less than a week after Montgomery had taken command of 8th Army, Churchill and Brooke were treated to one of his best performances. Brooke has described how dumbfounded he was 'by the rapidity with which Montgomery had grasped the situation facing him, the ability with which he had grasped the essentials, the clarity of his plans'. We may perhaps speculate as to whether this effect was produced not so much by *what* Montgomery said, as by the way in which he said it. What he said was a reiteration of what many others had said before–that Rommel was expected to attack in such and such a way, that the attack would be broken up with artillery and tanks, that Rommel would thus be obliged to withdraw, and that his own offensive would take a certain form. All this Dorman-Smith and Auchinleck had already expounded. But Montgomery was a consummate master at putting over both himself and his intentions in a manner which could not fail to impress. It was all so clear and simple. There seemed to be no doubt about its succeeding. The effect was not unlike that of

Nelson's explaining his renowned 'touch' to his captains. Although Montgomery has often deprecated Napoleon's decision to march on Moscow, he has always agreed, as the Emperor himself proclaimed, that one of the qualities a general needs is eloquence such as appeals to soldiers. In fact, it was precisely this that was needed in 8th Army in August 1942. The men had been puzzled and confused. Now, Churchill recorded, 'a complete change of atmosphere has taken place...the highest alacrity and activity prevails...I am satisfied that we have lively, confident, resolute men in command working together as an admirable team under leaders of the highest military quality.'

Churchill added that the army would eagerly meet an enemy attack, and this was true for a fresh, invigorated sense of purpose and confidence was abroad. New leadership could take some of the credit, but another cause was that in one respect the pendulum had already swung decisively in favour of the British. The battle of supplies and reinforcements had been nearly won. In August alone the Middle East received, for example, nearly 400 tanks, 500 guns, 7,000 vehicles and 75,000 tons of stores. Between January and August reinforcements of men for all three services totalled almost a quarter of a million. Moreover on 10 August a convoy of 14 merchant ships, Operation *Pedestal,* passed Gibraltar and with a strong escort headed for Malta. Only four of the supply ships reached the island, three with foodstuffs and one, *Ohio,* with the vital fuel, but they were enough. Malta was saved. Meanwhile Rommel's supply situation was steadily worsening.

He pointed out that in the Panzerarmee during the first three weeks of August, German units alone had consumed twice the amount of supplies which were shipped or flown across the Mediterranean in the same three weeks. Such statistics require little elaboration. Nor was the trouble confined to petrol and ammunition. All German units were short of men and equipment. Rommel calculated that he needed 1,500 trucks, over 200 tanks, the same number of troop carriers, and 16,000 men. He got none of them.

The battle of Alam el Halfa, therefore, when it came was fought by Montgomery with great advantages. Rommel was

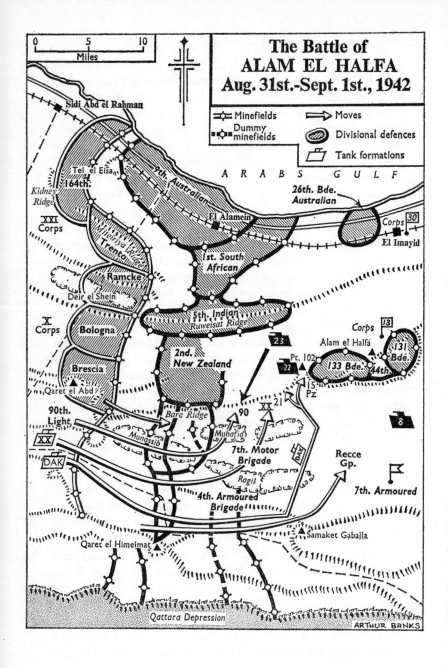

The Battle of
ALAM EL HALFA
Aug. 31st.-Sept. 1st., 1942

Minefields — Moves
Dummy minefields — Divisional defences
Tank formations

ARABS GULF

Sidi Abd el Rahman

Tel el Eisa
164th.
Kidney Ridge
9th. Australian
26th. Bde. Australian
El Alamein
Corps 30
El Imayid
XXI Corps
Miteiriya Ridge
Trento
1st. South African
Ramcke
Deir el Shein
X Corps
Bologna
5th. Indian
Ruweisat Ridge
Corps 13
Alam el Halfa
131 Bde.
23
Pt. 102
133 Bde.
144th.
22
2nd. New Zealand
Brescia
Qaret el Abd
90th. Light
Bare Ridge
Munassib
Muhafid
90
21
15 Pz
8
DAK
7th. Motor Brigade
DAK
Recce Gp.
Ragil
7th. Armoured
4th. Armoured Brigade
Samaket Gaballa
Qaret el Himeimat
Qattara Depression
ARTHUR BANKS

short of petrol and ammunition. He tried to fight an armoured battle without assured supplies of these two indispensable commodities. His opponents enjoyed an absolute air superiority; they succeeded in luring the panzers on to lines of concealed anti-tank guns and dug in tanks–the Afrika Korps' own favourite tactic; what is more the British managed to surprise Rommel with the depth and complexity of their defensive minefields. Michael Carver's lucid account of the battle ends by explaining that Montgomery won because he was able to make full use of his strength and depth and to exploit fully his own fire power in relation to his enemy's pinched manoeuvrability. Roberts, whom we last saw commanding a tank regiment, was in charge of 22nd Armoured Brigade, which Montgomery had posted at the western end of the Alam el Halfa ridge, and he describes the Afrika Korps' attack:

On they come, a most impressive array.... It is fascinating to watch them, as one might watch a snake curl up ready to strike. But there is something unusual too; some of the leading tanks are Mk IVs, and Mk IVs have in the past always had short-barrelled 75mm guns used for close support work and firing HE only, consequently they are not usually in front. But these Mk IVs have a very long gun on them; in fact it looks like the devil of a gun. This must be the long-barrelled stepped-up 75mm the Intelligence people have been talking about.

And now they all turn left and face us and begin to advance slowly. The greatest concentration seems to be opposite the CLY and the anti-tank guns of the Rifle Brigade. I warn all units over the air not to fire until the enemy are within 1,000 yards; it can't be long now and then in a few seconds the tanks of the CLY open fire and the battle is on. Once one is in the middle of a battle time is difficult to judge, but it seems only a few minutes before nearly all the tanks of the Grant squadron of the CLY were on fire. The new German 75mm is taking heavy toll ... the situation is serious; there is a complete hole in our defences. I hurriedly warn the Greys that they must move at all speed from their defensive positions and plug the gap. Meanwhile the enemy tanks are edging forward again and

they have got close to the Rifle Brigade's anti-tank guns, who
have held their fire marvellously to a few hundred yards. When
they open up they inflict heavy casualties on the enemy, but
through sheer weight of numbers some guns are overrun. The
SOS artillery fire is called for; it comes down almost at once
right on top of the enemy tanks... But where are the Greys?
'Come on the Greys' I shout over the wireless. 'Get out your
whips.'

Roberts went on to describe how the Greys arrived just in time
to fill the hole and stabilize the position. It was 31 August. Domi-
nioni has described what it was like to be on the other side on
the same day and in particular how, from the Panzerarmee's
point of view, the whole battle got off to a bad start.

By this time the British minefields were very extensive, and
minefields, hindering and canalizing movement as they did, were
ideally complemented by the RAF who were able to rain down
bombs on the Italian and German tanks as they struggled through
the imperfectly cleared lanes. Artillery concentrations and a judicious mixture of anti-tank and anti-personnel mines added their
part. The Panzerarmee's progress was so slow that the whole plan
was thrown out of gear, and even when it did get through and
out into the open, it was to learn that Montgomery's recipe for
success, whether in defence or attack, was to impose *his* battle on
the enemy.

The battle lasted for a week, but Rommel, shorter and shorter
of supplies, pounded by the RAF and concentrated artillery, never
able to muster sufficient armoured strength to counter Montgomery's persistent reinforcement of the Alam el Halfa position,
began to withdraw on 3 September. Rommel's repulse was a notable example of the cumulative effects of simultaneous operations
by land, sea and air forces. By sea and air he was starved of supplies, the RAF technique of pattern bombing was a new one,
whose development was greatly to influence the conduct of subsequent battles, and Montgomery's tight control of his forces,
whilst obliging the enemy to attack him ensured that the balance,
by which he put such store, was preserved. This principle was to

loom large in the planning of his next encounter with Rommel.

8th Army had been at bay for two months and had come off decisively best. Before long roles were to be reversed and the British would let slip the dogs of war, but with Montgomery in charge they would not be allowed very far off the leash. If Alam el Halfa were a turning point, it was not that it was a major battle. The Axis casualties were about 3,000, the British less than 2,000; the Germans lost 38 tanks and 33 guns destroyed, the British had rather fewer guns and more tanks put out of action; both sides together lost about a hundred aircraft. No important ground was gained or lost by either side. It was not in this way that the British achievement could be measured. It was rather that what Montgomery had said would happen, did happen. 8th Army's confidence in itself was completely re-established. Confidence in its new Commander was almost as great as his own. The Royal Air Force had demonstrated both by the superiority it had won and the bombing technique it had developed how huge a contribution it could make to the disruption of the enemy's armoured strength. Morale was higher than ever before. It had been an *Army* battle, its course predicted (albeit with help from those who came before), preparations and concentrations for it perfected, and then control of it tightly executed. The nature and conduct of desert battles had changed. There was to be no more failure and no more retreating.

Indeed it appeared that in the Mediterranean area the Axis powers had been contained, and now the Allies were about to seize the strategic initiative. In doing so there would come about the first great Allied enterprise with all the new influences which it brought to bear on how the final battle for North Africa would be fought. In the West there would be an amphibious operation larger than any yet mounted and wholly dependent on mastery of the sea and air. In the East where the British were enjoying to the full both material advantages and those of being close to their bases, there would be a major offensive on a narrow front against a skilful, determined enemy whose defences were in great depth. The timing and progress of each would both influence and be influenced by those of the other.

8. Alamein and after

No more manoeuvre—fight a battle.

Montgomery

Montgomery was very often to emphasize that his battles were fought according to a master plan. His first offensive battle as an Army Commander, however, succeeded not because he stuck rigidly to the master plan but because he created sufficient reserves to vary it. The extent of his material superiority was very great. When he began to prepare the second battle of Alamein he was able to count on having three corps, the 10th, 13th and 30th. With these corps 8th Army would muster some 195,000 fighting men disposed in three armoured divisions, seven infantry divisions and a number of independent armoured and allied brigades. On the other side the Panzerarmee would have a fighting strength of about 100,000, half German, half Italian. Their total of 12 divisions* sounded far more formidable than it was since every one was short of men and equipment. Equipment itself told a similar tale. Reserves aside, the British were to have 435 armoured cars compared with 192; 1,029 tanks (excluding light ones and including 250 of the new Shermans) compared with 496; over 900 guns compared with 200 German and about 300 Italian; almost 1,500 anti-tank guns, the majority being 6-prs, compared with 550 German and 300 Italian. In the air, leaving transport aircraft out of it, Tedder had 530 serviceable aeroplanes as against 350. Logistically the two sides were even more unevenly matched. 8th Army really had everything it wanted, and more. The Panzerarmee's condition was very different. General

---

* German: two armoured, two motorized; Italian: two armoured, one motorized, four infantry, one parachute.

Stumme's complaints to OKH had, like Rommel's, been frequent and vehement. Yet no number of protests, however carefully and convincingly argued, could alter the circumstances which had brought about this disparity of supplies–British communications, whilst lengthy, were sure and along them flowed steady reinforcements of men and material; the far shorter Axis supply line across the Mediterranean was uncertain and getting more dangerous every day. So that even *before* the battle of Alamein got under way, and once it started the Allied air effort was greatly intensified, the Panzerarmee had only enough fuel for eleven days' *normal* consumption–let alone battle requirements–and ammunition for a mere nine days. As Montgomery was planning for a twelve-day battle, a battle moreover in which material was to be the major consideration, it is clear that Stumme and later when he returned, Rommel, was handcuffed from the start.

In his eminently readable examination of Rommel as a military commander, Ronald Lewin compares his position before Alamein with Macbeth's at Dunsinane–'tied to a stake'. It is in two ways hardly a just comparison. In the first place, just as Macbeth *chose* to fight the boy Malcolm there–'our castle's strength will laugh a siege to scorn'–so Rommel was determined to wrest every advantage from the Alamein position, as it was the strongest one available to him. What is more he did all in his power to strengthen and deepen its defences. He had himself dissipated his mobile strike forces at Alam el Halfa. Now he hoped that 8th Army would do the same. Secondly, so little was Rommel in fact tied to a stake, in spite of Hitler's crass intervention on 3 November, that as soon as he became aware on the following evening of the danger of being encircled, he at once escaped from it, having already obtained Hitler's authority to do so, and then proceeded to conduct a masterly withdrawal. Both these points had great influence on Montgomery's handling of the situation, and the first of them made it inevitable that he would plan for a deliberate battle of attrition. It was in *this* respect that Rommel was tied. He either had to accept and fight such a battle, and by virtue of numbers alone, lose it, or give up the benefits of favourable ground and not fight it at all.

Corelli Barnett, whose heroes are understandably O'Connor and Auchinleck (both clubbable men), gives Montgomery little credit for originality or innovation. He points out that Montgomery's two claims in these respects, the creation of a *corps de chasse*, and the selection of a northerly point of attack, had both been thought of and indeed done before. This is true, but what Barnett perhaps overlooks is that after more than two years of war in the desert there were no real innovations to be found. It was in application and perseverance that Montgomery displayed his genius and difference from his predecessors. Most of the other major offensives by the British had been characterized by great 'swans' into the desert with resultant action and reaction, the scales finely balanced, and with the single exception of O'Connor's bold exploitation of mobility, leading usually to a disappointment brought about by Rommel's speed and decision. Montgomery's offensive was to be slow, methodical and final. The second battle of Alamein was thus quite different from any other battle which up to that time had been fought in North Africa. The very antithesis of the *blitzkrieg*, it was a set-piece conventional affair with troops allotted for clearing obstacles, breaking into the enemy defences, destroying them, and breaking out again, with lines to be reached at certain times, distinct phases, massive artillery plus air support and so on. It was in short a First World War push with a difference, the difference being that the ground which was won was kept and the lives which were lost were not uselessly thrown away. Montgomery, although new to desert fighting, determined to conduct one of the most difficult of military operations, a night attack, and having done so, adhered to the two first requisites of night fighting in the desert or anywhere else. Like Samuel Butler's two great rules of life, one was general, the other particular. The first was simplicity, the second preparation. It is the second of these, the steps he took to prepare properly, which now demand our attention.

His charter was clear. It was to destroy the enemy forces opposing 8th Army. To do so he intended to trap the Panzerarmee in its positions as they were. Any who escaped westwards would be dealt with later. In his meticulously detailed account of the battle

General Carver tells us that the preparations for realizing this ambitious resolve rested on three foundations–security, training and reorganization. It would not be unfair to add a fourth–Montgomery's own remarkable impact on officer and soldier alike. The grip which he imposed on 8th Army was far tighter than any that had gone before. It was complete. It says much for his leadership that his own undiluted confidence in victory was passed on and actually held by most of the men in his army. By going everywhere, seeing everybody and, what is more, expounding his ideas with such crystal clarity, he inspired in his subordinates interest, enthusiasm and conviction. Nothing quite like it had yet been seen in the desert. The first of Montgomery's three foundations, security, was achieved by minefields. Training and reorganization were more complex, and were of course subject to the details of his plan. The master plan was in origin simple enough. In the north 30th Corps was to break the enemy's defences, cut two lanes in the minefields, and allow 10th Corps with all its armour to pass through, choose ground controlling the enemy's supply routes and thus oblige the Panzer Divisions to attack it under circumstances, both of numbers and ground, favourable to 8th Army. Meanwhile in the south 13th Corps' attack would at once prevent Axis concentration against the northerly sector and allow light armoured forces to penetrate the enemy defences and move on El Daba. In essence the plan, as opposed to its execution, remained unchanged although Montgomery modified and extended 30th Corps' task to undertake what he called crumbling operations designed to widen the breach in the defences and systematically eat away the enemy's holding troops.

As at one time Auchinleck before him had done, Montgomery insisted that divisions should be fought as divisions. Moreover all armoured divisions were to have one brigade of motor or lorried infantry, and integration between infantry and tanks was to be the rule. 23rd Armoured Brigade, for example, attached one regiment to each of the divisions in 30th Corps, except 4th Indian which had none, and the New Zealanders who had 9th Armoured Brigade as a whole. Once 8th Army had been reorgan-

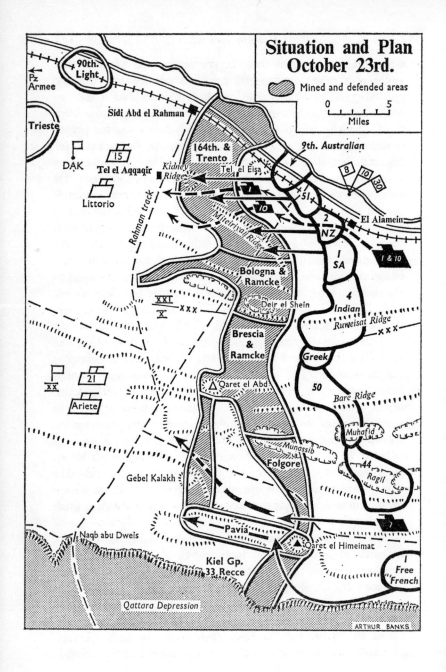

Situation and Plan October 23rd.

Mined and defended areas

0 ——— 5
Miles

90th. Light

Pz Armee

Sidi Abd el Rahman

Trieste

DAK

15

Tel el Aqqaqir

Littorio

164th. & Trento

Kidney Ridge

Tel el Eisa

Rahman track

Miteiriya Ridge

Bologna & Ramcke

9th. Australian

8 10 30

51

7

10

2 NZ

El Alamein

1 SA

1 & 10

4 Indian

Ruweisat Ridge

XXI
X   XXX

Deir el Shein

Brescia & Ramcke

Greek

50

Bare Ridge

21

XX

Ariete

△ Qaret el Abd

Muhafid

Munassib

Folgore

44

Ragil

Gebel Kalakh

Naqb abu Dweis

Pavia

△ Qaret el Himeimat

7

Kiel Gp. 33 Recce

1 Free French

Qattara Depression

ARTHUR BANKS

ized, training in earnest could begin. Those divisions not in the
line were able to train as divisions. The others had to carry out
their preparations brigade by brigade as relieved. Every unit re-
hearsed its part in the coming battle, although for the obvious
reason of maintaining security, it was not aware that this was so.
Major emphasis was laid on the very difficult problem of passing
large numbers of men and vehicles through the narrow gaps in
minefields at night. On the success of this technique, all would
depend. For the principal qualification of the master plan, indeed of any plan made in the face of the Panzerarmee's defences,
was precisely that posed by the need to clear ways through the
minefields and get tanks out the other side. It was this single
problem which caused more trouble and recrimination than any
other in the whole battle. All the practice and rehearsal, therefore, all the prodding and lifting drills, the gap-making parties,
traffic control and so on, together with new items of equipment
such as Polish mine detectors and flail tanks–all centred on this
first step to success. The very codeword for the attack, *Lightfoot*,
underlined the matter with grim humour. Furthermore this cru-
cial prologue to the operation did much to determine its timing.

Montgomery was adamant that the battle must start on the
eve of a full moon, for the hazardous business of negotiating
minefields could be done neither by daylight nor in complete
darkness. September was far too early. October then, in his view,
it had to be. It is fortunate that two of the other influences at
work–the timing of Operation *Torch* and the further relief of
Malta–were not wholly out of tune. Of course, the Prime Minister raged and composed acrimonious telegrams. But the facts
were that *Torch*'s D Day had been fixed for 8 November and
Malta's fuel and food would last until late November and early
December respectively. This meant that the British must have the
Benghazi airfields back in their hands by early November. If,
therefore, Montgomery were right in his estimate–'whole affair
about 12 days'–a successful attack on 23 October would mean
that pursuit into Cyrenaica should have begun exactly then. It
would no doubt be a 'damned nice thing', but it would do.
Churchill capitulated. In Alexander and Montgomery he had,

although he did not yet know it, found a pair of victorious generals after his own heart. It is worth remembering how felicitous were the command arrangements before Alamein compared with those on some previous occasions. Wavell, rock-like though he was and blessed with the vigorous O'Connor as a subordinate, independent in mind and activity, had too many campaigns to manage, and had lost O'Connor, Neame and Gambier-Parry at a stroke; Auchinleck chose two 8th Army Commanders, sacked them both and then took on the Army himself in addition to all his wider duties. How different was it now. Alexander had been freed of responsibility to the east and south, and he had total confidence in Montgomery who reciprocated this confidence absolutely. As for Montgomery, he had not only instituted the Chief of Staff system which has survived in the British Army to this day; he had selected his Corps commanders, men who, he knew, would fight the battle his way. Only Lumsden, commanding 10th Corps, was not one of his own men, and in the end he got rid of Lumsden.*

There was no comfort of this sort to be found in the Panzerarmee. Rommel himself described the affair as a 'battle without hope', and in any case Rommel was not there to start with. General Stumme could hardly aspire to the fame, experience and touch of the Desert Fox. Not all his tactical skill could alter the facts. Strategically the Axis had lost the initiative and that was that. It is interesting to record that even at this late stage† the German naval staff reiterated their ingredients for successful prosecution of the Mediterranean war–North Africa to be held from the Alamein position, air forces to be strengthened, Malta to be seized, an offensive against Suez to be eventually mounted. Rommel had no such illusions. He knew he could neither return to the offensive nor fight the sort of mobile battle at which he excelled. Instead the Panzerarmee must rely on the depth of its defences and aim to give back to the Afrika Korps its full freedom of

---

* Lumsden's alleged comment in the Cavalry Club on his return to England is worth recalling: 'There just isn't room in the desert for two —— like Montgomery and me.'

† An appreciation written in September.

manoeuvre. Having said as much, he retired to Germany for sick leave.

The battle itself had five parts–the break-in on the night 23–24 October; the crumbling operations of the 24th and 25th (the day Rommel returned) which did *not* clear the way for 10th Corps; Rommel's counter-attacks and Montgomery's change of plans from the 26th to 28th; Operation *Supercharge* on the night of 1–2 November which wore down the Panzerarmee to the point where they could no longer prevent a break-out;* and finally the break-out itself from 3 to 7 November. Montgomery, who like Napoleon thought morale the most important single factor in war, was well served by the morale of his soldiers in 8th Army, even without the undoubted enhancement of it which he himself brought about. The New Zealanders and Australians were tough veterans whom Rommel thought the best infantry he had encountered; 4th Indian Division and 50th Division had proved their worth time after time; the Desert Rats were there as usual; and there was 51st Highland Division eager for their first battle since the fall of France. One of their officers, Major H. P. Samwell, an Argyll and Sutherland Highlander, has described what the night of mines and wire, the 23 October, was like for a platoon commander who had never been in a battle before.

After a cramped and inactive day concealed in a slit-trench, he found great relief in all that had to be done as soon as it was dark. Commanders would come round and make last minute changes in the plan; the traditional hot meal was served, although excitement took the edge off many appetites; the Commanding Officer himself tried to speak to everyone and wish them luck. Samwell vividly remembered that the Colonel looked straight at him just as he was drinking water from an empty whisky bottle. Recalling the importance of conserving what was in his water bottle, he had sensibly made use of this alternative vessel. But the Colonel's look left him in no doubt as to what interpretation had been put on his practical economy. Worrying about it even took his mind off the forthcoming ordeal.

* Rommel put it thus: 'The battle is going heavily against us. We're simply being crushed by the enemy weight.'

He remembered moving to the start line–a piece of tape laid across the open desert–at about 9 pm. A full moon made it all seem terribly open. Then the guns began with a shattering roar, and so great was their impact that the ground shook beneath them. They could see shells bursting on enemy positions and starting fires which made it even lighter than before. They were glad that the enemy's guns were so long in replying and when they did, half-hearted at first. Some of the guns would never reply. They were already smashed to pieces.

Samwell found it all rather unreal, as if he were a spectator and not a participant, and only when he became aware of a change in the guns' behaviour–their own shells landing just in front of them–did he realize that the signal to advance was about to be given. Even then he felt detached and unflurried. Suddenly he found himself walking forward, almost casually, without having been conscious of getting up to go. There they all were in line, strolling forward in the desert, with company commanders shouting through megaphones to keep the line straight.

He was surprised to find that he had a stick in his hand instead of a gun, but smiled to himself when he recollected that he was at least armed with a pistol and nine bullets. Then the enemy's machine guns started and tracer streamed away in front of him. Mortar shells began to fall amongst them and men fell with groans and shouts. He saw a strand of wire in front of him, and some sixth sense made him jump over it. The sergeant behind him did not, and disappeared into eternity with a blinding flash. Now they were running, dim enemy figures appeared from trenches at which he vaguely fired with his pistol.

The line had broken up into blobs of men all struggling together; my faithful batman was still trotting along beside me. I wondered if he had been with me while I was shooting. My runner had disappeared, though; and then I saw some men in a trench ahead of me. They were standing up with their hands above their heads screaming something that sounded like 'Mardray'. I remember thinking how dirty and ill-fitting their uniforms were, and smiled at myself for bothering about that at this time. To my left and behind me some of the NCOs were rounding up prisoners and kicking them into some sort of formation. I waved my pistol at the men in front with their hands up to sign them to join the others. In front of me a terrified Italian was running round and round with his hands above his head screaming at the top of his voice. The men I had signalled started to come out. Suddenly I heard a shout of 'Watch out!' and the next moment something hard hit the toe of my boot and bounced off. There was a blinding explosion, and I staggered back holding my arm over my eyes instinctively. Was I wounded? I looked down rather expecting to see blood pouring out, but there was nothing–a tremendous feeling of relief. I was unhurt. I looked for the sergeant who had been beside me; he had come up to take the place of the one who had fallen. At first I couldn't see him, and then I saw him lying sprawled out on his back groaning. His leg was just a tangled mess. I realized all at once what had happened; one of the enemy in the trench had thrown a grenade at me as he came out with his hands up. It had bounced off my boot as the sergeant shouted his warning, and had exploded beside him. I suddenly felt furious; an absolute uncontrollable temper surged up inside me. I swore and cursed at the enemy now crouching in the corner of the trench; then I fired at them at point-blank range–one, two, three, and then click! I had forgotten to reload. I flung my pistol away in disgust and grabbed a rifle–the sergeant's, I think–and rushed in. I believe two of the enemy were sprawled on the ground at the bottom of the square trench. I bayoneted two more and then came out again. I was quite cool now, and I started looking for my pistol, and thinking to myself there will be hell to pay with the quartermaster if I can't account for it. At the same time I wondered when I had got rid of my stick, as I couldn't remember dropping it. I felt rather sad; it had been my constant companion for two years at home. I had walked down to the pictures with my wife and had put it under the seat, and on leaving I had forgotten it, and had had to disturb a whole row of people to retrieve it. I started then to wonder what my wife was doing at that moment.

Next they consolidated for a quarter of an hour before the advance continued. Samwell found his company commander and gave him a report. Suddenly the Colonel appeared, said a word of praise, and made off again. The company commander asked what it had all been like, commented on the 'pretty sights' of bayoneted men that had been left behind, confessed that he had not yet fired a shot. He agreed to give Samwell the reserve platoon to help reorganize. After that Samwell found himself on the move again, with a piper playing nearby, then shells started to land amongst them, and all at once he realized they were their own shells. They were going too fast. He pulled his men back and tried to find Company HQ and the companies on his left and right. He could find nothing at all.

My first feeling on realizing that the company on my right had carried on without me was one of intense irritation, but when I discovered there was no one on my left either, my anger turned to fear. For the first time that night I was afraid; a nauseating wave of terror went right through me as I realized I was quite alone with the remains of two platoons; my company commander and Company HQ had disappeared together with the wireless; the 'pilot' officer must have gone with the other company (we were sharing him). Instinct told me that I had gone too far to the left. All this time we had been steadily advancing again, and I started to swing to the right. I was still scared stiff, not at the shells that were exploding round us, but at the thought of being all alone, cut off from the battalion and even my Company HQ. I was to find—and so was the battalion later—that the failure of the unit on my left to keep up was to cost us dearly. We came to another enemy position; they surrendered without fighting, and we didn't waste time mopping up. I was so anxious to make contact with someone again. It appeared that many of the enemy at this position scuttled down the trenches to the left and remained in the gap where the unit on my left should have been, until we had passed, and then filtered back and shot up the reserve companies and Battalion HQ who were coming up behind. I was to be blamed for not finishing them off, but if I had attempted to chase them right across a battalion front I should have been hopelessly lost, while at the same time failing to secure my own objective.

Then up came part of the reserve company. What a joy to have someone else in a position of responsibility to talk to. Together they sorted out where they were, where they ought to be, and before long moved to the final objective, and captured some more of the enemy. They began to dig in. Samwell got through to Battalion HQ on the radio and reported. By dawn the battalion was firm in its positions. He was elated when he found that all was well. There was occasional small arms fire to be heard, but nothing more. Stand-to at dawn had been early and Samwell was tired out. Handing over to the sergeant-major, he fell into a slit-trench already occupied by two signallers, and went to sleep. He had earned it.

It would be hard to better Samwell's portrait of the confusion, loneliness, excitement and inexorable progress of battle. Yet if the fighting were hard for the Scots, how much more so was it for the Italians who opposed them. As the Count of Sillavengo has told us, 2nd Lieutenant Torelli was in the line almost opposite the Argyll and Sutherland Highlanders. They failed, as it were, to meet by a mere few hundred yards. By the morning of 26 October, when Montgomery was having second thoughts, Torelli's battalion was still hanging on to its position south-west of the Miteiryia Ridge. Torelli was soon 'to lose his liberty and become a mere number', his life 'a dreary succession of identical days. Such a life is not worth writing about.' But before this dip in his fortunes he recorded in his diary the story of his own capture.

Before the British actually closed with his position, there were the normal bombardments, and then the plain in front of him seemed to be full of enemy tanks. As there seemed to be nothing likely to stop them, Torelli went through the business of destroying maps and papers. In his diary he wrote that his conscience was clear and that he was ready to accept death, wounds or capture–hardly the sort of entry which might be made by an Anglo-Saxon.

When the attack on his battalion finally struck home, it seemed far from grim or relentless or frightening. There was an air of untidiness, chance, almost farce about it. As Battalion HQ was overrun, he and his comrades turned their guns on it–Italians and British alike. Then the British turned on his own group, and in the fight he noted how much more deadly British hand-grenades were compared with their own. At last two enemy soldiers seized him, and they rolled about on the ground, the two British Tommies 'splitting their sides with laughter, drunk as lords.' Later, when he and his fellow prisoners were taken to the rear, he observed the familiar scenes of a battle lost and won, the wounded behaving with startling differences, those badly hurt quiet and stoical, those with scratches squealing and moaning, some vomiting, some writhing on the ground, their uniforms personally soiled. He had seen it all so often before.

So much for the dog fight; 30th Corps' job was to make the hole and to do this there was bound to be close and bloody fighting. The controversial aspect of the battle was not this, but 10th Corps' role in it all. Whilst much was made of its being in Churchill's words 'a mass of manoeuvre', it was not in this fashion that in fact it fought. In his memoirs Montgomery explained that whereas up to *his* time, plans had been made with the object of destroying the enemy's armoured force first, so that when this had been done, the rest could be dealt with at leisure, he had decided to turn the process inside out. First he would destroy the infantry formations, and hold off the enemy's armour whilst doing so. Then, once this had been accomplished, he would tackle the enemy armoured formations with his own integrated groups of all arms.

Although it might be argued that since the enemy's infantry defences *had* to be tackled first in order to get through to the panzers, Montgomery had no choice in the matter, what is true is that his employment of the armour did bring in a new and tighter

control, which whilst resulting later in a pursuit condemned by
Alexander Clifford as a 'dull and measured affair', at the same
time prevented a repetition of the disastrously confused and uncoordinated encounters during the spring battles before Tobruk's
fall. General Leese maintained that Montgomery's handling of
armoured brigades and divisions was wholly different from what
had gone before. Swanning was out, and had been replaced by
properly coordinated use of tanks, artillery and infantry. The
armour was not to advance without proper support. Indeed where
possible, rather than advance at all, it would persuade the Germans to advance against it.

This was not to say that Montgomery could not, as we shall
later see, make sacrifices of the armour when he judged the situation to justify them. But he did at least try to ensure the effective
cooperation of all arms. In this resolve, however, he was frequently to fail. When he altered his plan for *Lightfoot*, the idea
was for 30th Corps to destroy the Axis infantry whilst 10th Corps
held off the panzers, that is exactly in accordance with his own
professed concept of how to fight a modern battle. But he had
further stipulated that if 30th Corps did not open the gate adequately, 10th Corps would have to *fight its own way through*, a
proposition so altered and unattractive that neither Lumsden nor
his armoured divisional commanders thought it sensible or possible. So strong indeed was both the dissent of the armoured
commanders and the scepticism of 30th Corps' divisional generals, who simply did not believe in 10th Corps' ability or determination to break through, that Montgomery had to complement
his 'no belly-aching' decree with orders that the operations would
be executed precisely as he had directed. They were not; and the
but partial success of *Lightfoot* led to a second great infantry
effort, *Supercharge*, which did eventually clear the way for armour. The armour itself bore some of the blame for earlier failure
because they did not make full use of artillery and infantry support which was available. As a result they emerged unsupported
from narrow minefield gaps and came under concentrated anti-
tank gun fire. In ensuring that the westerly limits of their minefields were so effectively covered in this way, the Axis forces had

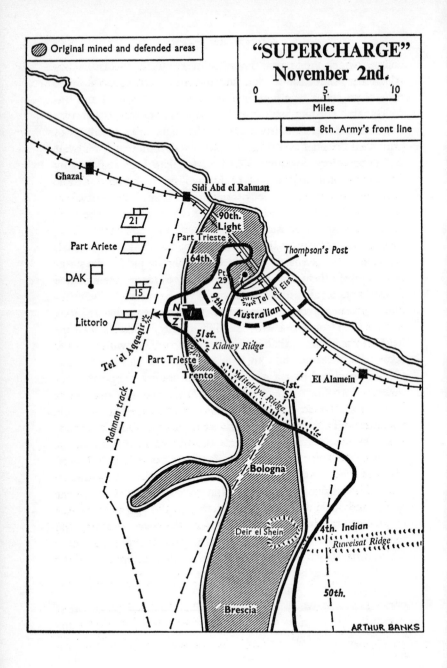

"SUPERCHARGE"
November 2nd.

Original mined and defended areas

0   5   10
Miles

8th. Army's front line

Ghazal

Sidi Abd el Rahman

90th. Light

Part Trieste

164th.

Part Ariete

DAK

Littorio

21

15

Thompson's Post

Pt. 29

9th. Australian

Tel el Eisa

N
Z

51st.

Kidney Ridge

Tel 'el Aqqaqir

Part Trieste

Trento

Miteiriya Ridge

1st. SA

El Alamein

Rahman track

Bologna

Deir el Shein

4th. Indian

Ruweisat Ridge

50th.

Brescia

ARTHUR BANKS

fully exploited the advantages of real depth. Even the final stages of 8th Army's break out on 2 November brought about a repetition of just these circumstances.

The 3rd Hussars, part of 9th Armoured Brigade, were given an unenviable task towards the end of *Supercharge*. Together with their companion regiments, the Warwickshire and Wiltshire Yeomanry, they were to exploit the successes of 151st and 152nd Infantry Brigades, push on towards the Sidi Rahman track and hold the door open for 1st Armoured Division. When the Commanding Officer of 3rd Hussars, Sir Peter Farquhar, heard what his regiment was required to do, he suggested to Montgomery that it was suicidal. He recalls that the Army Commander answered: 'It's got to be done and, if necessary, I am prepared to accept 100 per cent casualties in both personnel and tanks.'* Farquhar subsequently commented: 'I have always admired Montgomery for this frank reply–tough but typical of him. There was, of course, no more to be said.' The 3rd Hussars, like the other regiments, carried out their duty with great gallantry and suffered heavy losses in doing so.

Farquhar ordered the regiment to advance at 6.15, and they moved off on the right of the Wiltshire Yeomanry. At first all was well, but as the two leading squadrons got to the Rahman track, they were heavily engaged by anti-tank guns whose task was made easier by seeing their targets silhouetted as they came out of the dawn light. There seemed to be guns everywhere, but the 3rd Hussars 'pressed on relentlessly, just as their ancestors had done at Chillianwallah.'† Farquhar found his regiment down to seven tanks, and when the radio broke down, had to go round on foot to give orders. But what mattered was that they held fast, long enough to allow the 2nd Armoured Brigade to come up. At 10 o'clock that morning what was left of the 3rd Hussars assisted the

* 9th Armoured Brigade lost 75 per cent of its tanks and 50 per cent of its tank crews.

† In fact the British cavalry disgraced itself at Chillianwallah in a battle against the Sikhs in 1849. Because of some misunderstanding which led to confusion and panic, a division of cavalry stampeded to the rear. But the 3rd Light Dragoons' (as 3rd Hussars then were) part in it was an honourable one.

Queen's Bays in defeating a counter-attack by 15th Panzer Division. The regiment may have suffered great losses, but they had inflicted them too, knocking out 5 tanks, 4 field guns, 15 anti-tank guns and capturing 300 of the enemy.

Much more important, they and their sister regiments had done what Montgomery had wanted. They had forced the door open. A wedge some two to three miles wide had been driven into the enemy's position, and because of it 1st Armoured Division was able to come through and go on exerting the sort of pressure which eventually pushed the door right down. In spite of being reduced to a squadron* the 3rd Hussars continued to fight that afternoon, and in the morning, after leaguering for the night, were up at the front again. It seemed that the Germans had suffered even more heavily. When General Freyberg, commanding the New Zealanders, came up with Farquhar to examine the battlefield, he made a comment, which coming from such a soldier must have warmed those who heard it. 'Your regiment is magnificent,' he declared. 'The Hun is beaten—it is now the pursuit.'

In fact there was still some hard fighting to be done before Rommel ordered a general withdrawal on 4 November. Even when the pursuit did come, it was so only in name, not effect. In effect it was a following-up. The battle of Alamein did not destroy the Panzerarmee, but inflicted such great losses on it that it was on the defensive for the rest of the campaign. Michael Carver's view is that, of the 100,000 in the Axis forces, about half were casualties, that is, 30,000 taken prisoner and 20,000 killed or wounded. Moreover the Panzerarmee left about 1,000 guns and over 400 tanks on the battlefield. 8th Army lost 13,500 men killed, wounded or missing, 100 guns destroyed and 500 tanks unfit for action, but of these 350 were repairable. Although Rommel did not fight another serious defensive action until Mareth, four months after his disengagement from the Alamein position, the mere circumstance of his being able to fight it at all says much both for the skill of his retirement and the deliberation of 8th Army's operations from Alamein to El Agheila. There were

---

* The 3rd Hussars lost 21 officers, 98 soldiers killed, wounded and missing.

perhaps three reasons for it in addition to Montgomery's fundamental principle of no advance without security. Firstly on 4
November Lumsden with 10th Corps did not outflank the Afrika
Korps. He pushed against it. Bypassing the Afrika Korps had
proved unprofitable in the past, and Rommel was still Rommel
for all his losses. Secondly the dispersion of formations charged
with pursuit and encirclement, together with indescribable con-
gestion behind the front and inadequate traffic control or discipline, all added up to sheer slowness of movement. The rain on 6
and 7 November did not help, and lastly administrative arrangements were simply insufficient to ensure continuous re-supply of
petrol for the armoured divisions. But these disappointments
aside, what mattered was that as the familiar places were retaken,
Tobruk on 13 November, Gazala on the 14th, Benghazi on the
20th, it was for the third and last time. How had Montgomery's
handling of his first major offensive made certain that this was so?

Given that, in a conflict of attrition without cardinal errors on
either side, superior resources must in the end be decisive–and
the British advantage here both in quantity and quality was very
great–the main credit which should go to Montgomery is his sure
tactical grip in handling the battle. Of course it did not go exactly according to plan. But in essence the master plan worked.
A hole was driven through the enemy defences in such a manner
that, once it had been made, the Panzerarmee had no alternative,
short of allowing itself to be encircled and taken, but to retreat.
All turned on Montgomery's retention of balance, that is to say
his creation of reserves and use of them enabled him to take the
initiative and never let go of it. He chose where to strike, varied
the point of main effort, deceived Rommel as to where it was, and
thus by obliging him to react in a series of costly counter-attacks,
slowly but surely pushed the Panzerarmee off balance. 'The
Battle of Alamein', wrote Churchill, 'differed from all previous
fighting in the Desert. The front was limited, heavily fortified,
and held in strength. There was no flank to turn. A breakthrough
must be made. . . .' He went on to compare it with the offensives
of 1917 and 1918, their immense reliance on artillery and the
'forward inrush of tanks'. Whilst pointing out that there was also

a 'tremendous shield of minefields of a quality and density never known before', he does not mention that whereas in 1917 and 1918 tanks cleared lanes for the infantry, in 1942 infantry did the same for tanks. Nor does he draw attention to Montgomery's selection of night for the break-in. This, being a fundamental feature of both *Lightfoot* and *Supercharge,* was another important change in the nature and conduct of battle. The reason for it–how else to overcome the minefields which so dominated tactical thinking–was clear enough, and the success of Montgomery's methods speaks for itself.

Other features of this battle, whilst recurring ones, varied in intensity. Never had the Desert Air Force been so instrumental both in subduing Axis air activity and providing close support for 8th Army, so sustaining the already high morale of the soldiers. Never had the unceasing offensive against Axis shipping by air and sea alike been more effective (three issues* of petrol were available to the Panzerarmee before the battle when ten times as many were gauged to be the *minimum* reserve for waging it properly) or paid more decisive dividends.

Amongst all these developments one stands out–Montgomery's method of command. Gone were the doubts and uncertainties. Improvisation there was. But it went hand in hand with his own ideas about keeping balance. His calmness, his confidence, his refusal to be disturbed or ruffled, the habit of giving his orders personally to his corps commanders each morning and evening, all these had their effect. Montgomery does not want for detractors. But short of time, that all-important commodity, though he may have been–and when we consider that on 3 November, with *Torch* only five days away and with the fact that the Martuba airfields, 450 miles from Alamein, were deemed essential for the passage of the *Stoneage* convoy due in the Mediterranean on 16 November, itself the target date for capturing Martuba, the break-out had not even started, we see how short he was–his subordinate commanders were not harried. 'You always had a sense of time to spare', Leese later said. And the morale and confidence

---

* One issue of petrol was enought to move 100 km in normal, i.e. not fighting, conditions.

of commanders quickly made itself felt lower down. There was, of course, another major consideration as to the conduct of the battle. Rommel, who set the pattern of the defences before going on leave, had chosen to abandon his former partiality for mobile battles, at which he had so often worsted the British, because of his enemy's overwhelming superiority in numbers. Instead he substituted great depth of both mines and defended localities with guns dug in and tanks hull-down, a sandwiching of Italian and German troops, and an intention to counter-attack any penetrations rapidly and powerfully. But on his return he found that this last essential was unattainable. The Royal Air Force's supremacy, Stumme's penny-packet policy in distributing the panzers, lack of petrol and the need to react piecemeal to 8th Army's repeated and varied thrusts, robbed him of the ability to counter Montgomery's relentless pressure. 8th Army may have been wielded like a bludgeon, but at least it was an effective one. 'It may have been expensive and unromantic,' wrote General Carver, 'but it made certain of victory, and the certainty of victory at that time was all important. 8th Army had the resources to stand such a battle, while the Panzerarmee had not, and Montgomery had the determination, will-power and ruthlessness to see such a battle through.' Yet when the time came for him to give way, never did Rommel conduct so brilliant a withdrawal in the face of such uneven odds.

Whatever else might be said about the battle, its outcome had great impact. 'Seldom', says the *Official History,* 'can a communiqué have been more welcome to the Allies, nor, indeed, to the free world at large, than the announcement from Cairo on 4 November that the Axis forces were in full retreat.' Churchill rang the bells and understandably put it down as a 'glorious page in British military annals'. It was.

There have been many estimates as to what does or does not constitute a great general. One of the less obvious lists* of attributes, against which this judgment can be made, contains five—education, imagination, dedication, humanity and political acumen. In Montgomery's case his education, militarily speaking,

---

* By Major John Laffin in *The British Army Review.*

was thorough and his dedication absolute. Politically he was a child and his humanity, whilst prominent in presenting, and even committing, himself to his soldiers, did not stretch to recognizing the contribution which his predecessors had made to his own success. All this is clear. It is when we come to his imagination that our real interest is caught. If we think of imagination as a purely creative faculty, then we might suspect Montgomery to have been singularly short of it. If on the other hand we interpret it as the ability to think a battle through, weighing its ups and downs, its probabilities, its management, and then to present these imponderables—for if they were not imponderable, there would be nothing in generalship at all—in a clear and convincing fashion; if imagination is rather the trick of seeing things as they really are, and by doing so know how to grasp and keep the initiative, then we might concede his possession of it to have been superlative. The list, of course, is incomplete. General Carver's final assessment is that Montgomery's determination, realism and professionalism, together with the material superiority at his command, superiority of numbers and of fire power, were what won the day.* Many soldiers and observers of war have commented on the growing scarcity of men which becomes apparent as you advance from the rear areas to the front line, and General Carver also draws attention to the comparative fewness of those infantrymen, gunners, tank crews and engineers who actually did the 'bloody business'. It is about these men that we must allow him to have the last word on Alamein for this last word, coming from one whose part in it was so distinguished, perhaps gives in a nutshell what it was like to be there:

To the infantryman in the attack or sitting it out day after day in his slit trench in the front line; to the tank crew, grinding forward in the dark and dust among the mines, or trying to edge forward by day towards the ridge from which the anti-

* One of the most glowing tributes to Montgomery comes from Fred Majdalany who served under him in Sicily and Italy. Majdalany knew all about soldiering in war and had this to say: 'At a moment when the future of the western world was in the balance and history held its breath, he rallied his country's soldiers as Churchill had rallied its people.'

banged away, his cannon popping and snapping like a cap
pistol. Jerry seemed annoyed. Questing about, his turret rotat-
ing and turning with it the incredibly long and bell-snouted
gun, the German soon spotted his heckler. Leisurely, he began
to close the gap between himself and Daubin's light tank,
keeping his thick sloping frontal plates turned squarely to the
hail of Daubin's fire.

The crew of the m-3 redoubled their efforts. The loader
crammed what suddenly appeared to be incredibly tiny pro-
jectiles into the breach, and Daubin, the commander who was
also the gunner, squirted them at his foe. Ben Turpin could
not have missed at that range. Tracer-tailed armour-piercing
bolts streaked out of the muzzle and bounced like mashie shots
off the hard plates of the Mark IV.

The German tank shed sparks like a power-driven grind-
stone. Yet he came on, 150 yards away, then one hundred,
and seventy-five. In a frenzy of desperation and fading faith
in his highly touted weapon, Daubin pumped more than eigh-
teen rounds at the German tank that continued to rumble toward him. Through the scope sight, Daubin could see the
tracers hit, then glance straight up—popcorn balls, he thought,
thrown by Little Bo Peep. Fifty yards away, Jerry paused.
Daubin sensed what was coming and he braced himself.

The German loosed a round that screamed like an under-
nourished banshee. Ricocheting off the wadi bank a trifle
short, the shell showered sand and gravel into Daubin's open
turret hatch. How had the German gunner missed? Was he
addled? Was his gun useless at such short range? Impassively
the Mark IV continued to advance. Daubin wondered wildly
whether the tanker intended to use his gun tube to pry the m-3
out of its cozy terrain wrinkle. Was he planning to knock
Daubin into a corner pocket with a three-cushion shot? Instead, Jerry pulled to the right and mounted a small hummock
of ground. This destroyed Daubin's slight advantage of defil-
ade. Now the German was only thirty yards away.

It was time for Daubin to go. Gracefully if possible. But go.
Any way. If he could. Having made an estimate of the situa-

tank guns were firing; to the sapper clearing the mines, the anti-tank gunners and, to a lesser extent, the other gunners, it frequently seemed a chaotic and ghastly muddle. The area of the salient east of Kidney Ridge was the worst of all. The whole place was knee deep in dust. Nobody knew where anybody or anything was, where minefields started or ended. There was always somebody firing at something and usually somebody being fired at, but who and what it was and why was generally a mystery. To try and find out led from one false clue to another. The information one gleaned would probably be wrong anyway. In the end one gave up trying to 'tie everything up' and went one's own sweet way, hardening one's heart to the inconvenience, annoyance or anger it might cause to somebody else. The longer the battle went on, the less patient one became, the less inclined to obey orders and generally take trouble. The sudden glimpse of daylight, as the front began to break in the first few days of November, blew all this weariness of spirit away. Now it was a race for who should be first out, tempered by the feeling that, having miraculously survived the ever-present dangers of the battle among the minefields, it would be folly to fling away one's life too recklessly when victory was at hand.

Victory *was* at hand, and more victories were on the way. For as Churchill put it in his pithy, but hardly accurate, phrase : 'After Alamein we never had a defeat.'*

* Two days *before* Alamein, General Mark Clark had landed near Algiers from a British submarine in order to gauge likely French reactions to Allied landings there.

9. The end of the beginning

US ground forces must be put into position to fight German ground forces somehere in 1942.

Roosevelt

In his lectures on the Mediterranean Strategy, Michael Howard has traced with enviable brevity and lucidity how the decision for *Torch* came about. Although in the early part of 1942 the British and Americans were agreed that nothing should be allowed to interfere with Operation *Round-Up*–the invasion of Western Europe in 1943–studies by the British Joint Planning Staff as to the practicability of invading the Continent in *1942* (Operation *Sledgehammer*) concluded that what forces could be made available for it were such that they would quickly be eliminated by German formations already stationed there, thus not only condemning it as an operation in itself, but removing any chance of realizing its original purpose–relief of German pressure on Russia. General Eisenhower, who had already been appointed to command the United States troops which were assembling in the United Kingdom, did not at first agree, although he later conceded that these conclusions were sound. He was in any case powerless to alter the views of the British planners for at this stage of the United States' commitment the bulk of forces for *Sledgehammer* would have been British. There was still no thought of prejudicing *Round-Up* in 1943. Agreement that any side-shows must not be allowed to do this was unanimous. The very last thing that was to be contemplated was a landing in French North Africa. Landings in Brest, in the Channel Islands, in Norway–all were to be preferred to such a dispersion of effort and lengthening of communications. But war and strategy being, as we know, an option of difficulties, slowly but surely the easiest of these options became also the soundest.

Resurrection of the French North African idea, which had first been put forward by the British joint planners as early as December 1941, was set in train by President Roosevelt's determination to honour his perhaps hasty promise to Molotov, a promise which Germany's successes in her Russian campaign that summer made even more welcome, that a second front of some sort would be opened in 1942. When therefore it became clear that this could not be done in Europe, Churchill, as we have seen, renewed his proposal to Roosevelt in July shortly before departing for Cairo and Moscow. But even though the President was sympathetic, indeed enthusiastic, his generals were not. To Marshall and Eisenhower the proposal meant dissipation of resources away from the decisive arena in Europe itself and a postponement of *Round-Up* until 1944. Roosevelt overruled his military men, but even after his orders that *Torch* was to take place had been given, all was not plain sailing. There were still two profound disagreements between the Allied countries, first as to the strategic consequences of executing *Torch,* second as to the actual method of doing so. General Marshall in commenting on the first of these saw the operation as one which accepted the concept of a defensive circle round Continental Europe. The British Chiefs of Staff saw it rather as a means both of securing the Middle East, its oil and the Mediterranean sea routes (with all this would mean in terms of shipping released from the long Cape haul) *and* of closing the ring, not to stand on it defensively but, by tightening it, to throttle the Third Reich. The second disagreement emphasized that, in spite of their genuine wish to get to grips with the main bulk of the German armies in the west, the Americans were thinking circumspectly in that they wanted to land only on the Atlantic coast of Africa, then make their way slowly eastwards, whereas the British wanted Tunis and the straits there quickly, so proposed to land as far east as possible.

One thing though merited immediate accord and this was the appointment of General Eisenhower to Command *Torch.* His directive from the Combined Chiefs of Staff, dated 13 August, was based on agreement between Roosevelt and Churchill that a combined operation should be mounted against Africa as soon as possible so that Allied control of North Africa should extend from the Red Sea to the Atlantic. The operation was to be coordinated with Allied forces already established in the Middle East.

This directive envisaged three stages—getting established, exploiting to control all French North Africa, and then annihilating the Axis forces in the Western Desert. So far, so good, but where to land, that was still the question. The US Chiefs of Staff disliked the notion of committing their ships and men to the east of Gibraltar. Eisenhower, on the other hand, once converted to *Torch,* embraced it wholeheartedly, and with strong support from some of his British colleagues was anxious to go as far east as Bône. *Torch* had become a pet project for Churchill, and during this controversy he bombarded Roosevelt with his views. On 27 August he signalled the President compelling and prophetic reasons for landing well to the east.

His signal declared how profoundly disconcerted he and his advisers were by the memorandum which the US Joint Chiefs of Staff had sent two days before, and which by advocating landings too far west, seemed to him to rob *Torch* of all its promise. Algiers must, he urged, be captured on the same day as Oran. It was there, he believed, that the most friendly reception awaited the Allies, and even if it led to no more than the securing of Algeria, this would be a major strategic gain. But it might lead to more. With Algeria and Oran, the Allies could take on the Germans in a fight for Tunis—'even if they got there'. But to make the Germans a present of Tunis *and* Algiers was absurd. It had to be remembered that French cooperation, a principal feature of future campaigning, might depend on the occupation of Algeria, and its contribution to seizing Tunis and Bizerta—a necessary prelude to subsequent attacks on Italy. *Also sprach Churchill.*

After further exchanges it was agreed that there would be simultaneous landings at Casablanca, Oran and Algiers. The first under Patton and the second under Fredendall would be American; at Algiers the 1st Army commanded by Anderson would be a joint one. Settling *where* the landings were to be was to clear only the first hurdle. In deciding on an operation of this sort in such a part of North Africa and at such a time, the United States and Britain were making a total change in the nature and conduct of the campaign. It was to be a combined operation in two senses—first it was *Allied*; second it was amphibious. Unlike Egypt, French North Africa contained no great administrative complex of depots, storage installations, workshops, with well developed communications to serve the forward troops engaged in major, modern battles. All these things would have to be brought with the invading armies. And then the terrain was so different. The Atlas mountains and their subsidiary ranges stretched from Morocco to Tunis, and between Algiers and Bizerta these mountains ran close to the coast itself. Distances were great and communications poor. In short the logistic problems were immense. Nor were the tactical ones contemptible. Armoured troops, which had so dominated the fighting in Libya, would not find it so easy to manoeuvre in Algeria and Tunisia. Broken, rugged and sometimes forested hills with easily defended defiles and passes, heavily cultivated valleys which the winter rains would be likely to turn into bogs impassable for vehicles, it was country not exactly designed to facilitate the rapid advances of tank and motorized units. On the contrary it was made for defence. First, however, the Allies had to get ashore.

Eisenhower's great contribution to the Allied cause was that he was determined from the very beginning that his joint headquarters should be successfully integrated, would function 'as though its members belonged to in single nation', in fact that the two allies would be properly allied to each other. He made it work. The great need for harmony between a variety of commanders and staffs was aggravated by the extent and diversity of the cooperating forces. *Torch* was to begin with a landing from the sea. It was to be the first of many such enterprises and presupposed a degree of air and sea mastery in the Atlantic and Western Mediterranean which six months earlier could hardly have been countenanced, let alone furnished. Nevertheless the plan was daring. There were so many uncertainties. Would the French welcome

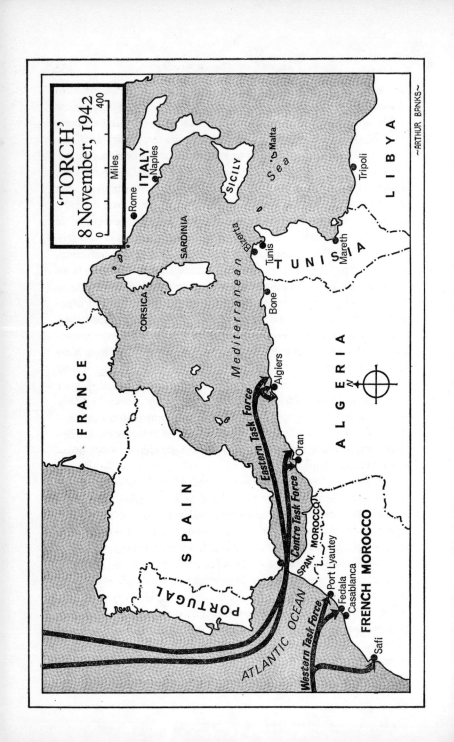

or resist the invaders? Would the Germans attempt to rush
through Spain and grab Gibraltar? Or would they content themselves with reinforcing Axis forces in North Africa, and if so, how,
in view of the Italian fleet's poor showing, would they do it? In
the event the Axis was taken completely by surprise. Even reports
of a great fleet* of ships in the Straits of Gibraltar on 5 November–the day Rommel began to withdraw his Panzerarmee from
the Alamein positions–did not click. It took a BBC announcement
on D Day to give the German naval staff Algiers as one of its
destinations. Interference from the Axis at this stage was therefore negligible. But their reaction, when it did come, was to be
swift, dramatic and eventually for them disastrous.

D Day had been fixed for 8 November, the earliest date consistent with preparation and training, a date, as it transpired,
which was auspicious for it found Rommel fully engrossed with
conducting his withdrawal from Mersa Matruh. Eisenhower has
described the tenseness there was while he waited in Gibraltar
for news of his great undertaking.

There was reason to be tense. It was after all the first joint
offensive which the Allies had been able to mount. Nearly everywhere else the story had been one of defence, and not always
successful defence. There had been too many Hong Kongs, Tob-
ruks, Singapores. Now assorted convoys of Allied ships were
ploughing their way through the Atlantic, some to brave the
Straits of Gibraltar where guns on either flank of the narrows
might speak with hostile voices. All three expeditions, one each
bound for Casablanca, Oran and Algiers, were running the
gauntlet of the U-boats and soon would come within range of
enemy air attack. Nor was this all. The very troops embarked
were about to undertake a complex operation, never before tried,
of landing on beaches which might be defended. Most of them
had never even been in action until this time. The ships that there
were, for all their numbers, were still not enough to carry that
preponderance of weight in supporting weapons which would
guarantee success. Eisenhower had plenty to occupy his mind.

In spite of scattered opposition all three landings went well. At

* 110 cargo and troop ships and more than 200 warships were used.

Algiers units of the 34th US Infantry Division and the British 78th Division landed in three sectors. In the west 11th Infantry Brigade completed its landings without opposition, and their objective, Blida airfield, was soon in Allied hands; in the centre 6th Commando captured Fort Duperré after it had been bombed, and 168th Regimental Combat Team occupied the high ground above Algiers itself. In the east there was also some fighting, but 39th Regimental Combat Team seized the airfields at Maison Blanche and Hussein Dey. By agreement with General Juin, Algiers was occupied by the British and Americans at 7 pm on 8 November. At Oran the main aims were similar–to secure the port, the town and neighbouring airfields. Again three sectors were chosen, but resistance here was much more coordinated, and it was not until noon on 9 November that Oran surrendered. Scuttled ships made the port unusable. Opposition was stronger still at Casablanca. Shore batteries opened fire on landing craft, which were handicapped by heavy surf, and on the beaches when troops were ashore. Fighting by French naval, air and ground units went on until 11 November, and only as a result of Admiral Darlan's general order to do so did Casablanca capitulate.

By this time therefore all lodgements were secure, and now came the second of Eisenhower's tasks–to drive on to Tunis. But this task was not to be so easily accomplished. On 9 November General Anderson had reached Algiers and taken command of 1st Army.

One of the groups he directed towards Mateur and Djedeida was Blade Force, made up of the 17th/21st Lancers in tanks, an armoured car squadron, field, anti-tank and anti-aircraft artillery, a company of the Rifle Brigade and other supporting units. On 25 November Blade Force was ordered to seize a road junction ten miles south of Mateur, and the 17th/21st Lancers were about to fight their first action of the war. C Squadron Leader tells us what his first experience of battle was like:

The CO told me to go down to the T-roads and contact Major Elkington, commanding the Rifle Brigade Company. I moved the squadron forward to a hull-down position about 800 yards short of the T-roads, and went forward in my own tank. Major Elkington said that the farm on the right was clear, and a carrier section of his was in it, but the farm on the left was held, with a gun firing from somewhere near it. I decided to seize the high ground above the farm on the right, as it appeared to overlook the farm on the left. I ordered the squadron to move up, and waited for them to get level with me. In moving up, two tanks, one from each Valentine troop, ran into the river and got stuck. The others came round by the ford, Crusaders leading. Just before they arrived, the enemy gun opened up, and bracketed the T-roads. I moved off hastily and saw the third round burst on the T-roads, so I put down a small and not very effective smoke screen to cover the squadron over the ford. The second Crusader—Sergeant Sorrell—was hit by an HE shell which blew its track off. I saw it running wildly in a circle with its rota-trailer behind it. I was afraid the crew had been concussed, but later they told me it was merely to avoid being hit again!

Two Crusaders reached the hill above the farm (Morton and Sergeant Smith). The former rounded the hedge to find an Italian self-propelled gun turning the other corner about seventy yards away. Morton's gunner fired a burst of Besa by mistake, and then hit it with his first six-pounder, smashing its steering and killing the driver. He then drove past it and shot it from behind, wounding the rest of the crew severely. Sergeant Smith dismounted and reported the tank quite out of the fight, he also went down to the farm which appeared deserted, but actually contained about thirty Italians, who surrendered later. Stanford's troop went round to the back of the other farm, and met another thirty Italians, who also surrendered. It was also held by some Germans who came to life and inflicted some casualties on the Rifle Brigade when they advanced to clear the battlefield. Dale, the carrier platoon commander, asked us to help them out. I therefore sent Lumley-Smith's troop across, and shelled it with the close-support tank and Besa'd it with the remaining tanks. The Besa set the haystack on fire, and the Germans came running out, until a message came from the Rifle Brigade to stop firing. The squadron rallied–refuelled from rota-trailers, made tea, collected prisoners, searched and set fire to the Italian tank, and were presented with a sheep by the grateful farmer. The total bag was four SP guns, about 100 Italians and 40 Germans, two good lorries and a great deal of equipment. Our casualties were nil, damage to tanks, one Valentine dented, one track blown off.

All things considered, it was a good start, and Blade Force continued to fight a number of successful encounters. But the forces at General Anderson's disposal for this first attempt to reach Tunis, principally 78th Division with elements of 6th Armoured Division and the US 1st Armoured Division were insufficient to overcome Axis resistance. At this early stage the Germans were still enjoying superior air power and the persistently far better gun-armour combination of their tanks. Their Pzkw IV with its powerful 75mm gun was formidable enough. Soon the dreaded Tiger, the Pzkw VI, mounting the deadly 88mm was to make its début.

The 17th/21st Lancers was not the only regiment being blooded during these first battles for Tunis. Another was the 1st Armoured Regiment of the US 1st Armoured Division, and one of its units advanced on the right of Blade Force. This was the 1st Battalion, equipped with the M-3 tank, which 8th Army called the Honey, and commanded by Lieutenant-Colonel Waters who had already made clear to his men that successes against the French in getting established ashore counted for nothing, and that they would have little to congratulate themselves on until they had shown what they could do against the Germans. Opportunity was not long in coming. The battalion acquitted itself well in a battle–the first of the war between American and German tanks–with a number of Mark III and Mark IV panzers. 2 Lieutenant Daubin had an unenviable encounter with a Mark IV :

Within gun range of the column, Daubin found partial cover in a small wadi, a dry stream bed that extended the protection of its low bank. Singling out one German tank as his own, he

tion and held a staff conference with himself, he decided that he was in a predicament known in the trade as 'situation doubtful'. A rapid retrograde movement to an alternate firing position was in order. Because his driver was half buried in the brass of expended shells and unable to receive his foot and toe signals, Daubin crouched behind him and yelled into his ear. He wanted the driver to pull back with all possible speed, to zigzag while backing, and to keep the front of the tank facing Jerry. 'Yes, sir,' the driver said clearly, without a trace of excitement in his voice. . . .

As the driver jockeyed his gears, Daubin began to feel that everything was going to be all right. The M-3 lurched backward and across the wadi, then up the bank. A distinct feeling of relief came over Daubin. He climbed into his turret and straightened up for a quick look out of the open hatch. At that moment, death, inexplicably deferred, struck. The slug that was doubtlessly aimed at the turret struck the vertical surface of the armoured doors and caved in the front of the tank. The driver was instantly killed. Blown out of the turret by the concussion, Daubin was thrown to the ground . . . he became aware of his M-3. Sheathed in flame, the tank was still moving, backing out of the wadi, continuing to retire. He watched it go, until it was out of sight.

It was this sort of reception which made impossible rapid achievement of Eisenhower's second task.

Admiral Cunningham, commanding the Expeditionary Force, maintained in his despatch that bold as the plan had been, it had not been bold enough, and that had the Allies landed forces as far east as Bizerta and Tunis, with missions amongst others of capturing the airfields there, the Axis would have been forestalled and success complete. 'We failed,' he wrote, 'to give the final push which would have tipped the scales.' General Anderson was of similar opinion. He believed that had American or British troops got to Tunis or Bizerta before the Axis, the French 'would have swung to our side' and that therefore some forces for just this purpose should have been landed well to the east either on the first day of *Torch* or the next. But having decided against this course of action, the Allies had heavy Axis reinforcements to reckon with. It was to be the old desert story of who could build up faster. As a result Tunis did not fall until May of the following year. It would be unsound perhaps to make too much of this failure to exploit *Torch* to the full from the very start. For almost every single man and machine which Hitler and Mussolini despatched to Tunisia was a hostage to fortune.

Hitler's reaction, although it was ultimately damaging to his own position, was remarkably prompt and violent. His occupation of Vichy France led to the scuttling of the French fleet at Toulon. But far more positive a step was that of sending troops, rapidly and in large numbers, to Tunis. By the end of November there were 15,000 German soldiers there including Parachute and Glider Regiments, Panzer Grenadiers, reconnaissance companies, and several Panzer Regiments some of which were equipped with the new Pzkw VI, the Tiger tank, mounting the famous 88mm gun. The whole of 10th Panzer Division would soon arrive, plus two other German and two Italian divisions. General Nehring, temporarily in command, determined to prevent the Allies from reaching Bizerta or Tunis. That the Germans had been able to reinforce so strongly that they were in a position even to attempt this was an astonishing tribute to the use they made of their own transport aircraft and their ally's shipping. Kesselring's Fliegerkorps II had been substantially strengthened and the transport fleet had been more than trebled. What is more the Luftwaffe units in Tunis itself were building up, and by mid-November Fliegerführer Tunis had 81 fighters, including some of the new FW 190s, and 28 dive bombers at his disposal. On 8 December General von Arnim took command in Tunis.

The Allied attempts to bounce Bizerta and Tunis failed, and enemy counter-attacks pushed back their leading troops from the Tunis plain in to the mountains. This line was held by the Germans until the spring. Some of the ground lost included the renowned Longstop Hill, which had been captured by the Coldstream Guards and then taken over by 1st Battalion, US 18th Infantry. The 2nd Coldstream Guards did not have a comfortable ride to Algiers. As one of their officers recalled the battalion was jammed into two decks of the SS *Nea Hellas* at the bottom of a hold below the water-line.

Provided everyone took off all their equipment and removed their coats, the battalion was just able to sit down. Sleeping was a different thing, and at night hammocks seemed to be hanging everywhere, while floors and tables were crammed with sleeping soldiers. Worst of all was the air. There were no port-holes and no fans. The only way any air could enter the decks at all was through the hatch, and this was closed at night in order to black-out the ship. It then became intolerable, and only when a canvas shaft was linked up to the open deck could any fresh air get in. Many were seasick, and to accommodate them a few 40 gallon drums slid along the decks splashing their contents about. After such a journey the hazards of battle were almost welcome.

Before the 2nd Coldstream came into action, von Arnim, whose command now was called the 5th Panzer Army, had succeeded in stabilizing the line. But a few days before Christmas 1st Army made a new attempt to get on. The idea was that 6th Armoured Division and 78th Division with US combat teams were to capture Tunis, but first Longstop Hill had to be taken, and the Coldstream Guards were to do it. They were still there on Christmas Day.

After the orders had been given out on the morning of 22 December, the battalion prepared for a night attack. All the many things to be done, cleaning guns, issuing ammunition, trying to grab a little rest, occupied the afternoon. The time-honoured custom of a good hot meal before going into an attack was adhered to. Then off the battalion set, along tracks, railway lines and roads, with the dominating bulk of Longstop towering in the distance, faintly lit up by a moon which was sometimes visible through the drifting clouds. The first part of the attack went well, but once the summit of Longstop was reached by No. 1 Company, the whole world was illuminated by flares and tracer ammunition. Machine gun bullets and grenades flew at the guardsmen, killing both Company Commander and Company Sergeant Major. Yet courage and discipline prevailed. The summit was taken, and then came the grim business of trying to dig in on the rocky, stony ground with inadequate entrenching tools whilst mortars rained down. The Commanding Officer decided to order up another company, but his radio failed him, and a liaison officer stumbled round to find it. An hour wasted, and still another hour or more to go before the American unit would arrive to take over.

Strong German counter-attacks had succeeded in re-taking the Railway Halt to the east of the main feature. Nevertheless the battalion handed over to the us 18th Combat Team, and began to make its way back towards Medjez-el-Bab in drenching rain. No sooner had they had some food and a little sleep than No. 4 Company was ordered–*to go back to Longstop*. German reoccupation and use of a feature, the Djebel el Rahra, north-east of the main hill, had obliged the Americans to abandon all of Longstop except for its western and southern slopes. No. 4 Company reoccupied the col, and next day, 24 December, the whole battalion was ordered to re-take the objective. They did so except for Djebel el Rahra. Up the slippery, mortar-raked slopes of the hill there was only one way to keep the battalion supplied, and that was by using soldiers as porters. There were no mules. Vehicles could not get there. A complete company exhausted itself with this task. Casualties, in ground too rocky to provide protection from digging, were high, and evacuating them was a hazardous business. The whole battle was a foretaste of what some of the bitter fighting in Italy was going to be like. On Christmas Day another German counter-attack, supported by heavy mortars and armoured cars, was too strong. The battalion, threatened from the south, was in danger of being outflanked, and was instructed to withdraw. Longstop Hill was back in German hands, where it was to remain for many a month. The battle had cost 2nd Coldstream Guards nearly 200 killed and wounded; the 18th us Infantry had lost 350.

On Christmas Eve Darlan had been assassinated, and his death cleared the way for uniting the forces of French resistance under de Gaulle. But by this time the rains had set in properly. Three days of torrential downpours had put an end to manoeuvre off the roads. Eisenhower's signal to the Combined Chiefs of Staff on the same day as Darlan's murder explained that continual rain ruled out the possibility of an immediate attack on Tunis. Much more likely was a slow, methodical advance by the infantry. Meanwhile he would try to get together a force to operate strongly on the southern front.

Yet if the transformation of the Tunisian countryside into seas of mud put paid to bold enterprises there, on the seas themselves the Royal Navy and the Allied air forces were slowly establishing an ascendancy which they were never again to lose. Before they did so, however, the Axis had shown once more what could be done when Hitler, Canute-like, was resolved to try and turn back the tide. Donald Macintyre has reminded us that the Italian Navy delivered 90,000 tons of guns, tanks, fuel and food to Tunis in November alone, but of course they were 90,000 tons which Rommel did not get. Indeed the scale of reinforcement and supply which was made possible once the Axis really turned its attention to Africa invites conjectures as to what might have happened if Rommel had enjoyed comparable benefits. During the first few months of 1943 the German and Italian air forces flew over 7,000 sorties to Tunis with 14,000 metric tons of supplies and 40,000 soldiers. A further 50,000 troops came by sea. If Malta did not at first interfere with this new and short sea route, the island was doing great things against the old one to Tripoli. The Italian Navy regarded this route as so badly imperilled by Malta-based sea and air forces that traffic along it might just as well be discontinued. British Naval forces, 'Q' from Bône, 'K' from Malta, with the help of RAF torpedo-carrying Beauforts and Wellingtons fell upon the Italian convoys and blew them out of the water. Out of more than 200,000 tons of cargo sailed to North Africa from Italy and Sicily during December 1942, only a little more than half reached port. In January 31 out of 51 Axis ships on passage were sunk or damaged. The Italian man of arms has sometimes been maligned for lack of *il dono di coraggio*. We have seen already that when well led the soldiers of Italy fought to the last. The courage of these seamen in the face of such losses is beyond praise.

Yet however many of these Italian sailors might be suffering a sea change, the facts were that von Arnim was being kept supplied with enough and Eisenhower was waterlogged. It would have been hard to imagine Alexander, at the other end of Africa, talking of methodical infantry advances. Montgomery's advances might have been methodical, but they were highly mechanized, steady and sure. Indeed his recapture of Cyrenaican airfields, together with Axis preoccupation in Tunisia and Tripolitania, had had just the hoped-for effect in further relieving Malta, and on 20 November the four ships of *Stoneage* convoy reached the island safely, whilst two weeks later five more of another convoy arrived. From that time on, resupply was sustained.

The battles for French North Africa in November and December 1942 had been very different from those in Libya. The Allies had met either opposition which was French, half-hearted and hardly worth the name, or had been stopped dead by it as soon as it was German. There were no grand outflanking movements to be done here. It was a change indeed from the desert. But before long 8th Army too would encounter new tactical problems, for they were about to leave the Libyan desert behind them. It would mean amongst other things that the gradually wearying Desert Fox would win his last victory–against the 1st, not 8th, Army. Yet this would not alter the outcome in North Africa. The Axis powers were on a losing wicket, and were about to be hit for six out of the ground. 'This is not the end,' Churchill had warned an audience at the Mansion House on 10 November. 'It is not even the beginning of the end. But it is, perhaps, the end of the beginning.'

10. Tripoli, Casablanca and Kasserine

> It was at this point in time that the 18th Army Group came
> into existence, comprising all the land forces in North Africa–
> British, American and French–under my command. My first
> task was to reorganize the forces facing eastwards in Tunisia–
> the British First Army and the United States II Corps.
>
> *Alexander*

From November 1942 there was not one battle for North Africa
being conducted on land, but two, the first by Montgomery with
8th Army, the second by Anderson with 1st Army. Not for three
more months were their efforts to be concentrated and coordinated under a single command. Montgomery's advance from El
Agheila to Tripoli was conditioned by two circumstances. First,
he was determined not to allow Rommel to regain the initiative
as he had so devastatingly done in April 1941 and January
1942; this determination demanded of course the very build-up
of reserves and resources behind him which had been impractic-
able on those previous occasions. The second, consequential circumstance was how to resolve the huge logistic problem which
Montgomery's methodical yet persistent advance imposed on the
supply and transport organization. Despite, therefore, some ex-
travagant claims about the pursuit to Tripoli,* it was in fact a
deliberate following-up of the Panzerarmee together with repeated, unsuccessful attempts to pin it down on the coast road and
cut it off by left hooks. Rommel, no less formidable in defeat, carried out a series of skilful, rearguard actions, went on living to
fight again another day and even to win one more North African
victory.

When he halted his army at El Agheila on 24 November,
Rommel was already at odds with Kesselring, Mussolini and
Hitler as to future operations in North Africa. Rommel's view

---

* For example: 'The whole of 10th Corps thundered westward' (11th
Hussar history); 'The armour was going headlong' (Kippenberger).

was that to stand at El Agheila without substantial reinforcements of men, weapons, aircraft and supplies was to invite encirclement and liquidation. 'We either lose the position four days
earlier and save the army,' he said, 'or lose both position and
army four days later.' But by this time Hitler, like Napoleon before him, was making pictures, and would not listen to advice,
however sound, which involved abandoning the African theatre.
Nor did he reject this advice in a reasonable way. British generals
might be subjected to bullying telegrams from the Prime Minister or even to the spoken word in an atmosphere of brandy,
cigars and apparent ability to do never-endingly without sleep.
But none of them was ever required to tolerate the sort of treat-
ment which Rommel got from Hitler. When he gave it as his
opinion that if the army remained in North Africa, it would be
destroyed–the date was 28 November, the place Rastenburg–the
Führer turned on him in a rage and launched a tirade of abuse
and recrimination, with which, to Rommel's further aggravation,
all Hitler's staff, few of whom had ever been in action, seemed to
agree. When Rommel pointed out that only one third of the
Afrika Korps had weapons, Hitler burst out with the accusation
that the others had thrown their arms away. He could not see
that it was the British battering from the air plus the shooting of
their guns and tanks which had destroyed all these weapons, and
refused to countenance Rommel's protest that with the totally
inadequate supply of petrol he had had, the Afrika Korps' escape
had been almost a miracle.

In any case discussion was not Hitler's forte. He simply laid
down that it was politically necessary to hold the position in
Africa as it was, and that therefore there would be no withdrawal.

Montgomery gave Leese's 30th Corps the job of trapping
Rommel at El Agheila. Three weeks were allowed for re-grouping, getting supplies up and planning for the battle. 51st Highland Division was to pin the enemy on the coast road, whilst 7th
Armoured Division broke through further south and the New
Zealanders made a wider outflanking movement. The attack
started on 14 December, but failed to trap the Desert Fox. He

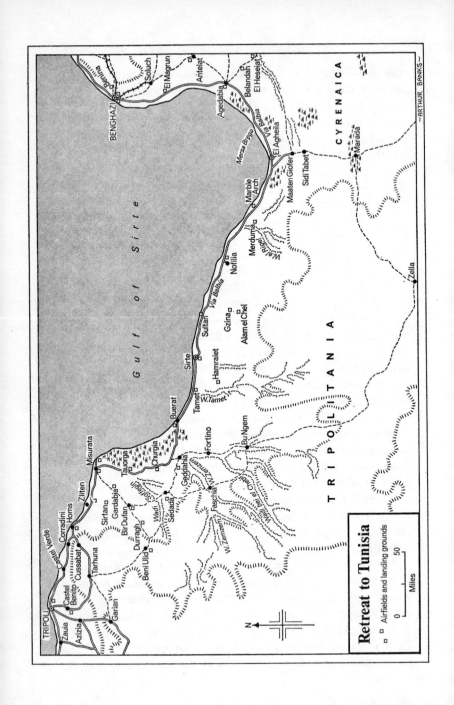

was far too wily for that. A wide encircling movement across un-known parts of the desert is slow work; withdrawal down a pre-viously reconnoitred, easily motorable road is fast. Nice coordin-ation of flank guards and rear guards, at which they were so ex-pert, gave the German troops who provided them both timely in-formation and the means to make a clean break without getting too committed or too closely pursued. Rommel's old subordinate, Heinz Schmidt, was with Special Group 288, and has recorded how he withdrew from the El Agheila position.

It was as early as 12 December that the withdrawal began. British preparations for a frontal attack were not hard to identify. Schmidt's group was given the task of flank and rearguard to the Afrika Korps, and by using mines, booby-traps and anti-tank ditches managed to slow up the British advance. Not until 15 December did the 8th Armoured Brigade catch up with them on the Marada road. Schmidt's unit lost a company in this engage-ment, and meanwhile the New Zealanders were left-hooking in an attempt to cut off the whole Group. They swung wide of the main position to come up some 60 miles west of El Agheila at the Wadi Matratin. Schmidt's rearguard, leap-frogging back along the road, found themselves still to the east of this wadi when the enemy were already in position behind them. But somehow the New Zealanders were not at their best, losing their way in the dark, and Special Group 288 managed to filter their way through by breaking up into small parties—though not without loss. Every-where they blew up bridges and culverts, and were generous in their distribution of mines. Following up needed a cautious hand, but by the evening of 16 December the two armies clashed again at Nofilia.

It was at Nofilia that the New Zealand Division supported by 4th Light Armoured Brigade had another shot at left-hooking in order to cut off the enemy rearguards of 15th Panzer Division. Kippenberger's brigade, as so often before and after, was in the thick of it.

From the top of an escarpment Kippenberger could see the coast road three miles away and the sea sparkling beyond it. Along the road to the west went German transport, escaping the net once more, while the rearguard was positioned to protect the southern flank and already was engaging Kippenberger's reconnoitring Bren carriers half a mile in front of him. While he called his battalion commanders forward for orders, he could see a comparable group of German officers standing on a knoll rather more than a mile to the *east* obviously discussing what to do about the advancing New Zealanders. As 88mm guns opened up at his carriers, Kippenberger decided to break the rules for once and without proper reconnaissance order an immediate attack by all three battalions in order to get astride the road and cut off as many enemy as he could. The battalions were to go forward as fast and as far as possible in their lorries and only dismount when the fire got too severe or the soft sand too difficult. Supporting artillery was already in action, but Kippenberger noted that he 'would have given a lot for a squadron of tanks.'

The 23rd Battalion charged forward in their trucks with the men being thrown about inside them and enemy shells pouring down on them. The sand was so heavy that unless a truck was actually hit, the shells did no damage. Although the other two battalions were also advancing, the German gunners stood fast and began to fire over open sights at the leading New Zealanders, who soon had to dismount from their trucks and continue the attack on foot. But the position was too strong to be bounced. The customary German teams of infantry, tanks, anti-tank guns and minefields held up both leading battalions, and then after dark slipped away. Kippenberger's cry for some tanks speaks ill of the grouping which had been laid down for what was essentially a series of encounter battles, a situation which calls for proper and strong integrated teams of all arms right at the front, able to strike quickly and powerfully, get and keep enemy rearguards on the run, and so avoid repetition of studied attacks which give the enemy the time they so urgently need during a withdrawal in order to prepare the next delaying position. Next day Kippenberger's brigade looked round the flank guard position which had held them up. It had been a fully dug battalion defence with supporting dug in anti-tank guns and tanks. After this the New Zealanders were to have a rest—but not the engineers. There were mines everywhere from Agheila to Sirte. Major Samwell, whom we last saw at Alamein, rejoined his battalion of Highlanders near Sirte on 12th January, just before Montgomery's announcement–'Tripoli in ten days'–and almost at once had a most unpleasant encounter with anti-personnel mines.

Whilst positioning his company he could not at first identify a number of explosions in the platoon areas, and on investigating found several men killed and wounded. Mortars, he thought. But on sending stretcher bearers over, they too were struck down with further explosions. Meanwhile he himself was carrying one of the wounded, a sergeant, back to Company Headquarters.

It was then that I realized we were in the middle of a concentration of anti-personnel mines. A cold shiver ran down my spine as I realized I had not only walked right through it, but had walked about in it while trying to patch up the sergeant and during the rests en route. It was hopeless to try and look for them in the dark, and the only thing to do was to carry on and trust to luck. It was a nightmare of a struggle back. The sergeant got heavier and heavier, and every step I took I expected to be my last. As I approached HQ someone came out to help me, but I shouted to him to stop where he was; the more people moving about, the more chance there was of standing on a mine.

I finally got my burden in, and immediately issued an order to everyone to stand where he was and not move. I had to find out how far the mines extended ... Having organized a mine-searching party to clear the area round Company HQ, I decided I should have to get through to the platoon beyond the minefield in order to warn them not to send men back until a path was cleared. No one except myself knew where they were, so there was nothing for it but to double back across the mined area myself. Crossing my fingers for luck I started back, and passing one of the stretcher-bearers on the way, I stopped only long enough to discover he was dead, and arrived safely at the platoon. The platoon commander had realized what had happened. He had actually been on his way to Company HQ when the first mines exploded, and had rightly decided that it was no use taking unnecessary risks, and had returned to organize a mine sweep of his own platoon area.

Once more I had to face that nightmare journey back. The problem was whether to crawl slowly feeling for mine-prongs, or just to dash across and trust to luck. I decided on the second alternative, and bounded across, keeping as much as possible to the same route as before. I got through safely, and after seeing the last of the wounded temporarily patched up and evacuated to Battalion HQ, Company HQ dug in, and the mined platoon settled in new positions, I turned in in the trench dug for me and my batman, who was already asleep in it. We were up early for stand-to the next morning; it had been after four o'clock before I had turned in and I felt dead tired. We had breakfast of bully and biscuits, washed down by half-cold tea made from the salt-marsh water. It was so filthy that I decided to shave in it instead...

Soon after that the race for Tripoli really did get under way, and Samwell remembered the Argylls' part in it. Looking round the desert for mile after mile the sight was uniform. Vehicles everywhere, of all shapes and sizes, galloping full speed across the desert, all bent on catching up with the enemy and at last getting him off balance. There was no question of stopping to sleep. They slept in their trucks with drivers taking it in turn, and the only reason for halting at all was to fill up with petrol. When they did halt, the lame ducks with engine trouble or those that had fallen out earlier with empty tanks caught up. Soon the countryside changed and in place of the desert, cultivated fields and white farmhouses–Mussolini's shot at building a second Leptis Magna– came into view. Not until they were almost at Homs did Samwell's battalion run into the enemy again.

As might have been expected the 11th Hussars were first into Tripoli. On their way through Castel Benito the leading armoured car crews read a message from the Afrika Korps scribbled on the white walls: 'Tommy, we shall return.' But underneath it a British infantryman, always ready to cap any sort of slogan, had written an Arabic word, which was a favourite with the soldiers: *Yimkin*–Perhaps! The 11th Hussars' leading cars motored on through Castel Benito and passed kilostone 23. What would be waiting for them on the last sixteen miles after an advance of more than a thousand–mines as usual, anti-tank guns in ambush, panzers, or what? In fact there was nothing. At 5 o'clock on the morning of 23 January 1943, the 11th Hussars entered a silent, darkened and, so it seemed, deserted city. So tense and unexpected an atmosphere was greeted in a way that perhaps only the British could have done. A grimy trooper stuck his head out of the turret of his armoured car and yelled 'Taxi!' The desert rats relaxed. The Tripolitanians no doubt wondered what sort of army had arrived.

It is an old administrative cry that whereas, whatever is happening in the battle, stomachs go on demanding to be fed, the nature of the battle itself determines whether petrol or ammunition is the principal headache. Since the thousand guns of Alamein had fired off so much ammunition, three months had passed, and with them the nature of the desert war had again been transformed. Fighting during the advances made possible by that famous victory, there had of course been. But after the break-out, 8th Army had really motored to Tripoli. General Alexander had almost fulfilled the task given to him by Churchill on 10 August 1942, and shortly was able to send his celebrated signal to the effect that His Majesty's enemies and their impedimenta had been eliminated from Egypt, Cyrenaica, Libya and Tripolitania. The motoring, however, had gone on for so long and over such distances that it had imposed an even greater burden on the logistic services than prolonged fighting near to the main base would have done. Such is the irony of military success. These services, aided irreplaceably by the Royal Navy and Royal Air Force, had shouldered this burden, and in delivering the goods had conspicuously demonstrated the brilliance of their planning and the dogged perseverance of those who did the donkey work. The *Official History* reminds us of General Surtees' admirable summing up:

In the rear services let tribute first be paid to troops in their tens of thousands–to the driver trundling his truck through hundreds of miles of nothingness day after day, cursing his 'V' cigarette, consoled by his brief 'brew-up' of tea; to the private cockily controlling a gang of skilled Egyptians in a workshop; to the sergeant confidently carrying out a charge which in England would have been given to an officer assisted by senior non-commissioned officers.

In the past 8th Army's advances into Cyrenaica had always been tethered by dependence on inadequate ports situated well behind their leading troops. But this time the port of Tripoli, great as a symbol of victory, greater still as a dispenser of supplies, was theirs. Yet to capture a major port was not to win the war of supplies. Victory parades needed to be tempered with this reflection. If the administrative difficulties of 8th Army were easing, so were those of Rommel, who was falling back with his Panzerarmee, smaller but still in being, on much shorter lines of communication, lines which were also for a time anyway much more secure. For the Axis were at last in firm control of what they had long been seeking–a short sea passage which they could guard, if not totally at least adequately, and this is what the routes from Sicily and Italy to Bizerta and Tunis, surrounded as they were by their own airfields, gave them. The battles for the Mediterranean at sea and for North Africa on land were as inextricably mixed as ever.

Whilst the Axis enjoyed passages to Tunisia varying in length between 120 miles from Western Sicily and 300 miles from Naples, the Allies were contesting the long sea route to Suez and even in the Mediterranean such distances as nearly 900 miles from Alexandria to Tripoli and 700 from Gibraltar to 1st Army's front. But the combination of the RAF, the Fleet Air Arm, the United States XII Air Force under General Spaatz, Royal Navy submarines and British laid minefields slowly turned the scales in the Allies' favour. Their success in attacking Axis shipping and protecting their own is strikingly advertised by comparing losses. One hundred and seven Italian and German ships of more than

500 tons, a total tonnage of almost 400,000, were sunk either at sea or in port during January and February 1943. Of this huge number about one half was engaged in supporting Tunisia. In the same period the British lost 21 ships or 100,000 tons. Apart from the Allies' growing supremacy in the air, the final relief of Malta, which was steadily being re-stocked, had again enhanced the island's offensive capability. By the end of February the battle of supplies, on which all else depended, had been lost and won. Although Hitler angrily dismissed repeated objections by Rommel and von Arnim that unless adequate supplies across the Mediterranean were guaranteed their campaigns could not be carried on, two generals from OKW, Warlimont and Keitel (the former called Tunisia a house of cards), both conceded that if North Africa was itself of strategic moment–and Hitler rightly feared that once it had gone the likelihood of Italy's continuing the struggle was re-mote–then only strategic decisions which ensured Tunisia's supply made any sense at all. While most of the German generals who knew anything about the matter were far from confident that the battle for North Africa could be supported much longer, the American and British leaders were deciding what to do when it was over.

Michael Howard has pointed out that at the Casablanca Conference the Mediterranean Strategy was 'born and legitimized'. The problem which faced the Joint Chiefs of Staff at Casablanca, recognizing as they did that there would be neither men nor material enough to engage in cross-Channel operations before 1944, was how to make use of North Africa to hasten Germany's defeat. Three particular objectives–to open the Mediterranean and release shipping, to divert German pressure from Russia and to oblige Italy to capitulate–were to be pursued *by invading Sicily*. Beyond that plans did not go. Of much more immediate consequence to what was happening in North Africa were the new command arrangements agreed to at the conference. Eisenhower became Allied Supreme Commander, North Africa; Alexander was to be his deputy *and* commander of a group of armies in Tunisia; Wilson was appointed to succeed Alexander in the Middle East; Tedder was to be Air Commander-in-Chief; and

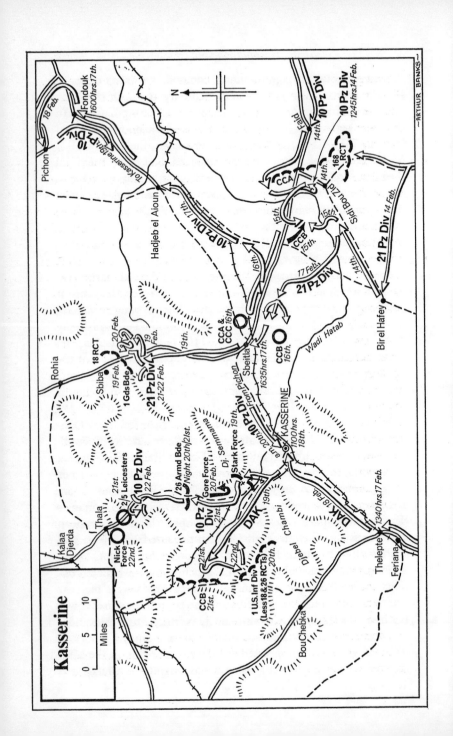

Cunningham would control naval forces in the Mediterranean. The boundary between the Middle East and North African theatres was settled as a line drawn from the Tunisian-Tripolitanian frontier to Corfu. In Tunisia General Anderson was to coordinate British and United States operations.

Allied changes in high command were matched by Axis ones. But if the Allies knew where they were going, at least for the time being, the Axis did not. Kesselring became Commander-in-Chief, South, and Kesselring amongst others was determined to get rid of Rommel. Although Rommel for a short time was in command of Army Group Africa, he was succeeded by von Arnim on 9 March when he left Africa to see Hitler. He never came back. Before he left, however, and in spite of the contradiction between Mussolini's chimerical ideas about reconquering Libya or thrusting deep into Algeria and Hitler's preoccupation with Russia, whilst admitting the African campaign's value in tying down Allied shipping, Rommel had time, like an eagle in a dovecote, once more to flutter the Allies in Tunisia with his last but one spoiling attack–Kasserine. After withdrawing from Tripoli Rommel had moved to the Mareth Line as his next main defensive position. Confident that Montgomery would continue his slow, albeit sure, progress, and concerned that an American advance from Sbeitla or Gafsa might cut off his withdrawal from Mareth, he determined to attack both Allied armies in turn, 1st Army to begin with, then 8th Army, in order to inflict further delay on the Allies and keep things going in Africa for a bit longer. On 14 February he attacked the Americans with 10th and 21st Panzer Divisions. Breaking through the Kasserine Pass on 20 February he turned both north to Thala and west towards Tebessa. But by the 22nd he had been halted and retraced his steps to have one more go at Montgomery. Rommel may have been between two fires, but he did his best to dampen them both down.

Heinz Schmidt, still with Special Group 288, was in the lead with his company in the advance from Gafsa to Feriana and Kasserine. He and his men were exhilarated at the thought of encountering Americans in battle for the first time. He had not yet grasped the fact that these new adversaries knew very little of war. His exhilaration was enhanced after a minor skirmish for an oasis when he and his soldiers found that the Americans had left behind some trucks full of rations and cigarettes. Next day Schmidt received orders from his commanding officer, Meyer, to take the lead with his company, supported by heavy *Panzerjäger*, self-propelled tank destroyers, in thrusting down the road to Feriana. They soon got within sight of the village, having been shelled and having seen a few American tanks. From Feriana came machine gun fire, and the battalion at once put into operation its drill for clearing villages.

The rest of the battalion detrucked swiftly and we went in, infantry-fashion, on a broad front. The sniping stopped. Out of the houses poured a number of Arabs–men, women, and children, waving and shouting in the false jubilation which these people always accorded any apparently victorious troops. Their sheikh recognized me as the officer in command and ran to me with outstretched arms. He gibbered words of greeting. But my right hand was on my automatic, just in case. He fumbled at me and tried to kiss my hands. When I pulled back in disgust, he grovelled on his knees and kissed my boots.

The Arabs...pointed out minefields, warned us that American artillery had only just pulled out, and said that there were still a number of heavy tanks on the far side of the village.

The minefield was newly laid, and the fresh-turned soil betrayed the presence of each mine clearly. We picked our way through gingerly, with sappers at our heels marking the track for the guns behind.

Beyond the minefield the road began to climb again. I was rounding a sharp curve when I sighted and recognized a Sherman tank on the road ahead, within attacking range. I jerked the wheel in the driver's hand and the vehicle swerved sharply towards the left bank of the road. The detachment manning the gun immediately behind me were swift in taking their cue. In a matter of seconds they had jumped from their seats, unlimbered, swung round and fired their first shell, while the Americans still stood immobile, the muzzle of the tank gun pointing at a hillock half-right from us. Our first shell struck the tank at an angle in the flank. The tank burst into flames.

We probed ahead and soon ran into fire from tanks and machine guns deployed on either side of the road. Sending a runner back to Meyer* with word of the situation, I deployed my company under cover of our anti-tank guns to attack the rise on our right...Steady fighting went on for an hour. Then thick columns of black smoke rose ahead, followed by explosions, obviously an ammunition dump. The enemy tanks ceased firing. We continued to advance...

Schmidt goes on to describe his group's encounter with the US 1st Armoured Division, the German attack on Sbeitla, the Americans' withdrawal and General Anderson's decision to call back into the line 26th Armoured Brigade, part of the British 6th Armoured Division, to help stabilize the dangerous situation developing at Kasserine. One of these actions was fought by Lieutenant Colonel Gore, commanding 10th Rifle Brigade. On 19 February with a mixed force from his own battalion, a squadron of 2nd Lothian and Border Horse, some anti-tank guns and F Battery 12th Royal Horse Artillery, Gore was given the task of preventing units of 10th Panzer Division from infiltrating round the flanks of the Americans holding the Kasserine Pass. His account of it shows not only what an untidy battle the whole thing was, but also how piecemeal and patchy 1st Army's reactions were. The balance, which comes from proper grouping, sensibly positioned and alert reserves, and clear, firm direction, simply was not there.

Colonel Gore got to the pass at about 4 o'clock in the morning of 20 February. He almost motored straight into the German positions, but having just avoided them, sent forward a carrier platoon to reconnoitre and make contact with the enemy. Once he had a clearer picture of where everyone was, he realized that the Germans already had the upper hand at the pass itself, and that it was up to him, with the few tanks and anti-tank guns he

---

* It is interesting to note that Schmidt had to send a *runner* back and apparently had no radio communication with his battalion commander.

had, to prevent a break-through right into 1st Army's lines of communications. With his mixed force he managed to stabilize the position, but the German self-propelled guns did a lot of damage and all his artillery observation officers were killed. The Lothian squadron fought until every one of its Valentines had been knocked out. By then it was dark and Gore was able to withdraw towards Thala and organize some sort of anti-tank defence with his remaining six-pounders and 4 Grant tanks which had been sent up to him. During the night German panzers set these Grants on fire with extremely accurate shooting, and, virtually down to his one company, Gore was obliged to move back again. But he had given the rest of 26th Armoured Brigade the time so vitally needed to form yet another line of defence, and throughout 21 February a desperate tank battle went on. It was renewed even in the night leaguer.

As it grew dark on the evening of 21 February the Lothians and the 17th/21st Lancers, after a day of fierce, uneven fighting, came into harbour near the Battalion.* Suddenly some tanks following behind them opened fire on 'B' and 'C' Companies. They were enemy who had passed through the Leicestershire Regiment, led, according to one story, by a captured Valentine, and motored into the harbour close on the heels of Brigade... One of these tanks, passing near a rifleman of 12 Platoon who was digging a slit trench, was invited by the digger 'to keep away from my ———— trench, you're knocking it in,' a remark which sent a revolver bullet whistling past his ear. Confusion in the harbour was extreme. The Germans shouted in good English 'Hands up—come out; surrender to the panzers.' It was almost impossible to distinguish which were our tanks in the dark until a gunner scored a direct hit on a German tank so that it went up in flames. By the light of this fire nine German tanks were soon ablaze and their daring attempt

---

* A member of 10th Rifle Brigade subsequently noted: 'Tunisia was a gentleman's war, and everybody packed up when the sun went down.' There were clearly few gentlemen about on the evening of 21 February. In the desert driving into the enemy's leaguer *by mistake* was not uncommon.

was thwarted. No German motor infantry were in evidence, although for the rest of the night alarms were many and firing profuse.

In fact the battle's crisis was over, and next day the Panzer Divisions, encouraged by demonstrations being made against the Mareth Line by 8th Army, began to withdraw. The United States troops had had a blooding from which they were greatly to profit. In his Papers, Rommel claims that unlike Kesselring he was able to appreciate early on both the fighting qualities of the Americans and their skilful handling of equipment. On the afternoon of 21 February he had watched an artillery duel between the Afrika Korps and Combat Command B of us 1st Armoured Division at Djebel el Hamra. Wooded hills restricted the panzers and the German columns stuck far too much to the valleys instead of advancing over the hills with infantry at the same time. The Americans allowed the enemy columns to advance until they had really committed themselves and then brought them to a halt with artillery fire from three sides. The veterans of two years' desert fighting were astonished at the accuracy and adaptability of the us artillery which put so many panzers out of action. Rommel registers too his view that although the American troops obviously were not yet as battle worthy as 8th Army, their quick tactical reactions, agile command arrangements and preponderance of equipment, particularly tanks and anti-tank guns, would make them formidable opponents in the mobile battles which were bound to develop once they broke out of mountainous country. Rommel described attacks by the us Air Force during the Kasserine encounters as surpassed in weight only by what his army had been subjected to at Alamein. He summed up his Kasserine offensive as a failure to exploit great initial success because of von Arnim's refusal to bring *his* forces to bear quickly enough and because of 'clumsy leadership by certain German commanders'.

Rommel was not the only one to be dissatisfied with his colleagues' leadership and his armies' command. It had been agreed at Casablanca that Alexander would command 18th Army Group in Tunisia, and Eisenhower's directive to him laid down first that from 20 February he would exercise command over the 1st and 8th Armies and any other formations which might be forthcoming, second that his task was to destroy all Axis forces in Tunisia. In the event Alexander took control some days earlier because of the alarming progress of Rommel's Panzer Divisions against 1st Army. He was extremely displeased with what he found, and in a signal to Brooke, the CIGS, he summarized what he felt to be a far from satisfactory situation. Units of different nationalities were all mixed up with each other. Formations had been split up and were not being commanded or fought properly. There was no policy, no plan of campaign. There was no grip or direction from the top. Worst of all the Allies had lost the initiative.

To the Prime Minister Alexander made it clear that victory was by no means just around the corner and that much was to be done before it would be. He then proceeded to give the orders necessary to tidy up the various formations' grouping, lay down a firm policy and get back the initiative. On 20 February he gave Anderson four tasks: to stabilize the southern front; to re-group his army into national sectors; to create a reserve; and to regain and keep the initiative. In fact Anderson had already given instructions designed to do all these things. Alexander's plan of campaign to carry out his mission of destroying the Axis forces in Tunisia was conditioned by the need to do it in time for a summer invasion of Sicily and was directed on the capture of Tunis. There were to be three parts; first to get 8th Army north of the Wadi Akarit, and this would mean two set-piece battles—one at Mareth, another at Wadi Akarit—whilst 1st Army would help by limited attacks to draw off enemy reserves and capture ground important for later advances; then both Armies would concentrate on capturing airfields in order to bring the ever-growing strength of the Allied air forces to bear as heavily as possible; finally, with all the striking power at their disposal, the Allied armies would close in for the kill.

Thus it became clear that the ultimate battles for North Africa were to be conducted in a far tighter and more centralized fashion than anything which had been seen before. Major-General

Fuller has called it a decline from generalship into ironmongery. Not again were field commanders to have the free hand that O'Connor had so enjoyed and justified, or that Rommel had made such brilliant and startling use of when, like Lear, with his good biting falchion he was making 8th Army skip. The United States' entry on to the stage made ironmongery an inevitable feature of future operations, and their generals had not yet had a chance to show what they could do. But Patton and Bradley were soon to demonstrate in their different ways what stuff they were made of and what generalship could do, while Montgomery's handling of Medenine was a model of defensive fire-power at its most destructive. At Mareth the Desert Air Force was to change the pattern once again and carry out a 'blitz' attack in close cooperation with 8th Army. Between them all they were about to start closing the ring.

11. The ring is tightened

In accordance with orders received Deutsches Afrika Korps has fought itself to the condition where it can fight no more.

On 23 February 1943 Rommel assumed command of Army Group Africa which contained the 5th Panzer Army under von Arnim in northern Tunisia and the 1st Panzer Army under Messe at Mareth. Three days later Rommel wrote to his wife:

> If only we could win a major victory here. I rack my brains night and day to find a way. Unfortunately the conditions for it don't exist. Everything depends on supplies–and has done for years.

He was already planning a spoiling operation against 8th Army, and noted that, if it should fail in its object of postponing the British offensive, the end in Africa would be close. At the same time Montgomery was preparing his attack on the Mareth Line, a position which Alexander judged to be as strong as Alamein. Like Montgomery's set-piece attack there more than four months earlier, this one was to be preceded by a defensive battle which took heavy toll of Rommel's panzer strength and made 8th Army even more confident than they already were. There were three corps available for Montgomery's offensive–30th, containing amongst other formations 4th Indian Division and 201st Guards Brigade; New Zealand which apart from the New Zealand Division had 8th Armoured Brigade and Leclerc's force from Lake Chad; and 10th Corps with 1st and 7th Armoured Divisions. Broadly the plan was for 30th Corps to attack frontally, the New Zealanders to do yet another, and very wide, left hook, while

10th Corps remained in reserve ready to exploit. The attack was to be mounted on the night of 20–21 March.

Two weeks before this Rommel had his last fling in Africa and attacked Montgomery at Medenine. By this time 8th Army, after stretching out to assist 1st Army in the last week of February, was re-balanced. Two armoured brigades, 51st Highland Division, the New Zealanders, 201st Guards Brigade–all had been brought up to strengthen the defences, and it was against these formations that the bulk of the panzers advanced. The defences were excellently organized and showed how much 8th Army had learned from the Afrika Korps about how to handle anti-tank guns, which were sited not to protect other units but to knock out tanks. 70,000 mines were laid to improve the effectiveness of a natural anti-tank ditch in front of the Highlanders. Armoured brigades were in depth behind, and the whole position boasted nearly 500 anti-tank guns, 300 tanks and 350 field guns. On 6 March 10th, 15th and 21st Panzer Divisions together with 90th Light and the Spezia Division assaulted this formidable array of defences. It was as well that they had given 8th Army time enough to re-organize. De Guingand, Montgomery's Chief of Staff, recalled in *Operation Victory*: 'Montgomery frankly admitted to me that, for once, through his action to assist First Army, he now found himself unbalanced. So we worked feverishly to prepare ourselves to meet this attack when it came ... By March 5th we were ready for the attack, and a very strong force was ready to receive it. Rommel had missed his opportunity, and we all breathed freely again.' But there had been a number of anxious days, and in its timing there was therefore another curious parallel between Alam el Halfa and Medenine. But its conduct was totally different for the attacking armour was stopped almost exclusively by anti-tank gun fire. When the attack did come, Kippenberger as usual was at the sharp end.

He was not content with viewing the opening rounds of the battle from his own headquarters, but went forward to his Maori battalion, where he was treated to what the battalion commander called 'the sight of his life'–the whole of 10th Panzer Division moving forward to attack. This attack, unlike some of the recent

Axis ones, was strongly supported by fighter-bombers which pressed home their strafing even in the face of powerful Allied fighters and lost heavily as a result. Kippenberger found 10th Panzer Division a fine sight. Some 50 tanks were rolling swiftly towards Metamaur, in companies line abreast, and behind them were hundreds of lorries with Panzer Grenadiers. As he watched the attack Kippenberger was struck with how badly coordinated it was–most unlike the Germans. It certainly did not get far. The combination of artillery concentrations on the debussing infantry and anti-tank guns at the panzers soon broke it up.

Kippenberger went on to record that along the whole corps front the defences were never in jeopardy. Casualties were negligible. By evening the Afrika Korps had withdrawn having lost over 600 men and 50 tanks. He called Medenine a model defensive battle, reminiscent of the earlier one in September. Everyone had felt ready, balanced and confident. There had certainly been no question of Montgomery's dancing to anyone's tune except his own. During the next day the officers of 8th Armoured Brigade held a discussion as to what 10th Panzer Division should have done. The commander running this discussion pointed out how completely the Germans had failed in what they had formerly been so brilliantly successful at–integrating the action of tanks, artillery and infantry. Things had come full circle since the battles of June and July when Rommel swept into Tobruk and beyond while 8th Army scrambled helter-skelter back to Alamein.

It was this which was the common experience of all those in 8th Army who witnessed and took part in the battle–surprise at the enemy's tactics. The 3rd Battalion, Coldstream Guards were mystified as to why Rommel sent his tanks against dug-in, prepared defences without close infantry support, and jealously watched the Scots Guards on their right knocking out tank after tank, a total of fifteen, while their own anti-tank platoon was able to get only one gun to bear. Its first shot sent a panzer up in flames. The Argyll and Sutherland Highlanders also enjoyed the unusual feeling of being attacked when everything was in their favour.

Samwell found this battle much more to his liking than some

others he had taken part in. He and his men were all ready for a 3 day battle, with plenty of food and ammunition, well dug in, a killing ground chosen, and they were confident that they could defeat any attack made on them. It was quite a new kind of war to sit comfortably protected and shoot at advancing enemy soldiers in the open. Too often in the past it had been the other way round. And when the enemy did come this was just how it was.

> They were a mixed bag of Germans in the khaki uniform of the Afrika Korps and Italians in their dark green tunics. They advanced by sections in close formation, and offered an admirable target. I took over a Bren gun myself, and, shouting to the others to hold their fire, waited until they were within four hundred yards; then I gave the signal, and we let them have magazine after magazine. All along the front we could hear the Brens and rifles cracking. Then enemy sections stopped, wavered, broke into a double, and pushed on, stopped again, and finally dived for shelter among some scattered olive trees. They must have suffered terrible casualties. We reloaded and waited; there was a long pause; over on our left in the direction of Medenine we could hear what we guessed was a tank battle in progress, the deep rumbling of the tanks and the sharp crack of the six-pounders. The guns would flare into a fury and then die down to an occasional shot...

Samwell's company was not affected by the bombs or the mortars which followed, but in the late afternoon he was invited by his company commander to lead a counter-attack against the enemy lodgements with *only one platoon* supported by two tanks. It is curious how often in war, with whole armies committed to a particular battle, a mere handful of men are required to do something which is of great moment and for which it might have been expected that the commanders who wanted it done would have made ready enough force to be sure of it. Samwell did not find his mini counter-attack as much to his liking as sitting in holes shooting at the enemy doing similar things. The tanks did not arrive in time, synchronisation of flanking attacks was bad, smoke obscured the battlefield, he and his men ran into heavy mortar fire, and all in all it was not an unqualified success. But Rommel's attack as a whole had petered out, and this was what mattered. Samwell's soldiers got an unexpected bonus from the affair–lots of American cigarettes and chocolate which the Germans had previously captured and then left behind. Chocolate was a luxury almost unknown and the cigarettes were even more welcome, as the battalion had reached the stage of cutting the dread 'v' ones into three, and having one third of a cigarette morning, afternoon and evening.

How unlike Rommel the whole escapade had been. But then, of course, the plan was not in detail his, nor was his own indomitable spirit properly behind it. He had taken no hand in the low level tactical arrangements. He was not leading at the front any more. That sort of personal grip and drive seemed to have gone. Fuel was low, ammunition too, and this last indispensable commodity had been ill distributed, while the British artillery freely fired off 30,000 rounds. It was all quite untypical of the Germans' normal flair for thorough organization. It was more like 8th Army in its salad days. That same evening Rommel called off the attack. Churchill noted in *The Hinge of Fate* that nothing like this power of anti-tank artillery against armour had before been seen. He called it Rommel's sharpest rebuff in Africa. It was certainly his last rebuff, or any other action, in Africa. He flew to Rome on 9 March, and von Arnim took over command of Army Group Africa. His old friend, Heinz Schmidt, called it a grievous blow to the Africa Korps. Schmidt saw Rommel only once more, months later, in Northern Italy, wearing a smart hat, surrounded by staff officers, and carrying the baton of a Field-Marshal. This, he thought to himself, was not the Desert Fox– 'dusty, with a scarf round his neck, his recognition flags, the dust goggles on his high-peaked cap'. All that was gone. But he was still Desert Fox enough to leave his glittering companions, to their astonishment, and chat to the still very junior Schmidt about the good old days in Africa when they had matched their wits against the 8th Army. Rommel's occupation was not yet gone, but he

could bid farewell to the tranquil mind and to content. His way
of life was falling into the sear, the yellow leaf.

Five days after Rommel's departure Alexander issued a further
and much more precise directive. 8th Army's job was to take
Mareth, whilst Patton's II US Corps would advance towards
Maknassy and Gabes; 8th Army was then to exploit to Gabes,
and final arrangements to polish off the Axis forces would be
decided as a result of these operations. In the meantime neither
Rommel in consultation with the Axis dictators nor von Arnim
with Commando Supremo could make them see that unless the
Tunisian front were shortened, penetration of it was bound to
take place and thus to eat up their resources and reserves. Kesselring laid it down that positions from Cape Serrat to Mareth
must be held, and von Arnim gave his own instructions accordingly.

Yet however stretched von Arnim's Army Group might be, the
battle of Mareth was no walk-over. It was a battle perhaps notable in two respects–in the way it resembled Alamein, and in the
way it did not. In the first place, as at Alamein, Montgomery
intended not merely to break the position but destroy the enemy
forces there, and like Alamein, he did one but not the other; like
Alamein too, he was obliged to switch his main effort when the
initial one bogged down *and* had the reserves to do so–even its
name, *Supercharge* II, was the same as at Alamein; the battle of
Mareth, again like its forerunner, was a great success but it was
not a *conclusive* victory. On the other hand, the Mareth position,
unlike that at Alamein, could be and was outflanked; there was
no long dog fight, no interminable thrashing around; it was altogether a quicker affair; and then heavy air support was used
for the first time in a *blitzkrieg* fashion. When Broadhurst, commanding the Desert Air Force, heard of Montgomery's intention
to switch the main thrust to the Tebaga Gap, he proposed to put
his bombers and ground attack aircraft together, concentrate
their fire power on a narrow front and so enable the ground
troops to break right through. 'You will have the whole boiling
match,' he said, 'bombs and cannon. It will be a real low-flying
blitz.' De Guingand has described how they were to be employed.

Forty light bombers would concentrate on a narrow front, where
the attack would be launched, and be timed to precede it precisely.
There would be five Spitfire squadrons as air cover to prevent
enemy interference, while no less than 16 Kittybomber squadrons
would range over the battle area for two and a half hours. There
would always be two squadrons up, bombing and strafing any
enemy they saw. One specially trained squadron of tank-busters
was to attack enemy panzers whenever and wherever they
appeared.

Implicit in such a plan was of course another change. It meant
attacking *by day*, whereas up to this time 8th Army's major assaults had been at night. Changes of this sort all contributed to
realizing that ever-to-be-sought characteristic of surprise. The
plan for bursting through the Tebaga Gap was broadly that the
New Zealand Corps would make the hole for 1st Armoured
Division to pass through, and although Montgomery made the
rather cumbersome arrangement of putting *two* Corps Commanders, Freyberg and Horrocks, in charge of the operation,
they soon came to an understanding as to who was to do what.
Kippenberger's brigade attacked on the right supported by tanks
of 8th Armoured Brigade. His account of the battle on 26 February tells us what a pitch of tank, artillery, infantry and RAF
cooperation—whose lack had so often been bewailed in the past—
had at last been reached:

Punctually at 3.30 p.m. the fighter-bombers appeared, squadron after squadron: all along the line of the forward infantry
little columns of orange smoke appeared indicating their positions, and this smoke steadily grew and spread. The bombers
made no mistakes and nothing was dropped on us, but for half
an hour they turned the enemy position into a pandemonium.
Very soon there were several columns of black smoke from
burning trucks or tanks. The whole narrow area between the
hills looked like a cauldron. I noted with concern that Hill 209,
the Maori objective on our right flank, was scarcely being
attacked. Otherwise the 'blitz' seemed likely to be an effective
preparation.

Under cover of the noise and smoke of this bombardment, in clouds of dust, the Sherman tanks of the Notts Yeomanry and Staffordshire Yeomanry rumbled up, passed on either side of Hill 201 and deployed along the infantry start-line. They were moving into position when the guns opened, firing for twenty-three minutes on the enemy positions, and at 4.15 p.m. the tanks moved majestically forward, followed closely by our little carriers. The infantry climbed out of their pits–where there had been nothing visible there were now hundreds of men, who shook out into long lines and followed on 500 yards behind the tanks. At 4.23 p.m. the barrage lifted a hundred yards–an extraordinarily level line of bursting shells–tanks and infantry closed to it and the assault was on.

From my battle headquarters in a hole on the northern slopes of Hill 201 we had a perfect view...

I went up in a Bren carrier just before dark... Just before going forward we had seen the awe-inspiring sight of the hundreds of tanks of 1 Armoured Division rolling in masses past the left of 201 and on through the gap made by the attack... About midnight we heard that 1 Armoured Division was through and heading for Hamma.

But von Liebenstein, the German commander in that sector, handled his forces boldly and skilfully. With his own 164th Light Division and parts of 15th and 21st Panzer Divisions, he was able to establish an anti-tank screen a few miles south of El Hamma and check the headlong rush of 2nd Armoured Brigade–which at times resembled its former one in the opposite direction between El Agheila and Msus in January 1942, with British tanks and German panzers pelting along parallel or even mixed up with each other. By sealing the breach, however, von Liebenstein gave 1st Panzer Army the very time that the British lost by pausing to lay on another door-opening operation. Once more the Afrika Korps slipped away–this time to Wadi Akarit. Once more 8th Army followed up.

The desert pendulum had at last stuck, pointing west. There were now only two more battles for 8th Army to fight, and by this time the Allied air forces were so strong–during March an average of more than 700 sorties were flown *every day*–that the Luftwaffe was unable seriously to challenge them for mastery of the air. Allied superiority was not confined to one particular sphere of operations. It was all-embracing. Attacks on Axis aircraft on the ground, in the air, neutralizing airfields, sinking convoys at sea, to say nothing of the support given to the advancing Armies. 'Never before,' said de Guingand, 'had our Desert Air Force given us such superb, such gallant, and such intimate support.' The Axis command was compelled to admit that they could put up no effective fight against such relentless concentrations.

While 8th Army was battling its way through the Mareth Line, Patton's II US Corps was not idle. Indeed they greatly helped Montgomery by drawing 10th Panzer Division away from Mareth. By 17 March II Corps had occupied Gafsa. Patton's unconventional and flamboyant methods were recalled by Alan Moorehead. When he first saw Patton he noted the weather-beaten face, the pearl-handled revolver and the remark he made to his ADC–'Go down that track until you get blown up, and then come back and report.' In fact the Germans had already evacuated Gafsa, and the Americans simply motored into it. El Guettar, 15 miles further east, was entered next day, and Maknassy on 22 March. A week later Alexander directed II Corps to drive forward to the Gabes road, a mission well suited to Patton's thrusting spirit. He in turn gave the job to the 1st US Armoured Division. The United States Official History shows how the Americans were to learn, as the British had before them, that armoured strength, however courageously pressed forward, could not prevail in the face of a properly organized anti-tank defence.

The task was given to Benson Force which contained two tank battalions, a reconnaissance unit, two artillery battalions, some engineers, two infantry battalions and a tank destroyer unit. The attack began on 30 March, but did not get far. It was a familiar story. The German artillery and anti-tank weapons, well sited, mobile and used in conjunction with minefields, were just too strong. By day the leading American tanks were knocked out, and the only way to get on was to clear lanes through the mines with infantry at night.

Even Patton was reluctant to order tanks to advance against such successful and expensive enemy tactics, although he toyed with the idea of sacrificing a complete tank company to blast a hole in the defences. Instead he instructed Benson to wait for air support and coordinate his attacks accordingly. In fact Benson made slow, costly progress in a series of tank-infantry actions, but the fact was that in ground so totally unsuitable for decisive fire and movement, sheer weight of artillery and numbers of tanks could not do the trick. Such skilled and determined resistance imposed on the Americans a bit by bit advance. There was no question of grand armoured exploitation.

The fact that Patton's Corps did not make much progress was less important than the threat which they offered to the right flank of General Messe's 1st Panzer Army, a threat which brought about the move of 21st Panzer Division to reinforce 10th Panzer Division opposite Patton, and so lighten the defensive capacity of Wadi Akarit, which Montgomery now had to overcome. The dividend of Alexander's ability to ring the changes, thrust right-handed, left-handed or both-handed as he chose, was about to be reaped.

8th Army closed up to the Wadi Akarit position on 29 March. Montgomery decided on yet another set-piece attack by 30th Corps with 10th Corps held ready to dash forward once the last natural obstacle to his breaking into the Tunisian coastal plain had been removed. His proposal to attack on the night 4–5 April fitted well with Alexander's plans for getting hold of the Gabes gap. Alexander intended first that Montgomery should be assisted once more by pressure from US II Corps, and then to use his main reserve, 9th Corps, to capture the Fondouk gap and get behind von Arnim's southern corps. As might have been expected at a time when things were going badly for them, Axis counsels were divided. Kesselring wanted to hold Akarit as the last defence line in the south, and beat off any threat to the area east of Maknassy-El Guettar with armoured counter-attacks. Mussolini, on the other hand, had already authorized withdrawal to Endfidaville.

Von Arnim meanwhile declared that without the fuel and ammunition, which, like Rommel before him, he so urgently needed—on 1 April he mentioned 8,000 and 10,000 tons for these two commodities as being essential requirements by German forces alone—defeat was unavoidable. He even admitted to 'squinting over his shoulder for ships'. Like Rommel he had to make do with promises. Nevertheless the Akarit position was held, and strongly. In addition to two Panzer Grenadier Regiments, 90th and 164th Light Divisions were in the line together with four Italian divisions. 15th Panzer Division was in reserve.

The ground was mountainous, and once again it was necessary to blast a hole through the defences. Manoeuvre by itself would not do the trick. Here in these mountains was to be seen yet another change in the conduct of a battle. Montgomery's recent *History of Warfare* contains a curiously relevant passage in which he discusses Greek tactical ideas in relation to mountainous country. He condemns the battles as mere slogging matches in which fire and movement played no part. There was no opportunity for manoeuvre, no master planning, no skilful generalship. This is not inapposite when we examine what happened at Wadi Akarit, except, of course, that there was, as customary in a Montgomery battle, plenty of fire—450 guns' worth—and that at the *lower* level, notably General Tuker's with his famous 4th Indian Division, generalship was sound. Tuker did not like Leese's Corps plan, which was to go for and seize Roumana, and pointed out that Djebel Tebaga Fatnassa, being the key to the whole position, must be taken first. Furthermore, since the enemy was weak in infantry, the very thing needed to hold these mountainous features, whereas 8th Army was strong, and his own 4th Indian Division peculiarly suited by temperament and training to mountain fighting, Tuker guaranteed that he would take Fatnassa. 50th and 51st Divisions could then capture Roumana and the positions between Roumana and Fatnassa. All this was good advice. It was adopted, and as things turned out the decision to attack Fatnassa first, then the other objectives, with three divisions at night with no moon and as early as 5–6 April surprised the enemy. Montgomery's signal to Churchill of 6 April contained this sentence : 'I did two things not done by me before, in that I attacked centre of enemy position, and in the dark with no moon.' The Nelsonian ace of using his subordinates' ideas was up Montgomery's sleeve too, and much of the credit both for the concept of this attack and its execution must go to Tuker and his magnificent Division.

1/2 Gurkhas were in the van of 7th Brigade and almost at once struck into the Italians of Pistoia Division. In helping to open the door which led to Axis defeat, Subedar Lalbadur won the Victoria Cross :

The dense darkness of that boulder-studded ravine hid a great feat of arms. Under command of Subedar Lalbadur Thapa, two sections of Gurkhas had moved forward to secure the only pathway which led over the escarpment at the upper end of the rocky chimney. This trail reached the top of the hill through a narrow cleft thickly studded with enemy posts. Anti-tank guns and machine guns covered every foot of the way, while across the canyon, where the cliffs rose steeply for some 200 feet, the crests were swarming with automatic gunners and mortar teams. Subedar Lalbadur Thapa reached the first enemy sangar without challenge. His section cut down its garrison with the kukri. Immediately every post along the twisted pathway opened fire. Without pause the intrepid Subedar, with no room to manoeuvre, dashed forward at the head of his men through a sheet of machine gun fire, grenades and mortar bombs. He leapt inside a machine gun nest and killed four gunners single-handed, two with knife and two with pistol. Man after man of his sections were stricken until only two were left. Rushing on, he clambered up the last few yards of the defile through which the pathway snaked over the crest of the escarpment. He flung himself single-handed on the garrison of the last sangar covering the pathway, striking two enemy dead with his kukri. This terrible foe was too much; the remainder of the detachment fled with wild screams for safety. The chimney between the escarpments was open, and with it the corridor through which 5th Brigade might pass. It is scarcely too much to say that the battle of Wadi Akarit had been won single-handed several hours before the formal attacks began.

By 0830 on the morning of 6 April most of Fatnassa was in the hands of 4th Indian Division. On their right 51st Highland Division's attack had also gone according to plan, and Roumana was captured. 50th Division's progress had been slower, but even so Horrocks, commanding 10th Corps, was sufficiently satisfied that a big enough hole had been made by 30th Corps for his own to pass through. He asked Montgomery for permission to do so, permission that was granted, yet it did not happen, at least not in time to finish off 1st Panzer Army at Wadi Akarit. Once again they were allowed to get away. German skill in plugging gaps with tanks and anti-tank guns obliged 10th Corps to pause, and as so often before the Axis commander authorized withdrawal just at the time when 8th Army issued orders for continuing the advance. It was a story often repeated during 8th Army's successful exit from Alamein. Time after time the door seemed to have been pushed open by one formation for another, and equally time after time they somehow or other did not manage to get through it. There were three explanations possible for such failure. Either the door had *not* been properly opened, or the exploiting units were not sufficiently pushing, or the problem of dealing with the enemy's rapidly thrown together anti-tank screen, well beyond the door, unsuspected, unanticipated and thus unplanned for, simply had not been tackled, still less solved. Of the three, the last is most likely to hold water. This omission reflected two weaknesses in the higher echelons of command–inability either to cope rapidly with the unexpected or to call for their almost overwhelming close air support at the critical moment which arbitrated between partial and complete success.

Yet Wadi Akarit had once more taken heavy toll of the Axis forces. Messe had withdrawn them back to Enfidaville, but in admitting to serious losses gave his view that it had not been *una bella battaglia*. From 8th Army's position in the ring, it might have been a good battle; the three divisions of 30th Corps had all fought well. But of them all it was the Indians' exploits in the mountains which rang loudest through the world. Even Tuker, who knew his men so thoroughly, marvelled at their skill and courage. Good battle though it was, however, it was another win on points. The knock-out eluded them still.

But the ring was tightening. It was Army Group Africa which was at bay now. 1st and 8th Armies had linked up near Gafsa on 7 April and again near Kairouan four days later. Their operations became even more closely reciprocal, and with the Axis forces thus besieged, one of the questions facing Alexander was with which hand the final blow should be delivered. Montgomery understandably enough wanted his own Army to be the one, and as he closed up to Enfidaville on 11 April, he sent a signal to Alexander asking for another armoured division so that he would be strong enough to direct the next main operation. He requested that 6th Armoured Division be put under his command at once. Alexander thought differently. He wished to make use of the easier country in front of 1st Army and go for Tunis from the west. By this means he hoped to cut the Axis forces in half, drive some of them to the south to be further mauled by 8th Army, and allow the remainder to be mopped up in the north. His reply to Montgomery, therefore, far from giving 8th Army another division, took one away. 1st Armoured Division was to reinforce 9th Corps for part of the main effort by 1st Army, while 8th Army exerted maximum pressure to help. Alexander's directive of 16 April laid down that offensive operations to destroy or take all enemy forces in Tunisia would now get under way, and that the pressure would be such that together with naval and air forces, no enemy would be able to withdraw by air or sea.

Alexander's plan was that, whilst 8th Army contained Messe's forces at Enfidaville, 5th and 9th Corps of 1st Army would conduct the main attack up the Medjerda Valley to Tunis; meanwhile II US Corps would make for Bizerta and the French for Pont du Fahs. 1st Army, in short, and more particularly 5th Corps, was to provide the relentless pressure, although before it was all over, 8th Army had to hand over still more reinforcements. Naval and air forces had a good deal to congratulate themselves on. It was not just that they were now required to

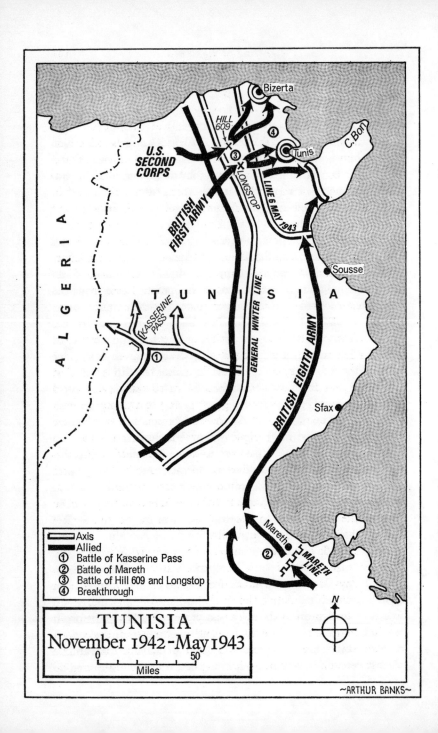

Bizerta

HILL
609

C. Bon

U.S.
SECOND
CORPS

③

④

LONGSTOP

Tunis

LINE 6 MAY 1943

BRITISH
FIRST ARMY

A L G E R I A

KASSERINE
PASS

T U N I S I A

①

GENERAL WINTER LINE.

Sousse

BRITISH EIGHTH ARMY

Sfax

☐ Axis
■ Allied
① Battle of Kasserine Pass
② Battle of Mareth
③ Battle of Hill 609 and Longstop
④ Breakthrough

Mareth

②

MARETH LINE

N

TUNISIA
November 1942 - May 1943

0   50
Miles

~ARTHUR BANKS~

prevent the enemy's withdrawal–a mission they accomplished with almost total success; it was that they had been of infinite consequence in bringing about the very situation where the enemy had no alternative, except annihilation, but to attempt the withdrawal which they were to prevent. All Hitler's efforts to increase the monthly tonnage of supplies to Tunisia failed. The principal reason for more and more sinkings was that the Allied air forces, notably those of the United States, had grown so strong that in March 1943 two thirds of the Axis ships sunk by air attacks were accounted for by US aircraft. Allied submarines also enjoyed many kills off Sicily and the west coast of Italy. Nor was this all. British and American aircraft were savaging the Axis air transport fleet. On 22 April, for example, out of 21 of the huge Messerschmitt 323s carrying ten tons of fuel each, losses from the interception of Allied fighters were so heavy–16 of them were 'hurled headlong flaming from the ethereal sky'–that Göring vetoed all transport flights to Africa, until Kesselring persuaded him to relax so absurd a ruling. But only a quarter of the former sortie rate was ever again realized. The effect of all this was that in March and April sea tonnages transported were 43,000 and 29,000 compared with an average of 60,000 to 75,000 in previous months. The measure of the shortfall becomes clear when we read that even these latter, higher figures were as much as 100,000 tons *per month* lower than what was actually needed. Air transport, which managed 8,000 tons in March, 5,000 in April, could not make up the sum. Some reinforcements of soldiers got to Africa, but far from being able to turn the Axis tide, they at once created the need for yet more supplies, and in the end simply swelled the Prisoner of War camps.

On the other hand Allied supplies flowed in with a regularity that spoke highly of their leaders' cooperation and machinery. Malta's days of starvation were over for good, and having been so instrumental in winning the battle for North Africa, the island was now to figure largely in the next great Allied enterprise in the Mediterranean–the invasion of Sicily. If by severing Axis sea communications, whilst preserving their own, Allied naval and air forces had made an overwhelming contribution to the armies' operations, their reward was in sight. The armies' clearing of the North African shores, the opening of the Mediterranean to Allied shipping, not having to sail to the Middle East and India via the Cape of Good Hope, the advantage gained from those precious commodities, time and tonnage–the value of these prizes was incalculable. Naval forces under Admiral Cunningham had yet one more great moment of triumph just ahead of them. They stopped the enemy escaping. The entirety of Cunningham's success is recalled for us on the last page of Heinz Schmidt's memoirs: *Six hundred and sixty three escaped.** They went by air.

Before they went, however, and before the gigantic haul of men and material fell into Allied hands, there were three weeks of hard fighting to be done. This was to be an Army Group battle –the first in North Africa. In fact it was a series of smaller ones. Alexander's general offensive, Operation *Vulcan,* allotted these tasks to his subordinates:

First Army will:
    (a) Capture Tunis.
    (b) Cooperate with 2 US Corps in the capture of Bizerta.
    (c) Be prepared to cooperate with Eighth Army should the enemy withdraw to Cap Bon Peninsula.
2nd US Corps will:
    (a) Secure suitable positions for the attack on Bizerta, covering the left flank of First Army.
    (b) Advance and capture Bizerta with the cooperation of First Army on the right flank...
Eighth Army will:
    (a) Draw enemy forces off First Army by exerting continuous pressure on the enemy.
    (b) By an advance on the axis Enfidaville-Hammamet-Tunis

* Heinz Schmidt himself got away because his year-old application for permission to marry was granted about two weeks before the Axis capitulated. Before he went he enjoyed a last coup. In answer to one of Kesselring's exhortations to hold on at all costs, he and a companion signalled: 'We will hold positions. Where is the alcohol?' Far from a reprimand, jerricans of Muscatel wine came up with the rations. On manoeuvres nowadays, the rum ration is bid for at the first drop of rain—but not always conceded.

prevent the army withdrawing into the Cap Bon Peninsula....

This was what was supposed to happen and very broadly it was
what did happen, but not without much shifting of weight, pausing, re-grouping and trying again. 8th Army took Enfidaville on
20 April, 1st Army re-took Longstop Hill on 26 April, and the 1st
US Armoured Division captured Mateur on 3 May. Then Alexander made his arrangements for the last attack. In the north
was the whole of II US Corps, in the south 8th Army less 4th
Indian Division, 7th Armoured Division and 201st Guards Brigade, and in the centre 1st Army, with 9th Corps comprising the
three formations taken from 8th Army, plus the 4th Infantry and
6th Armoured Divisions. It was 9th Corps under Horrocks which
was to deal the final blow. On 6 May, it did, supported by over
2,000 bomber and fighter bomber sorties and more than 1,000
guns. It was *blitzkrieg* on the grand scale. Ironmongery of this
sort could hardly miscarry. Tunis was occupied the same day,
Bizerta the next. Finally 6th Armoured Division broke through
the Hammam Lif to Hammamet.

8th Army's battle for Djebel Garci and Enfidaville preceded
Vulcan by four days, and in these actions 4th Indian Division
and the New Zealanders showed again what matchless soldiers
they were. At Garci 5th Indian Infantry Brigade was invited to
capture the Djebel itself, and during the savage fighting for it,
Jemadar Dewan Singh sustained one of the bloodiest and most
exciting encounters which even the famed Gurkha warriors could
boast. It was while he was scouting forward by himself:

I was challenged in a foreign language. I felt it was not the
British language or I would have recognized it. To make quite
sure I crept up and found myself looking into the face of a
German. I recognized him by his helmet. He was fumbling
with his weapon so I cut off his head with my kukri. Another
appeared from a slit trench and I cut him down also. I was
able to do the same to two others, but one made a great deal
of noise, which raised the alarm. I had a cut at a fifth but I
am afraid I only wounded him. Yet perhaps the wound was

severe, for I struck him between the neck and the shoulder.

I was now involved in a struggle with a number of Germans, and eventually, after my hands had become cut and slippery with blood, they managed to wrest my kukri from me. One German beat me over the head with it, inflicting a number of wounds. He was not very skilful, however, sometimes striking me with the sharp edge but oftener with the blunt.

They managed to beat me to the ground where I lay pretending to be dead. The Germans got back into their trenches. ... My platoon advanced and started to hurl grenades among the enemy. But they were also falling very near me, so I thought that if I did not move I really would be dead. I managed to get to my feet, and ran towards my platoon. Not recognizing me, I heard one of my platoon call: 'Here comes the enemy! Shoot him!' I bade them not to do so. They recognized my voice and let me come in.

My hands being cut about and bloody, and having lost my kukri, I had to ask one of my platoon to take my pistol out of my holster and put it in my hand. I then took command of my platoon again.*

Battles for Tunisian Djebels were apt to be costly, and the Garci-Enfidaville affair caused 8th Army many casualties. All battalion commanders in Kippenberger's brigade, for example, were wounded. Nor did 1st Army find the steep, bare hills north of Medjez, such memorable features as Tangoucha, Longstop, the Kefs and the Djebel Ang, easier going. 38th Infantry Brigade, part of the renowned 78th Division, had much savage fighting to do there. The brigade commander, Russell, described the battle area as a series of 'impossible fortresses'. When he later went over the battlefield accompanied by the Corps Commander, the general asked him how on earth the men had managed it. He found himself equally at a loss, but was convinced that it never would have been done at all but for first class troops led by the very best junior commanders.

---

* The Jemadar was shortly afterwards ordered, much against his will, to the battalion first aid post.

Brigadier Russell might have added that his brigade was composed of Irish riflemen and fusiliers.

Further north II US Corps advanced and went on advancing. The US 1st Armoured Division, off the leash at last, swept into Mateur on 3 May, with its eye on Ferryville and beyond, whilst the 9th Infantry Division was directed on Bizerta. Perhaps the most spectacular and tactically valuable stroke was that of the British 6th Armoured Division in penetrating the German defences at Hammam Lif and driving on to Hammamet, so frustrating enemy hopes of evacuation from the Cap Bon Peninsula. Even before this was done, scenes of victory, so often to be repeated in the towns of Europe, were being enacted. A troop leader of the 17th/21st Lancers remembered being amongst the first British soldiers to reach St Germain. The fact that the enemy were only 2,000 yards away and sending shells at them and that he in his tank was firing back did not deter the French civilians. They climbed on to his tank, put flowers round it, thrust roses and bottles of wine at him. One girl even embraced him from behind while he was giving a fire order to his gunner. Outside the tank delighted watchers picked up the empty shell cases as they were thrown through the revolver port and sent a flow of wine bottles back in. Flags waved, tricolours were unfurled, women wept, firearms were discharged in the air. The hysteria of liberation took over.

This *was* the beginning of the end in Africa. On the afternoon of 7th May the leading armoured cars of 6th and 7th Armoured Divisions, the Derbyshire Yeomanry and 11th Hussars reached the centre of Tunis. It was fitting that the 11th Hussars, who had begun the battle for North Africa, should be in at the kill. The effect of 6th Armoured Division's break through to Hammamet was vividly, if somewhat imaginatively, described by Alan Moorehead :

They roared past German airfields, workshops, petrol and ammunition dumps and gun positions. They did not stop to take prisoners–things had gone far beyond that. If a comet had rushed down that road, it could hardly have made a greater impression. The Germans now were entirely dazed. Wherever they looked, British tanks seemed to be hurtling past. Von Arnim's guns would be firing south only to find that the enemy had also appeared behind them–and over on the left–and on the right. The German generals gave up giving orders since they were completely out of touch and the people to whom they could give orders were diminishing every hour. In what direction, anyway, were they to fight? Back toward Zaghouan? Toward Tunis? Under the German military training you had to have a plan. But there was no plan. Only the boats remained –the evacuation boats which had been promised them. The boats that were to take them back to Italy. In a contagion of doubt and fear the German army turned tail and made up the Cape Bon roads looking for the boats. When on the beaches it became apparent to them at last that there were no boats–nor any aircraft either–the army became a rabble. The Italian Navy had not dared to put to sea to save its men. The Luftwaffe had been blown out of the sky. In other words, the Axis had cut its losses and the Afrika Korps was abandoned to its fate.

On May 10th I set off up the Peninsula through Hammam Lif to see one of the most grotesque and awesome spectacles that can have occurred in this war–an entire German army laying down its arms.

One great change, which augured well for the future, had marked the conduct of battle in the closing stages of the North African campaign. Von Gause, Chief of Staff, Army Group Africa, put his finger on it when he said that singleness of aim and unity of effort were what at last had become principal features of Allied planning. All was directed to clearing Africa, so that a second front somewhere in Europe could be opened in 1943. Alexander's grip of 18th Army Group had at length done the trick.

Yet in spite of it and in spite too of overwhelming material superiority, the actual operations were modest in concept, cautious in execution and hesitant in the seizure of opportunity. Differences in equipment, temperament and experience of the three main Allied armies made for methodical, rather than bold, ideas. It was an affair of bit by bit, not the one irresistible stroke. Nonetheless, attrition on land together with mastery of communications, at sea and in the air, had told its tale.

On 13 May 1943 two signals, amongst many others, were despatched. One from Alexander to Churchill declared that the campaign was over, and that the Allies were masters of the North African shores. The second one was from Headquarters Afrika Korps to Army Group Africa and OKH:

> Ammunition shot off. Arms and equipment destroyed. In accordance with orders received DAK has fought itself to the condition where it can fight no more. The German Afrika Korps must rise again.

Whenever the battle for North Africa is thought of or talked over or written about, it does rise again. Its creator and commander, Erwin Rommel, made some memorable comments on the conduct of war. One of them that sticks was that if you were going to take on the whole world, you had to think in continents. Africa was now firmly in Allied hands. What, asked Churchill, to whom the redemption of this continent had been so great a goal, should we do with our victory?

12. The spoils of opportunity

I will in no circumstances allow the powerful British and
British controlled armies in the Mediterranean to stand idle.

Churchill

Troilus and Cressida has got plenty of good stuff for the soldier.
Ajax's bragging and Achilles' sulks are alike to be eschewed,
degree to be preserved; and although the spoils of opportunity
which Ulysses talked of were very different from the tactical ones
which Rommel had so often seized in the desert, and from the
strategic ones which the Allies were now to enjoy, he also made
it clear that only perseverance keeps honour bright. If there were
a single feature in the British conduct of the battle for North
Africa, which might be lifted from all the others, it was perseverance. Wavell's perseverance in building the logistic foundation
was what made a campaign possible in the first place; Auchinleck's perseverance in the face of disaster was what saved the
8th Army and Egypt; Montgomery's perseverance in directing a
battle of material was what crippled the Panzerarmee. Not for
the British–O'Connor's offensive always excepted–the brilliant
spoiling attack and alarmingly rapid taking of tides at the flood
which so characterized Rommel's reign. No, for them it was dogged persistence in defence and slogging step-by-step gains in
attack. Yet for all this consistent pattern in the panorama as a
whole, changes in the nature and conduct of battles were, as we
have seen, continuous and radical.

Indeed in the three years that it had taken the British to advance from Egypt to Tunis, it would have been surprising if this
had not been so. For much of that time, in fact for nearly all of
it except the first British conquest of Cyrenaica, the man who
called the tune in one way or another was Rommel. Others might

come and go. Rommel had made his everlasting mansion in the desert. Churchill acknowledged his greatness as a field commander. 'We have a very daring and skilful opponent against us,' he declared to the House of Commons early in 1942, 'and, may I say across the havoc of war, a great general.' Seven months later he was insisting that nothing mattered but beating him. In bringing this story to a close, therefore, some of Rommel's retrospective deliberations might have a claim to first place.

He put the cause of his victories down in large measure to British mistakes, mistakes whose origin dated back to many years before the war, such as their rejection of the whole concept of mechanized warfare as expounded by Fuller and Liddell-Hart; he considered that the British paid far too little attention to proper training both before and during the war, and in particular to speedy, adaptable movement of motorized forces, and its corollary–close, personal command. He was always critical of British command arrangements, above all of their not choosing tank specialists as Army commanders in a conflict where the handling of armour was paramount. His point about training was endorsed by many British generals, notably Auchinleck who said that instead of training for war in peacetime, the British merely played at it. Then there was the question of equipment. Rommel–and his views were totally supported by the soldiers who had to use them–regarded British tank and anti-tank guns as having far too short a range, and to start with no proper HE shells. He believed too that British commanders did not commit their forces to battle in the tactical way which mobile warfare demanded. In the end what this amounted to was that the British seemed unable to get their *grouping* right. Grouping, after all, was essentially bound up with organization, which in turn depended on and influenced how command was to be exercised.

'Probably our most fundamental and important advantage over the enemy in North Africa', Rommel wrote, 'was that when my army arrived in Africa in 1941, it was in a better position to benefit from further training on modern lines than were the British. My officers, particularly the younger commanders and General Staff Officers, were up to date in their thinking and not hampered by the conservatism of the British officer.' His final desert opponent, Montgomery, might have been cautious, but then, as Rommel himself conceded, he could afford to be, and his conservatism was guided solely by experience. Rommel respected Montgomery's thinking and praised him in that he made no strategic mistakes. The same could not be said of Rommel himself. He might have accused with reason the German and Italian supreme command for having squandered and thrown away their opportunities in North Africa, but he must bear the responsibility for rejecting Kesselring's wiser counsels in June 1942 and insisting on his 'try-on'. On the other hand when that gamble had ended with the persistent coming up of 'zero', and roles were reversed–Rommel advising Hitler to cut his losses in Africa, Hitler adamant in hanging on and reinforcing–he was right to comment : 'As a result of the senseless sacrifice of so many German and Italian troops in Tunisia, it became impossible to beat off the landings in southern Italy.' The thought of an additional 250,000 properly equipped and supplied troops available to defend Sicily and the toe of Italy must give us pause.

But it was as a brave and brilliant tactical commander in fluid, mobile battles that Rommel's place in military history is sure. His flair for sensing where and when the enemy was weak and uncertain, his instinctive concentration and personal grip at the front during critical times, his implacable drive, his chivalry, above all his opportunism–these are the things for which the Desert Fox will be remembered. The ultimate spoils of opportunity– Cairo and the Canal–were never his, although there were moments when it looked as if they would be, and the soldiers of the Afrika Korps anticipated them enough to send radio mesages to Egyptian daughters of the game to make ready for them. Rommel's secret was, of course, that he kept his own eye and finger on what was happening at the sharp end. 'I tried all possible methods of establishing close signal communications with the fighting troops', he wrote, 'and concluded that a headquarters near the front, equipped with radio and protected by a strong bodyguard, gives the best results.' It was a method which seemed to have little appeal to the higher British commanders.

Rommel then was a consistent agent in devising and conducting battles from the Axis pavilion. The British had more captains to choose from and to dismiss. No contrast could have been greater than that between the early, impoverished days of Wavell –when he told Western Desert Force to 'make one man appear to be a dozen, make one tank look like a squadron, make a raid look like an advance'–and the ironmongery at the disposal of Alexander and Eisenhower. From first to last the ebb and flow of battle washed over some memorable men and unforgettable events. O'Connor's audacity, the surprise he thus achieved, his exploitation of it which was of the boldest sort, his mastery of tactical method–taking enemy camps in rear, breaking into the fortresses of Bardia and Tobruk, the grand outflanking sweep across the desert and the slender trap which closed on an entire Italian army–he set the stage for harnessing mobility and concentration to singleness and simplicity of purpose. The novelty of his tactics multiplied their power; the cooperation of his tanks, artillery and infantry showed at once how effective and indispensable it was; his devastation of passive defensive measures showed how worse than useless they were.

So well did O'Connor demonstrate what could be done with boldness and agility that Rommel, taking a leaf from his book, executed a Beda Fomm in reverse and took all Cyrenaica back. *Blitzkrieg* and dynamic leadership in the van of strong and mixed panzer groups brought a new set of rules to desert fighting. Indefensible petrol dumps, which simply robbed armour of its mobility, were shown to be worth nothing; but a Tobruk, a fortress gnawing at the Axis vitals, a Malta on land, this was a different thing altogether. Next the weight at Auchinleck's disposal together with his superior logistic resources brought about a series of furious and costly armoured battles notable for Rommel's daring raid to the frontier and Auchinleck's phlegmatic decision to stand firm. Clearness of aim on the British side–to destroy the Afrika Korps–was not enough; it had to be matched by concentration and integration of forces if it were to yield conclusive dividends. 8th Army's subsequent dispersion, unreadiness and lack of fast, firm and sound management gave Rommel his greatest chance of all. A spoiling attack which ended in the enemy's being routed and losing Tobruk was to reap the spoils of opportunity all right. Yet just as 8th Army had overreached itself in *Crusader,* so did Rommel after capturing Tobruk. Stalemate at Alamein was the sour prize. Minefields then took command of the desert. Getting through them and on from them was for Montgomery to do, and just as 8th Army was making its way once more, and finally, towards the frontier with Cyrenaica, the Allied armada of *Torch* began to set its cargo of guns, tanks, soldiers and supplies ashore. Roosevelt's pledge to fight the Germans somewhere on land in 1942 was realized. Yet such was the resilience of the Axis powers that another six months were to pass before Alexander's *Vulcan* captured a quarter of a million men and freed North Africa. Throughout it all the Royal Navy and the Allied air forces had given every form of support to those who fought the battles in the sand. Malta had not just stood firm. It had struck mortal blows. Between them they had won the struggle for communications; they had robbed the enemy and given to their own the indispensable sinews of war. These sinews had found most typical expression in the tank, racing across hard desert, grinding its way through soft sand, blowing itself up on mines, victim to the 88mm or 6pr gun, target for the low flying fighter or bomber, symbol of the Afrika Korps or the Desert Rats. O'Connor had had but a few regiments; Alexander had been able to muster division after division, so much so that in ringing the changes for his last decisive blow he was able to take two armoured divisions from one of his Armies and give them to another. This was weight-shifting indeed.

And what had it all led to—the possession of North Africa? There were two great dividends. The first of them could hardly be better put than it is by the *Official History:*

It was of course here that Italy was defeated, and for nearly two years this was the only theatre with a land front on which British and German troops were in contact. So it was mainly here that the techniques of land warfare were kept constantly up-to-date, the intimate tactical cooperation of land and air

forces evolved and perfected, and the conduct of large and in-
tricate landing operations put to the practical test. Thus the
Mediterranean and Middle East was the workshop in which
the weapon of invasion was forged and the trial ground on
which it was proved; it was here that the highest commanders
learned their business of handling it...

Had the Eastern Mediterranean arena not been successfully
held during the lean years (in which case, for want of bases, no
British fleet or air forces could have even disputed the control
of the Mediterranean sea communications) the task of the Allies
in gaining a foothold in Europe would have been rendered
immensely more difficult; indeed it might well have proved to
be beyond their powers.

So much for the first of the prizes; what about the second? Churchill was not slow to answer his own question–what should we
do with our victory? Michael Howard's lectures on the Mediterranean Strategy show how the British attitude changed as Axis
resistance in North Africa crumbled. Enthusiasm for exploiting
success threw to the winds former caution about landing operations in Italy. The Americans, on the other hand, with their eyes
firmly on the original and main ball, persisted in their view that
the invasion of Western Europe must take priority over everything else. So far did this latter view prevail that in the end substantial forces from Alexander's armies in Italy were actually
taken away from him to land in southern France at a time when
he, Alexander, was riding on a wave of optimism as to thrusting
through the Ljubljana gap on Vienna. Yet no responsible com-
mentator would now suggest that the correct strategic decisions
were not taken. As a distraction from other fronts, as a commitment which Germany could not afford to ignore, the campaign in
Italy played its part. Professor Howard maintains that for Churchill and 'perhaps for the commanders of the victorious British
armies in Africa, the impulse to carry the battle into Italy was
emotional as well as strategic'. Certainly these armies did not
stand idle.

But the strategy towards which their work was directed was

again opportunistic. They were on the threshold of Italy and to Italy they went. The spoils of opportunity were to be less spectacular for the right-handed push, which Churchill had spoken of, than they were to be for the left-handed one. The strategic concept itself was nonetheless in being. Right up until the actual launching of *Overlord,* delays in its D Day were accepted by the Americans in order to allow one more advance, one more prize, one more attempt at something conclusive in Italy. The Mediterranean Strategy might have been a subsidiary one, but it was still an irreplaceable stepping stone to victory in the West.

One further word must be said about Churchill, for if any one man was the architect of victory in North Africa, it was he. His passionate concern with winning the desert war is easily understood when we remember that it *was* the one place where British troops were engaging the German Army. We may therefore forgive the stream of minutes and telegrams which so plagued commanders on the spot, particularly when we recall that some of his minutes, many of them marked with his bright red label, ACTION THIS DAY, were addressed to others. 'They galvanized with a sense of personal responsibility, and a sense of the urgency of the perils through which the country was steering, the Ministers and civil servants to whom they were addressed. "It was as though the machine had overnight acquired one or two new gears, capable of far higher speeds than had ever before been thought possible."' To Churchill's drive and vitality, the 8th Army, commanders and soldiers alike, owed the tools with which they finished the job. Moreover, however much Churchill might argue with the Chiefs of Staff and his other military advisers, he did not in the end overrule them. What exasperated him time after time was what seemed to him to be the Desert Generals' failure to cap strategic opportunity with tactical success. But the truth was that the battle for North Africa was marked on the British side by strategic vision linked to tactical deficiency, and on the Axis side by tactical brilliance manacled to strategic blundering. Through it all the courage and devotion to duty of the individual soldiers, sailors and airmen of both sides shone undimmed.

Tacitus, it will be remembered, rounded on the war-mongers and peace-brokers alike for turning everything into a wilderness—*ubi solitudinem faciunt, pacem appellant*. 'Where they make a desert, they call it peace.' We can perhaps be kinder to those who fought the battle for North Africa, for at least the wilderness was there already, and give them as their epitaph—*ubi solitudinem invenerunt, bellum fecerunt*. 'Where they found a desert, they made war.'

BIBLIOGRAPHY

Alexander, Field Marshal the Earl, *The Alexander Memoirs, 1940–1945,* Cassell, 1962

Barnett, Correlli, *The Desert Generals,* Kimber, 1960

Blumenson, Martin, *Rommel's Last Victory,* Allen & Unwin, 1968

Bolitho, Hector, *The Galloping Third,* Murray, 1963

Bradley, General Omar N., *A Soldier's Story,* Eyre & Spottiswoode, 1951

Bryant, Sir Arthur, *The Turn of the Tide,* Vols I and II, Collins, 1957 and 1959

Caccia-Dominioni, Paolo, *Alamein, 1933–1962,* Allen & Unwin, 1966

Carver, General Sir Michael, *El Alamein,* Batsford, 1962; *Tobruk,* Batsford, 1964

Churchill, Sir Winston, *The Second World War, passim,* Cassell

Ciano, Count, *Diary, 1939–1943,* Heinemann, 1946

Clarke, Brigadier Dudley, *The Eleventh at War,* Joseph, 1952

Clifford, Alexander, *Three Against Rommel,* Harrap, 1943

Connell, John, *Auchinleck,* Cassell, 1959; *Wavell,* Collins, 1964

Crisp, Robert, *Brazen Chariots,* Muller, 1959

Davy, George, *The Seventh and Three Enemies,* Heffer, 1952

de Guingand, Major-General Sir Francis, *Operation Victory,* Hodder & Stoughton, 1963

Eisenhower, General Dwight D., *Crusade in Europe,* Heinemann, 1949

Farran, Roy, *Winged Dagger,* Collins, 1957

Fergusson, Sir Bernard, *Wavell, Portrait of a Soldier,* Collins, 1961 ffrench Blake, Lieutenant-Colonel R. L. V., *A History of the 17/21 Lancers,* Macmillan, 1962

Fuller, Major-General J. F. C., *The Second World War,* Eyre & Spottiswoode, 1948

Hastings, R. H. W. S., *The Rifle Brigade in the Second World War,* Gale & Polden, 1950

Howard, Michael, *The Mediterranean Strategy in the Second World War,* Weidenfeld & Nicolson, 1968

Howard, Michael, and Sparrow, John, *The Coldstream Guards, 1920–1946,* O.U.P., 1951

Howe, George F., *US Army in World War II, passim,* Department of the Army, Washington

Kippenberger, Major-General Sir Howard, *Infantry Brigadier,* O.U.P., 1949

Lewin, Ronald, *Rommel as Military Commander,* Batsford, 1968

Liddell Hart, Captain Sir Basil, *The Tanks,* 2 vols, Cassell, 1959

Macintyre, Donald, *The Battle for the Mediterranean,* Batsford, 1964

Macmillan, Harold, *The Blast of War,* Macmillan, 1967

Majdalany, Fred, *The Battle of El Alamein,* Weidenfeld & Nicolson, 1965

Montgomery, Field Marshal the Viscount of Alamein, *Memoirs,* Collins, 1958; *A History of Warfare,* Collins, 1968

Moorehead, Alan, *Mediterranean Front; A Year of Battle; The End in Africa; Montgomery,* Hamish Hamilton

Nicolson, Harold, *Diaries and Letters,* 3 vols (ed. Nigel Nicolson), Collins, 1968

Official Histories. *United Kingdom History of the Second World War,* H.M.S.O., in particular vols. dealing with the Middle East and the Mediterranean and Grand Strategy

Patton, General George S., *War As I Knew It,* Houghton Mifflin, 1947

Rommel, Erwin, *The Rommel Papers* (ed. B. H. Liddell Hart), Collins, 1953
R.U.S.I. Journal, passim

Samwell, Major H. P., *An Infantry Officer with the 8th Army,* Blackwood, 1945
Schmidt, Heinz Werner, *With Rommel in the Desert,* Harrap, 1951
Scott Daniell, David, *4th Hussar,* Gale & Polden, 1959
Stevens, G. R., *Fourth Indian Division,* MacLaren, 1948

Tuker, Lieutenant-General Sir Francis, *Approach to Battle,* Cassell, 1963
Times Literary Supplement, passim

Verney, Major-General, *The Desert Rats,* Hutchinson, 1954
von Mellenthin, Major-General, *Panzer Battles, 1939–1945,* Cassell, 1955

Wheeler-Bennett, Sir John, *King George VI,* Macmillan, 1958
Wilmot, Chester, *The Struggle for Europe,* Collins 1952
Wood, Herbert Fairlie, *The King's Royal Rifle Corps,* Hamish Hamilton, 1967

Yindrich, Jan, *Fortress Tobruk,* Benn, 1951
Young, Brigadier Desmond, *Rommel,* Collins, 1950

INDEX

The numerals in **bold type** denote the figure numbers of the illustrations.